TERROR AND TOLERATION

Terror and Toleration

The Habsburg Empire
Confronts Islam, 1526–1850

Paula Sutter Fichtner

REAKTION BOOKS

For Waltraud and Walter, in gratitude

Published by REAKTION BOOKS LTD
33 Great Sutton Street
London EC1V 0DX, UK

www.reaktionbooks.co.uk

First published 2008

Printed and bound in Great Britain
by Cromwell Press, Trowbridge, Wiltshire

British Library Cataloguing in Publication Data
Fichtner, Paula S.
    Terror and toleration : the Habsburg Empire confronts Islam, 1526–1850
    1. Muslims in popular culture – Austria – History
    2. Austria – History – 1519–1740 3. Austria – History – 1740–1789
    4. Austria – History – 1789–1900 5. Austria – Relations – Turkey
    6. Turkey – Relations – Austria
    I. Title
    943.6'03

ISBN-13: 978 1 86189 340 6

Contents

A Note on Usage

Of the many vexed terms in the Western historical lexicon, the word 'Turk' is certainly among the more troubling. Officially at least the Ottomans never applied it to their territories or their subjects. The latter were known as people of the 'Well-Protected Domains' and the polity in which they lived the 'Sublime State'. For the sake of style and contemporary authenticity, I have chosen to use the terms 'Turk' as understood by Europeans in the period which this essay covers and 'Ottoman Empire', 'Ottoman lands', 'Ottoman domains', 'Ottoman holdings' and the like when speaking of Ottoman dynastic territories. I have also made use of the term 'Porte', shortened from 'Sublime Porte' in passages that refer to Ottoman government institutions themselves.

I have also tried to keep 21st-century readers from mistaking the 'Habsburg empire' for the 'German', or 'Holy Roman Empire'. The Habsburgs were in fact emperors over the many quasi-autonomous principalities that constituted 'Germany' from the fifteenth to the early nineteenth centuries. At the same time, however, they were assembling a proprietary dynastic state that took in a few German lands, chiefly the constituent provinces of modern Austria, but also many non-German regions, Hungary, the modern Czech Republic, Slovakia, Slovenia, Croatia and Poland among them. 'Germany' and 'German empire' here mean the area more or less covered geographically, though not administratively, by today's Federal Republic of Germany. 'Habsburg empire' and, from 1806 to 1867, 'Austrian empire', refer to the multinational state that ruled much of east-central Europe until 1918.

All dates are contemporary to the period under discussion. Given names are generally rendered with their English equivalents; transliterations of Muslim names follow accepted current use when these are available. At the risk of offending some national sensitivities, I have generally used current place names, with historical equivalents in parentheses when called for. Cities that are very well known to the English-speaking world,

Vienna or Prague, for example, will not appear as 'Wien' or 'Praha' though because Budapest is a comparatively modern amalgam of two municipalities, the Hungarian city occupied by the Ottomans will be 'Buda', as it was throughout much of the early modern period. I have also retained the use of 'Constantinople' at the expense of Istanbul. It was a name with a numinous hold on Western minds in the period covered here, and it is with those feelings that this study is concerned. Indeed, the Ottomans used 'Istanbul' and the Turkish version of Constantinople interchangeably. Modern Turkey made the former name official only in 1930.

Introduction

Just as the day broke on the 15th of July, with us still fast asleep, the enemy arrived at our market square. On the cry and report from the lookout, we quickly gathered in and around the church, where the walls protected us. The enemy completely occupied the market, and it was therefore impossible for anyone to ward them off. Thus, we left ourselves to God's mercy.

The enemy had assured us of our personal safety, even in writing, so that should any other groups [of them] appear, we were to present the document and nothing evil would befall us. Thus, in the name of God, we opened up [the church]. We mingled with them, and they with us, without the slightest fear . . . We brought them food . . . Once they ate their fill, leaving very little for us, they called out, bring the arms! . . . Two Turkish pashas sat at the cemetery gate, listed all of the males among us, then ordered us at the church to raise our right hands. We bade one another farewell. The enemy, in the meantime, each with a saber on his side [and] another weapon in his hand, stood ready to our left. We never imagined that they would slaughter us on the spot, but thought that they were going to take us to Vienna, to use us as storm troops and to dig trenches. Once they saw that all of [our] men were out of the church, their commander gave a hand sign . . . after which they fell upon and hacked away at us hideously, an act of cruelty that left us all falling atop one another, screaming for mercy the whole time.[1]

The year was 1683. The scene was Perchtoldsdorf, a village just outside Vienna. The armies of the Ottoman empire, having failed to take the Austrian capital in 1529, were on their way to try again. Why they did what they reportedly did in Perchtoldsdorf is unclear. Nevertheless,

9

The Defence Tower of Perchtoldsdorf, 1521.

such encounters and reports of them had terrorized central and east-central Europe for decades. Almost 100 years before, Ottoman raiders had apparently done much the same thing with the German-Hungarian population of Mór (Germ.: Falckenmor), not too far from the fortified town of Komárom. Surrounded by the Muslim enemy, the townspeople promised generous tribute in return for personal safety. They turned over horses, a respectable sum of gold, and finally a good supply of bread and wine. The Turks waited until Christian supplies began to run low. They then assembled all male inhabitants outside of the town, counted them, then ordered that they swear to pay a yearly tax of one Hungarian gulden each. The Turks then slipped into the streets. The pasha leading them ordered that all who remained inside – children, the elderly, nursing infants – be killed. Only nubile females came away with their lives, though only if they would service the enemy's pleasure. The women, however, were so overwrought with grief at the loss of friends and family that no man could approach them. Frustrated and angered, the pasha ordered the breasts of some to be cut off. The town walls served as gallows for all who remained.[2]

About a month and a half after the Perchtoldsdorf episode, however, fear of Turks and Muslims in central Europe began to subside. On 12 September, Ottoman forces now besieging Vienna retreated in front of an international Christian coalition that had been organized by the house of Habsburg, a German-Austrian dynasty that ruled a good part of central Europe. One decisive victory inspired others. By 1700 the Turks had withdrawn well south of the Hungarian Danube, their threat to central Europe ended.

The excesses of war and self-defence have tormented humankind from the beginning of time, and the grisly details of Christian–Ottoman conflict in central Europe are not unique. But it was repeated encounters with what Perchtoldsdorf exemplified to many that made the Muslim Turks 'the terror of the world' for Europeans and turned the word 'Europe' into a geographic synonym for Christendom. The line between religious and dynastic territoriality was indistinct; Hungarians regarded the integrity of their faith and the preservation of their kingdom as identical causes. On the way to Bohemia after spending more than two years in Ottoman prisons, a young Czech nobleman, Wenceslaus Wratislaw of Mitrowitz (Václav Vratislav of Mitrovic), crossed what to him was a religious border and not a political one.[3] When the sultan's forces fled in disorder from Vienna in 1683, the entire continent, along with the British Isles, rejoiced in relief. Given their own expansionist leanings, the Austrian Habsburgs (emperors over Germany's territorial principalities as well as rulers of their own extended empire in east-central Europe) were ordinarily suspect among other monarchs. At this moment, however, the regime in Vienna was applauded throughout the continent for driving Christendom's foe from their capital city. Christian and Muslim, in short, had been locked in a struggle with only one acceptable outcome: undisputed possession of the lands that each side associated with its faith.[4]

Both the Habsburg government and the Roman Catholic Church that it was defending had worked for two hundred years to create military and political infrastructures to contain a dangerous, resourceful and persistent foe. They also spent much effort on cultivating habits of popular thought and behaviour that would stiffen the public will to resist. Imaginations worked overtime in Vienna and elsewhere in the monarchy's lands to find language that discredited the 'Other'. Out of such policies came a psychological and intellectual template of stereotypes calculated to inspire Christian hatred of Muslims and readiness to fight them without question.

While clergyman often chastised imperfect Christians, they saw Muslims as barbarian non-believers whose social and sexual customs were often ridiculous and occasionally animalistic. Turks reportedly reduced churches and chapels to stables, foddered animals with communion wafers, covered iconic tableaux with manure, then trampled and destroyed them. They stuffed votary candles with gunpowder that would explode when penitent pilgrims lit them.

The education of people writing and telling these tales determined the quality of expression, but their basic standpoint remained the same well into the eighteenth century, regardless of social class or learning. A pre-Lenten carnival parade in Hernals, today the seventeenth district of Vienna, featured a mule with a rider representing Kara Mustafa, the Turkish Grand Vizier who retreated ignominiously from the siege of the city in 1683. *Türkenrennen*, in which historically-costumed cavaliers speared and shattered likenesses of the dreaded enemy, entertained diplomats in Vienna in 1814. The occasional Turkish or 'Moorish' heads still peering from above or alongside entrances to Austrian taverns and inns were often souvenirs of these games, scooped up from an arena in the Imperial Winter Riding School after audiences had left. Contemptuous renditions of Turks and their faith lingered on in popular song and the Austrian theatre. 'Oh my dear Muslim, everything is all over' ran a parody of the German drinking song 'Ach du lieber Augustin' in Friedrich Radler's summer theatre comedy *Die Türken vor Wien* that was performed well into the twentieth century.[5] Political and administrative anarchy is called 'Turkish management style' in the modern Czech language.

Aristocrat, well-to-do burgher, artisan and peasant in the Habsburg lands all had some preformed idea of the fearsome Turk and what to expect from him. They also had well-developed convictions about the worthlessness of Islam and the need to identify with their Christian leaders. The Habsburgs had other dangerous foreign enemies: the French almost constantly, later the Russians, and now and again Bavarians and Prussians. But none of these threatened both the house of Austria's state and its religious establishments like the Ottomans and their hegemonic ambitions.

The 9/11 attack on the World Trade Center in New York City prompted many Austrians to reflect on the history of their country's problematic relations with Muslims. Some frankly declared that their culture and its dominant Roman Catholic faith never had been reconcilable with Islam and never would be. Probably the most incendiary remarks in this vein came from Kurt Krenn, then bishop of the diocese of St Pölten in Lower Austria, whose general conduct had long been subject to wide public criticism. Though he disavowed using force against Muslims, he called their religion inherently aggressive, political and impervious to civil niceties. Pointing to the growing Islamic community in his country, he announced that Austrians, who had already survived two Turkish sieges, were now in the midst of a third.

Such intellectual crudity in the twenty-first century embarrassed local liberals and even many on the right. Norbert Leser, a noted Austrian conservative and Catholic philosopher, carefully distanced himself from Krenn's generally bizarre thinking. Nevertheless, on the matter of Islam, he thought the clergyman had something to say. Christianity was, in Leser's opinion, the superior faith. The Christian faithful, he said, follow a son of God rather than a prophet whose word is spread through fire and sword. Their understanding of man as fashioned in the image of God has been a key source for contemporary notions of human rights. Leser openly acknowledged that Christians had often behaved reprehensibly towards unbelievers and one another, but these episodes were largely offset by the positive ideals embodied in their creeds. Furthermore, anti-Muslim sentiments still echo loudly in Austrian right-wing politics today. 'Home instead of Islam' – *Daham statt Islam*, as it more or less rhymes in local dialect – was one of the many slogans of the Freedom Party in the national elections of 2006.[6]

Nevertheless, much has changed in central European perceptions of the Turks and Islam, at least when one looks at the long conflict between the two factions in historical perspective. Today's Hungarians can be downright irreverent. A good example is the central square of Győr, a medium-sized city in north-western Hungary that was one of the most contested sites of the Habsburg-Ottoman wars. Named after one of modern Hungary's great reformers, Count Stephen Széchenyi, the square is dominated by a column topped with a gold-crowned statue of the Virgin. Its legend recalls the liberation of Buda from 'Ottoman power' in 1686 with the help of that Virgin and Emperor Leopold I. In urban central Europe, however, where space is always at a premium, the square often functions as an open-air market. The monument and the low wall around it are hung with signs advertising wares of various kinds and their prices.

Perchtoldsdorf treats its deadly encounter with the Ottomans more sombrely, yet, in its quiet way, more provocatively. The town itself, immaculately manicured and dotted with wine gardens, is a showcase for the prosperity and pleasures of contemporary Austria and not to the horrors that took place there more than three centuries ago. Drily worded descriptions of the massacre of 1683 are displayed on low retaining walls around one end of the town square, which is dominated by a 60-metre-high defensive tower, the tallest such structure in central Europe when it was finished in the early sixteenth century. The plaques are seated so low, however, that even alert tourists miss them. That the perpetrators belonged to what Austrians and Czechs of the early modern era routinely called the 'hereditary enemy' is clear, but not stressed. St Augustine's church, which dominates the complex, does have a so-called Turkish window from the late nineteenth century that shows Turks slaughtering helpless Christians. The bright green banner of Muhammad the Prophet behind the Ottoman commander identifies the religion of his force. But no additional commentary is provided.

Nor are visitors urged to stop at the nearby town hall to view an impressive contemporary wall-painting of the event, along with an early eighteenth-century commemorative tablet. The latter makes plain how raw feelings were about the Turks even after 1683. 'Barbaric' is the adjective of choice in a text that emphasizes Ottoman destructiveness, untrustworthiness and blood-lust. The tone of these lines, however, contrasts markedly with the explanatory brochure given to tourists to guide them around the commemorative installation both indoors and outside. Low-key and quick to point out where legend and historical record part company, it says more about mankind's willingness to make up its collective mind on the basis of fact rather than editorials about Turkish bad behaviour. If the purpose of the Perchtoldsdorf complex was meant to reinforce the ethnic and political identity of Austrians by inflaming memories of collective past suffering, it is not very effective.[7]

Nevertheless, the few painstaking corrections made to the 1683 story of Perchtoldsdorf indicate that some Austrians still recall the details of the bloodbath. What differentiates them from their countrymen of three hundred and so years before is their concern to recall the episode as accurately as possible. Scrupulous factuality, they seem to believe, is rhetorically more compelling than one-sided sensationalism. Psychology may be playing a role here. As history widens the spread between then and now, Austrian memories of alleged Ottoman atrocities are fading proportionately. While large numbers of Austrians oppose the entry of Turkey into the European Union, many do not, and are eager to assure Muslims throughout the world that their country will no longer knowingly misrepresent the historical relations of both communities.

Discarded memory in itself can be a form of forgiveness, though the results might be embarrassing. One of Vienna's leading daily newspapers in 2002 gave 1783 rather than 1683 as the date of the Ottoman siege of the city.[8] Contemporary material and intellectual values, along with practical political circumstances, however, have undoubtedly quickened the pace of change far more. It has become necessary, even fashionable, for contemporary Austria to look at Turks and Muslims more dispassionately. Austrian democrats, regardless of their party affinities, are often uneasy about their past links to a dynastic empire that may have ended the Ottoman threat to the West, but was itself unashamedly militaristic and monarchic. Liberals and leftists generally often associate hostility to Muslims with religious Austro-Fascists who tried to firm up Austria's resistance to Nazism in the 1930s by recalling the Catholic defeat of the Turks and Islam. Indeed, as late as 1983, the tricentenary anniversary of the European victory over the Turks before Vienna, the Austrian Federal Press (*Bundesverlag*) published a volume entitled *Besieged by Turks – Relieved by Christians.*[9]

Not all publications in 1983 on the subject, however, exploited Christian–Turkish polarities. The introduction to a major collection of essays about the Habsburg–Ottoman encounter edited by the director of the Museum of the City of Vienna did not use the term 'Muslim' once. And the tendency to soft-pedal historical enmity has continued. Contemporary demographics alone in Austria have forced politicians and their constituents to re-evaluate the centuries-old tensions between Christian and Muslim. The Turkish and Muslim population is burgeoning, especially in Vienna. Almost 8 per cent of the city's residents are now Muslims. The census of 2001 found that around 4.2 per cent of the entire population of Austria are Muslim. Of these, the overwhelming majority are Turks, with Bosnians in second place and peoples from a variety of nations from the Middle East making up the rest. Austria has recognized the Islamic religious community as a public corporation in Austria since 1979. Elected officials have often more than gone out of their way to acknowledge their respect for the Islamic faith. Though Austrian political leaders in high places admit that relations between the country's Christian heritage and new Islamic presence are not always cordial, the mayor of Vienna now holds a ceremonial fast-breaking meal during Ramadan for Muslims. Children from Muslim households are entitled to religious instruction in public schools at state expense. The major political parties in Vienna worry about equipping immigrant children with German-language skills and not about excluding them from the country altogether.[10] During the year-long festivities in 2006 surrounding the 250th birthday of Wolfgang Amadeus Mozart, a company from the opera in Istanbul put on the composer's *Abduction from the Seraglio* as an exploration of Christian–Muslim relations. The orchestra used authentic Turkish instruments to render their effects more authentic than Mozart's Westernized approximations of them.

It would therefore be easy to conclude that contemporary political, social and economic pressures alone have muted hostility to Turks and Muslims in Austria and Hungary too. The historical record, however, argues that these changes are only one part of a long, uneven and intricate process. Central Europeans have been shedding much of their stereotypical antipathy to Turks and Muslims which has persisted for more than three centuries. Even in the ideologically torn Austria of the 1930s, the general public was not much interested in coalescing around memories of the one-time Islamic enemy. The former Habsburg government, which vanished in 1918, had made its accommodations to Islam as administrative needs dictated. In 1874, a law governing religion in the Habsburg lands had already extended specific protections to Islam. The incorporation of Bosnia into the Habsburg empire in 1912 had brought around 600,000 Muslims into the dynasty's lands who were quickly put to use in state service and elsewhere. The imperial *Islamgesetz* (Islam Law) of that same year was the first formal concession in Europe that allowed Muslims to worship freely and to manage their own religious affairs. Only World War I aborted plans to build an elaborate mosque in the Habsburg capital.[11] Long before this, Hungarian nationalists were worrying far more about the threats to their national identity posed by Slavs, Germans and Romanians than those posed by the Turks who had once occupied the kingdom. Hungarian rebels, along with social and national dissidents throughout the Habsburg empire, actually took asylum in Constantinople during and immediately after Europe's revolutions of 1848.[12]

Even more striking was an earlier methodological profession of faith made by an Austrian scholar, Joseph von Hammer-Purgstall, as he introduced his monumental history of the Ottoman Empire in 1827: 'love for the honourable and the good, with loathing for the shameful and bad, without hatred for Greek or Turk, without prejudice for Muslim or Christian, with a love of legitimate (*geregelte*) power and well-ordered government, for cultivation of law and the arts of war, for institutions of public benevolence and the expansion of learning, with hatred, on the other hand, for disruptiveness and oppression, cruelty and tyranny.'[13]

By the standards of his day, Hammer-Purgstall was a liberal. At the same time, he was a product of a society innocent of the moral acrobatics that often go with academic and political discussions of the non-Western 'Other' in Europe and North America today. Open warfare with the Turks was still too close to his past and that of his contemporaries for them to have forgotten the documented viciousness of a dreaded foe. He was clearly ready, however, to renounce simplistic stereotypes of Ottoman Turks and Islam. He was also among the leading 'Orientalists' of the first half of the nineteenth century, trained at the Oriental Academy founded in 1754 to prepare linguists and diplomats for Habsburg service in Constantinople and the East generally.

Orientalists in our own time are in bad repute, thanks largely to the efforts of the late Edward Said. His very influential *Orientalism*, first published in 1978, argued to passionate effect that most nineteenth-century orientalist discourse was intended to whitewash Western imperialism and to construct the term 'Islam' in ways that aroused Western dislike and contempt. The book has been questioned part by part many times. One of its chief weaknesses is that it is drawn largely from French and British experience. The work begins in earnest only with Napoleon's invasion of Egypt in 1797, a moment when the Ottoman empire no longer directly threatened the West. Europeans found it much easier, therefore, to construct dismissive images of Muslims and all subject peoples throughout the East. Humanists of the sixteenth and seventeenth centuries, on the other hand, along with non-academic contemporaries who figure in this essay, were often living in deep and immediate fear of an enemy that closely identified itself with Islam and conquered in the name of its prophet. As the Ottomans reeled off one victory after another, Europeans had no reason to believe that they would end up on top in the scenarios of dominance and subordination that colonial relations suggested to later Frenchmen and Britons. Indeed, the peoples of early modern Europe often had to persuade themselves that Christian belief was indeed superior to all others. Defending central Europe and its faith required them to find fault with Islam, wherever and however they could; describing Turks, their behaviour and their faith in the darkest terms imaginable was one way of doing this.[14]

Said admitted that he neglected German scholarship on the East, but did nothing to remedy the lapse. A closer look at Hammer-Purgstall and at some of the people who taught, admired and read him closely might have tempered the thrust of *Orientalism*, to the advantage of scholarship generally. Hammer-Purgstall was well aware of Ottoman decline, even as he published the bulk of his immense corpus between 1800 and 1850. Nevertheless, he clearly appears to have thought that scholarship was more than an instrument of power.

What prompted even one person in the Habsburg empire of the early nineteenth century to reject emphatically the negative and often wildly distorted images of an enemy that had terrorized his compatriots to varying degrees for almost two centuries and to turn scholarship into an end unto itself? And what kind of cultural conditioning had persuaded him to simultaneously endorse open-mindedness towards a deeply alien 'Other' and the liberal ideals of his own time that in turn had roots in the European Enlightenment?

Historians today, this writer among them, willingly accept the idea that culture itself is not fixed but, in the words of Said himself, 'dynamic and ceaselessly turbulent'. Any given complex of circumstances will often include quite dissonant elements.[15] The processes of change and continuity run parallel to one another; human beings are constantly sorting through and recombining materials from both dynamics, often inconsistently. They change their minds often, sometimes quite radically, sometimes incompletely. The results are left for historians to organize as coherently as they can.

It is such accommodations and turns in the mental and spiritual culture of the Habsburg empire that we shall be tracing. After looking at why many people in the lands of the house of Austria cultivated and believed baleful images of the Turks and their faith, we shall turn to the question of how and why many people rethought, reconfigured and even discarded these notions. Readers should keep in mind that there were always two sides to the vast historical story that runs beneath this one. Ottoman Muslims and European Christians both had a hard job distinguishing between self-defence and aggression when each were fighting for land and faith. This particular study focuses on Christians, particularly Roman Catholics, in central and east-central Europe, not because their convictions about innocent suffering at Ottoman hands were uniformly accurate or justified, but because many in the Habsburg domains were able to move beyond the negativity of victimhood over time. The theme is not one of oppressed Christians and ruthless Muslims, but the factors that persuaded some central Europeans who had been deeply conditioned to think one way about an 'Other' to change their minds. Indeed, the following essay is based upon the author's belief and hope that the process is not unique to one culture and time, but that humankind generally alters its opinions about other cultures more according to circumstance than to deeply-rooted psychological predisposition. That something like this took place in the Habsburg lands is remarkable only because it unfolded among a group of people who had been thoroughly trained to fear and loathe a Muslim enemy until well into the modern era. If the prejudice of 'us versus them' ever had a homeland, it was Ottoman-threatened central Europe.[16] Reactionary archbishops notwithstanding, most Austrians today, along with Hungarians, Czechs and other nations once part of the Habsburg empire, have ceased associating Turks and Muslims with the vilest traits that humankind has to offer. While they do worry about the potential threat that Islamic fundamentalism poses to hard-won democratic values, political and educational authorities in central and east-central Europe, they generally want to accommodate, even to absorb, Muslim communities into the general body politic.

As a practical case-study in the possibility and process of cultural revision, this essay should reassure those in liberal Western societies who fear that racial and ethnic stereotyping will necessarily poison their cultures forever, even when it is in response to unusually dangerous and stressful situations. Recent scholarship has done much to discredit the idea that two very different cultures living in close proximity to one another will inevitably go to war.[17] Less attention has been given to the role of circumstance creating cultural oppositions. That such negative views may have some basis in experience rather than ignorant bigotry may make them more resistant to change but not permanently immune to it either. One of the underlying premises of the present text is that hateful depictions of an aggressor, especially a highly alien one, are often not 'imaginary resolution of real anxieties' but quite realistic appraisals of what that enemy might do.[18] At the same time, the example of the Habsburg empire's relations with the Turks and Islam over time and amidst changing situations argues that such thinking can be reversed, even in the precincts of 'priests, academies, and the state' where, according to Said, established cultures entrench and defend themselves.[19] It can even be replaced by the habits of evaluating information independent of psychological or societal agendas that twist fact to suit preference. One can learn, particularly in the story of Joseph von Hammer-Purgstall and Austrian Orientalists who followed in his path, how one can approach the culture of an inimical 'Other' empathetically, yet critically, and why it may be a good idea to do so.[20]

Past and present really are different, and one generation's response to specific issues is never completely applicable to the challenges facing another. Nor is cultural change always benign. That some people in the Habsburg empire dramatically revised their visions of Turks and Muslims does not guarantee that others, even faced with similar circumstances, will behave the same way. But one can ill afford to overlook the suggestions of prior experience, especially in times when ready solutions to difficult problems in cultural relations do not seem at hand. It is in this spirit that what follows should be read.

East-central Europe *circa* 1570.

CHAPTER 1

An Enemy Real and Imagined

A CONQUEROR IN THE EYES OF OTHERS, 1400–1500

Christians in central Europe had formed opinions about Islam long before the Ottoman Turks threatened to overrun them. Few of these views came from direct experience. Muslim settlements did exist in Hungary after the tenth century, but they were small and far apart from co-religionists throughout the world. As time went by, whatever Arabic these people knew vanished along with the rudiments of their faith. By 1300, most of these communities had apparently turned Christian.[1]

Notions about the Islamic conquest of the Iberian peninsula in the early eighth century and the medieval crusades in the Levant and Holy Lands left more lasting marks on the imaginations and historical memories of Europe. The latter, which began at the end of the eleventh century, were a major factor in turning the Muslim into the 'normative enemy' of Christendom. But these views neither closed the Christian West from the East, nor the other way around. An extraordinarily lively and unforced exchange of ideas and goods between Arab and Christian went on all around the Mediterranean basin throughout the Middle Ages and the Renaissance.[2]

Should Europeans acquire some learning about Islam and its prophet, their approach to Muslim culture could be quite appreciative. Observations and commentaries of medieval and Renaissance merchants and travellers could be quite enlightening, at least for the literate of the time. European scholars and thinkers sincerely admired the work of their Arab Muslim counterparts. By the fifteenth century they clearly realized that Islam and Christianity were closely related.[3] One of Renaissance humanism's true luminaries, Nicholas of Cusa, who lived in fifteenth-century Vienna for a time, aspired not only to a union of Eastern and Western Christendom, but of Christians and Islam. Having carefully compared the Koran and the New Testament, he concluded that the two faiths differed in significant matters. Muslim scripture, he declared, was fundamentally flawed. Nevertheless, Islam to Cusa was more a Christian heresy than a wholly alien religion. Both certainly agreed on an all-important basic truth – the existence of a single God.[4] A lull in the Christian–Muslim conflict during the latter decades of the fifteenth century and a lively spurt in trade between the sultan's holdings and the West may have inclined Western thinkers to make room in their own cultural heritage for Islam. A handful of contemporary humanists laboured to fit the Ottomans and their rulers into Biblical and the European classical traditions, as well as into known political systems on the continent. Turks became the offspring of the Trojans and their rulers as variants of the despots of Renaissance Italy. These efforts were only abandoned in the late eighteenth century.[5]

It was, however, the expansion of the Ottoman Turks and the religious mission that many sultans publicly assigned to themselves that hardened European hostility to Muslims for centuries to come. Originally at home in the Eurasian steppes, the point of departure to Europe and the Middle East for several Turkic peoples, the Ottomans adopted Islam in Anatolia where they became dominant. Appearing towards the middle of the fourteenth century in today's Greece and Bulgaria, their forces set about harassing rural outposts of Byzantium, the last segment of the Roman empire to withstand its general collapse in the West. Byzantine rulers often willingly

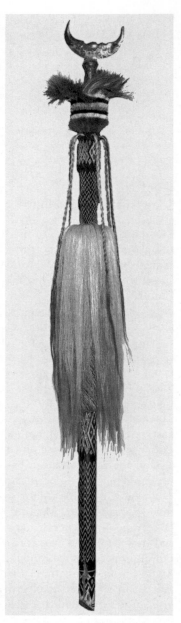

The Horsetail Standard of an Ottoman Commander, second half of the seventeenth century.

co-operated with the Ottomans to mutual advantage in the Mediterranean and the Near East. The Ottomans themselves were often quite solicitous of their Christian subjects, especially when they, like all rulers in early modern Europe, had great need for soldiers, taxpayers, even talented officials.

Sultans, however, had territorial designs on Christian Europe and the Muslim Middle East that made the Turks and Islam more than objects of intellectual curiosity. In the course of the fifteenth century they conferred upon themselves titles associated with universal rule – *kaysar, basileus* and *padishah* among them. Ottoman rulers aspired to rule from Constantinople long before one of the most successful among them, Mehmet II the Conqueror, took the city in 1453.

To fifteenth-century Europeans, Constantinople meant many things. It was the seat of Eastern Orthodoxy, a renegade version of Christianity in Western opinion. The city was also a major commercial hub, strategically positioned to control the extensive maritime commerce in the eastern Mediterranean and the Aegean. Italy's great trading city-states, Venice and Genoa, had extensive business interests there. Mehmet's triumph, however, turned the city into an emblem of the Turkish threat to Europe. Even the most broad-minded Christian intellects found it hard to qualify the perils that Ottoman conquest posed for their faith and material well-being. Throughout the Western reaches of the continent, Muslim Turks were quickly labelled as bestial idolaters whose military forces seemed unstoppable. Their only possible moral equivalents were the Greeks, commonly thought in the West to be too avaricious and treacherous to have defended the Byzantine capital vigorously. In fact, Greeks did seem willing to co-operate with the new rulers in Constantinople. Many of them quickly accepted Mehmet II's invitation to return to the depopulated city. Mehmet also appointed at least two nephews of the late Emperor Constantine XI as Ottoman administrators, and former Byzantines continued to work at the sultan's court into the sixteenth century.[6]

European leaders recognized the danger posed by the invasion, particularly those whose lands were uncomfortably close to the path of Ottoman conquest up the Danube valley. The medieval kingdom of Hungary was especially vulnerable. To counter the peril, kings and princes at the centre of the continent repeatedly urged their nobilities and common folk to commit themselves to one more crusade against Islam, this time embodied by the 'Turk'. These appeals occasionally worked – the Hungarian-led defence of Belgrade in 1456 was a prime example – but Christians were reluctant to co-operate with one another. Political fragmentation and self-destructive local rivalries in the Balkans and south-eastern Europe made Ottoman expansion all the easier.

Christendom's highest ecclesiastical authority in the West, the Roman papacy, had often exploited the weaknesses of Byzantine rulers and the Church that they theoretically supervised. The split between East and West in the Christian world had taken place in 1054, the product of intractable differences in theology and ritual as well as conflicts over rights to Church lands in southern Italy. Rome, however, continued to claim undisputed primacy over Christian believers. Even as Mehmet II gathered his forces before Constantinople in 1453, Pope Nicholas V demanded that Constantine XI redouble efforts to reunify Byzantine Catholics with the Western Church.[7]

Pleased though they may have been to see their competition in the East diminished, Nicholas's successors took great alarm at this new thrust of Islam into Europe. Dealing with it effectively was another matter. The four-teenth- and early fifteenth-century Western Church was wrestling with its own schism. For roughly forty years after 1378, the papacy had two seats, one in Rome and another in the southern French city of Avignon. Only after a church council decided in 1417 to recognize a single pontiff in Rome was it possible to mount a serious defence against the Turks.

The actual collapse of Byzantium, however, moved the papacy to sound the alarm about Islamic conquest to all of Christendom. Entire populations were alerted daily about the perils that awaited them. Pope Calixtus III issued a Bull in 1456, calling the faithful to repentance and prayer. Homilists, he advised, should alert congregations to the dangers of the man he called 'Muhammad the Son of the Devil'. Churches were to ring their bells to remind parishioners that they could be future victims of the Turks. Known to Germans as *Türkenglocken* (Turkish bells), they tolled three times every afternoon and night between noon and half-past twelve, summoning Christians to repeat the Lord's Prayer three times fol-lowed by three Ave Marias to immunize themselves against Islam. Calixtus III's immediate successor, Pius II, preached anti-Turkish sermons all over Europe in what turned out to be a disappointing effort to recharge the crusading energies of the continent.

The preachers of central Europe quickly made the 'Terrible Turk' a central homiletic theme, especially when major Ottoman offensives loomed. Insofar as language went, they pulled no punches. In Vienna at the mid-point of the fifteenth century, a Franciscan Minorite, Johannes Capistrano, called Muslims 'dogs', with Muhammad himself the 'giant dog' among them. The bishop of Esztergom in Hungary, János Vitéz of Zredna, sermonized vividly on the cruelty of the Turks, their sacrilegious beliefs and their wild hordes. In 1462, George Podiebrady, the king of Bohemia, proposed a general league of European princes to drive the 'Turk' from Christendom. The results of these efforts, however, were disappointing.

Rome endorsed Podiebrady's idea, but the response of Europe's rulers was tepid. The papacy contented itself with verbal combat, eloquently publicizing the occasional Christian victory over Ottoman troops and working very hard to keep fear of the Turkish threat alive in popular consciousness, perhaps even in the military plans of sovereigns.[8]

Popes of the Middle Ages had never been confident that they could defend themselves against Muslim expansion; their Renaissance counterparts and their advisers were equally uneasy, particularly when they were consulting the works of those Byzantine historians who had nervously anticipated Muslim takeover for decades. Out of this mixture of fear and loathing came a strident model for Catholic homiletics intended to rally all classes of the faithful in the defence of Christendom and its institutions. Should Islam prevail, as the rhetoric of the time went, learning and culture would vanish. By 1500, Turk and Muslim were generally two sides of the same repellent coin for Europeans. To become a Muslim was, for the next 200 years, to 'turn Turk'. Whether Turkish ambitions were fuelled by religious fervour or lust for 'plunder, slaves, and booty' – an ongoing debate among Ottomanists even today – was beside the point. Whatever their motives, the Turks were unsettling intruders upon the European scene. A staggering mass of Christian scriptural scholarship flooded the continent in support of a single proposition: Islam was a false and evil faith. Neither the creed nor the polity that the sultans and their officials were constructing around it had any place in a Christian West governed by Christian rulers.[9]

Christian moral lapses, often contrasted sharply from the pulpit with the perceived devoutness of Muslims, had contributed to this state of affairs. On the other hand, surrendering to the sultan was out of the question. Following religious services, the clergymen of central Europe might read out state mandates to save both the continent and the world from the Turks. A handful of European scholars continued to explore Islam and its culture during the sixteenth century. Arabic, it was noted, had affinities with Aramaic and Hebrew and was therefore one more key to unlocking the subtleties of biblical scripture. Merchants and the simply curious continued to visit the Middle East and to report quite factually on the peoples and customs of the region. But ignorance and fear led most Europeans to think of Muslims and their faith in terms of negative and distorted stereotypes. Muslims were idolaters who rejected the Trinity; Muhammad himself a kind of wizard. Muslims accepted polygamy, homosexuality and paedophilia. Islam's notions of Paradise were inexcusably erotic. When waging war against Muslims in the fifteenth century, Christians were therefore not only defending their lands and persons, but their beliefs from doctrines wholly antithetical to their own.[10]

The European advance of the Ottoman Turks slowed or even halted several times. Sultans often had to redeploy their forces in other parts of their imperium. Anatolia and Persia, along with Venice, which exercised considerable influence in what are now Bosnia and Albania, were especially problematic. But 'the Turk', either singly or collectively in contemporary understanding, always came back to the continent with the same agenda: the destruction of Christianity. When churches became mosques as they often did, the message was clear even to Europe's illiterate. The peoples of the Christian south-eastern Europe were the among the earliest to see that faith and land were at stake. Frightened inhabitants of Carniola, today part of Slovenia, pointed out to Pope Sixtus IV in 1474, that the sultans' military triumphs only strengthened a 'Muhammadan foe' of Christendom.[11]

Encouraged as they were to focus on allegedly irreconcilable differences between the two faiths, Europeans did not spend much time mulling over doctrinal commonalities with Islam. But neither did the Ottomans seem to be agents for a religion of peace, especially when they publicly described the goals of their campaigns. Indeed, between the fourteenth and the mid-sixteenth century, sultans and their legal advisors constructed a theory of universal sovereignty that effectively grounded the right of conquest in religion. Ottoman rulers proclaimed themselves *ghazis*, holy warriors against the infidels, in this case Europe's Christians. Their official documents openly proclaimed their global aspirations and listed recent conquests to drive the point home.[12] A formal subcategory of armed jihad or struggle, these offensives were to spread Islam throughout the non-Islamic world, the 'House of War' to observant Muslims. Such enterprises were a sacred duty that conferred a kind of religious authority upon the Ottoman sultan. A victory or *ghaza* was a sign of divine favour, placing the man who led it in the line of succession from the Prophet and his proximate religious and political heirs. A military strike did not have to be large to meet this purpose; simple but nasty raids – the kind used to intimidate the Byzantines over decades – would do.

Well into the eighteenth century, the Ottomans endorsed this mission as much for political reasons as religious ones. To legitimize their preeminence on the Anatolian plateau, they had declared themselves the territorial heirs to the Seljuk Turks who had arrived in the region in the eleventh century and subjugated much of it. Lacking dynastic justification for their conquests in Europe, Ottoman rhetoric called upon religious prescript. Citations from the Koran and references to acts of Muhammad frequently justified renewing hostilities, even if armistices and other diplomatic agreements were cast aside in the process. Current or future campaigns were presented as holy causes. Officials at the Porte distinguished

Christian and Muslim both on the battlefield and in more civilian settings as sharply as did any European. The Turkish language version of a peace in Hungary between the European and Ottoman forces in 1606 referred to the Christian enemy's threats to 'our Islamic faith and state' and spoke of tax payments from Hungarian peasants to 'Muslims'.[13]

Ideals of heroic self-sacrifice in battle against Christians took roots in Ottoman literature and thought in the fifteenth century; indeed, martyrdom was held out as one of possible rewards of participating in such conflicts. Once under Ottoman control, territories became a sultan's dynastic holdings as well, giving him two very serious reasons to defend them. The common folk of Constantinople were just as swept up in the religious fervour associated with the run of Ottoman victories during the fifteenth and sixteenth centuries. Raucous public celebrations in Constantinople accompanied news of the Christian defeats, foretelling, it was thought, the moment when the sultan would bring Islam to the entire world. Well into the modern era, Westerners reported that Turks took up arms vigorously to defend their religion. Indeed, remarked an Austrian observer, the sultan's forces responded far more willingly to such challenges than did their Christian counterparts.[14]

Ottoman apologists made it clear, however, that all this bloodshed would come to a good end. Because wars of aggression against true believers were proscribed, a universal Islamic government would realize humankind's dream of world peace. In the fifteenth century one did not even have to accept Islam to qualify for protection from a Muslim ruler. Subjects had only to acknowledge his supremacy and pay his taxes. On the other hand, the non-believers who governed the extra-Muslim world and the loyal among their subjects had bleak futures: conflict halted only by opportunistic truces that did not last for very long. The Koran did forbid outright terror and plunder, but only within its domain, the House of Islam. Enslavement of infidels and confiscation of their possessions were permissible. Prisoners taken in a holy war faced death or indefinite servitude.[15]

A CONTEST OF DYNASTIES AND RELIGIONS

By the reign of Süleyman the Magnificent, the ruler of the Ottoman empire from 1520 to 1566, the cause of militant Islam and the expansion of the Ottoman holdings were synonymous for Turkish rulers and their officials and Europeans generally. Christian rulers, however, were also eager to enlarge their domains. Especially prominent among them was the house of Habsburg – the house of Austria, as it was known from the middle of the fifteenth century – whose patrimonial holdings in what is now modern Austria put them on a collision course with the sultans in Constantinople. Unlike the Ottomans, who had only one religious mission built into their territorial drive, the Habsburgs, within the first decades of the sixteenth century, had two: the defence of Christian central Europe against Islam, and the defence of Christian unity (understood in Vienna as the Church of Rome) against Reformation Protestantism. Both motifs remained closely attached to the dynasty's public image and private convictions until it passed from the world political scene in 1918.

Originally from south-western Germany and Switzerland, the Habsburgs, whose original lands were in Alsace, southwestern Germany and Switzerland, came to Danubian Austria in the latter third of the thirteenth century. It took some time for them to achieve real eminence in the region. The patriarch of the house in central Europe, Rudolph 1, was German king from 1273 to 1291. Theoretically eligible to hold the office of Holy Roman Emperor, he was never crowned to that office in Rome. Nor, for that matter, were most of his family members who, like Rudolph, held both titles. But the thorniest problem to afflict his house in the late Middle Ages was fraternal squabbling over the territorial legacies of their family. Not until around 1460 did the Habsburg emperor Frederick III win effective control of both the imperial crown and the bulk of his family's Austrian possessions: the duchies of Austria above the Enns river and Austria below the Enns, with the city of Vienna embedded in the latter; Carinthia and Styria, two sizeable provinces to the south and south-east; and a string of lands along the Dalmatian coast. To the west lay the silver-rich county of the Tyrol, though it remained for Frederick's son, Emperor Maximilian 1, to reclaim the province for the principal male line of his house. The imperial title remained with them to until the beginning of the nineteenth century when Napoleon Bonaparte terminated the office as part of his rearrangement of German government. The Austrian lands were theirs, along with titles to other lands in central and east-central Europe, into the twentieth century. But these changes were far in the future. With a sizeable segment of fifteenth-century central Europe under either their titular or actual control, however, the fifteenth-century Habsburgs were well-placed to be leading players in the dynastic power politics of the continent for centuries to come.

Direct Habsburg-Ottoman conflict began even as Frederick III and Maximilian 1 were consolidating their positions in their Austrian patrimony. Ottoman skirmishing parties, appeared in and around the Habsburg holdings during the first decades of the fifteenth century. Their boxlike formations, their swarming advances on their targets and what to Christians seemed to be wanton destructiveness were unfamiliar and frightening for that reason alone.[16] Moreover, these marauders seemed bent on disrupting Christian institutions and practice. One of the earliest of these attacks was in 1478, at Reifnitz near Lake Wörth in Carinthia, where raiders broke up processions and Church festivities. In that same year, Turkish contingents crossed the border between what is today Slovenia and Carinthia in an expedition that gave rise to the kind of imagery Austrians would use for centuries to describe how badly these Muslims from the East could behave. They reportedly took prisoners, slit open their bodies, stuffed them with gunpowder, then set them on fire. Turkish forces also came close to the Styrian capital city of Graz, where bewildered inhabitants had no idea of how to deal with such intruders.

Frederick III's son, Emperor Maximilian I, one of the few genuinely imaginative rulers that the house of Austria ever produced, toyed with the idea of a crusade against the Turks through a good part of his life. The project spilled over into his poetic fantasies as well. *Theuerdank*, an allegorical recreation of his young manhood that he both sponsored and oversaw, includes, among other achievements, the liberation of Jerusalem from a presumably Muslim enemy. The same work put an Ottoman twist on a disputed epigraph scribbled by his late father, 'A.E.I.O.U.' Conventionally thought to stand for 'Austria Will Triumph in the Entire World' (Lat.: *Austria Erit in Orbis Ultima*), Maximilian read it as 'Austria Has Been Chosen to Vanquish the Ottoman Empire' (Lat.: *Austria Electa Imperatorum Ottomanicum Vincet*). At one point, Maximilian considered gathering the several Austrian lands into an independent kingdom that might be better positioned to resist Ottoman aggression.[17]

All of these schemes fell through. Maximilian bitterly laid much of the blame in 1518 on fellow Christian princes who wished his dynasty and its holdings no good, even if the target of his planning was an acknowledged enemy of their faith.[18] But both Maximilian and his father had done much to develop a territorial base that improved the capacities of their house to resist whatever enemies came their way, Christian or Muslim. Maximilian had married Duchess Mary of Burgundy, heiress to the greater part of the Netherlands, one of the most economically productive regions of Renaissance Europe. He also arranged the union of their son, Philip, with Princess Juana of Castile, the third child of Isabella of Castile and Ferdinand of Aragon. An improbable series of deaths that struck her elder siblings and their offspring made Juana heiress to the Castilian crown, though she never actually ruled the kingdom. That role fell to her eldest son, Charles, who ruled Spain from 1516 until 1558. When Maximilian I died in 1519, his awkward and ungainly grandson became Emperor Charles V.

To Europe's other rulers, the territorial appetites of the house of Austria looked as menacing as the Ottoman advance. Worse yet, Charles and his immediate successors in Spain were in a position to draw upon formidable wealth from their New World colonies to underwrite Habsburg interests. Though the territorial princes of a yet-to-be-united Germany never funded imperial military campaigns happily, they did occasionally give their emperors significant support. Most exposed to the Habsburg colossus in the making were the kings of France; decades of French–Austrian conflict ensued. The Ottomans, however, had just as much reason to worry. Charles v loomed as a major competitor both on land and at sea, and the Porte undertook few military and naval campaigns before ascertaining what the emperor might do.

Nor was Charles the only Habsburg of his generation to be set up for conflict with the Ottomans. Habsburgs from the fourteenth century on had tried to secure their place in central Europe through succession agreements with the kings of Bohemia, today the heartland of the Czech Republic, and Hungary. None of these schemes had materialized, but Juana and Philip had produced a second son for his grandfather to marry off, Archduke Ferdinand i. In 1512, Maximilian arranged a future wedding of the nine-year-old with the daughter of the ruler of Bohemia and Hungary, Princess Anna. He also ordered in his testament that Charles turn over the Austrian patrimony of his house to his younger brother.

Ferdinand had hoped to rule Spain, and the Austrian lands were no more than his consolation prize. Their economic potential was limited; worse yet, they were exposed to Ottoman invasion. Süleyman the Magnificent had been moving up the Danube very successfully. Belgrade had fallen to him in 1521, and he had trained his sights on Hungary, which had been challenging the Ottoman presence in Europe for decades. Control of it would help to pacify the sultan's northern and western borders, where both Hungarian and Ottoman raiders harassed local populations regularly.[19] One of the most gifted and ambitious rulers in Ottoman history, Süleyman took his forces into Hungary in August of 1526, where he routed a royal army at Mohács, in the south-west of the kingdom. The childless Hungarian king, Louis ii, fled from the battle but drowned in a marsh where his horse fell from under him.

Hungarians had been trying to reduce their vulnerability to Turkish attack for more than a century. At the outset of the fifteenth century, their kings were exploring a possible anti-Ottoman alliance with Asian rulers and the Tartars of the Crimea.[20] Their clergy had adopted quite early what would become the standard perceptions of the Turks. A fifteenth-century archbishop of Esztergom with humanist leanings, János Vitéz, eloquently condemned what he saw as Ottoman cruelty, the undisciplined hordes that accompanied their armies and their blasphemous treatment of things Christians held as sacred. Mohács, unsurprisingly, became a defining catastrophe of Hungarian history right after the battle took place. Christians, as we shall see, were not beyond beheading their Muslim opponents, but the behaviour of the Turks after Mohács still shocked those who witnessed it, if only because, as a later Habsburg officer noted, Vienna might suffer the same fate. The Hungarian commander-in-chief, Pál Tomori, the archbishop of Kalocsa, was decapitated then impaled before the sultan's tent, and not only, as Süleyman disclosed in his victory letter, because the cleric-combatant opposed the sultan's offensive. The Ottoman leader explained that he was also waging holy war to shelter his peoples from the licentious infidels who were their neighbours. Such punishment was justified by his goal, or so he implied.[21]

The Habsburgs had their own interests in Hungary and the kingdom of Bohemia immediately to the north. The Austrian dynasty had long sought to secure their eastern borders by winning these crowns. Unfriendly princes in the neighbourhood were dangerous, especially when they were like the sixteenth-century kings of Poland who were ready at times to protect their extensive realm to the south and east by striking bargains with the Ottomans. The Turks were a problem for them too, and they were not beyond arranging mutually beneficial alliances with the Porte.

The unfortunate Louis of Hungary, Ferdinand i's brother-in-law, was also ruling Bohemia at his death. He therefore left two vacant thrones and an opportunity that the Habsburgs had been anticipating for almost two centuries. It was also, for Ferdinand, an emergency; Süleyman had intended to push on to Vienna in 1526. Though the sultan aborted this plan, he was very likely to return.

Ferdinand soon established himself politically in Bohemia, where the royal estates chose their king. Hungary, also an elective monarchy, was far more problematic. A fraction of the Hungarian estates did accept him but not before some of their colleagues chose a native candidate, John Zápolya, the duke or *voivode* of Transylvania. A Hungarian land to the far east of the kingdom, it remained a bone of contention in Habsburg–Ottoman relations until the beginning of the eighteenth century. It did not take long for the duke to reveal why the house of Austria wanted control of the region. Defeated by Ferdinand in battle in 1527, Zápolya offered both himself and his principality in vassalage to Süleyman, who closed the deal swiftly. Though internally quite autonomous, Transylvania became a prized protectorate of the sultan, to be defended by him against Habsburg aggression as well as any local figures, including seditious Turkish governors (*beg*) who attacked it. For their part, the princes of the land threaded their way between the competing powers as their interests saw fit. Protestants, who would eventually become a majority in the province, lived and worshipped more freely under the arrangement than their counterparts in lands ruled directly by the house of Austria.[22] Hungary was split into three unstable spheres: Transylvania, which the sultan understood to be most of the eastern part of the realm, royal Hungary to the north and west and under Habsburg control, and central Hungary north and south of the Danube, an area that gradually fell to the Turks. The sultan's forces occupied Buda and Pest after 1541.[23]

Even with one additional crown and a good claim to another, Ferdinand would be hard put to defend them. A good part of Ferdinand I's career in Austria and as German king and emperor – titles he assumed in 1558 – was therefore spent scrambling to mobilize his lands politically, fiscally and militarily against his religious and territorial opponents from Constantinople. His Ottoman opponents had a far more organized and responsive system of taxation, particularly for military purposes. By 1500 their troops were largely under a form of contract with the sultan, whereas Ferdinand more or less raised forces anew each time he began his campaigns. His Austrian lands had been shouldering the expense of Habsburg military ventures for some time; their young ruler would have to supplement these revenues to hold off an enemy with deeper resources than his own.[24]

While Ferdinand's supporters in the Hungarian estates never expected him to finance the liberation of Hungary alone, they did hope that his brother, the German emperor and ruler in Burgundy and over the New World, would contribute heavily to the effort. But Charles v would never commit himself fully to the project. As king of Spain he had his own problems with the Ottomans in the Mediterranean. Though he occasionally responded to calls for help in central Europe, he was not always forthcoming. Ferdinand, a figure of far less prestige, often acted as his brother's representative in Germany and used the opportunity to make appeals for support from Germany's princes. Should they refuse, as they sometimes did, or simply not fulfil their promises, he borrowed. His successors did the same thing through the next century or so.

Religious upheaval in German-speaking Europe itself also complicated the Habsburg struggle with the Ottomans. The Protestant Reformation, unleashed in Saxony in 1517 by Martin Luther, threatened all heads of state to a certain extent. It would take almost two hundred years for most European monarchs to accustom themselves to the idea that confessional pluralism among their subjects was not the equivalent of sedition and disloyalty. Indeed, from this perspective, Ottoman sultans were far more comfortable with religious difference than their Christian counterparts. But the often outspoken Luther also viewed the Turks in ways that indirectly challenged the house of Habsburg, as German emperors, Austrian territorial rulers and now kings of Hungary and Bohemia. Though the German reformer had no great regard for either Islam or its Ottoman advocates, he found the latter very useful for his own polemical purposes. Believing in the sinfulness of all of Europe and the falseness of papal teaching about redemption, he argued that the Turks had been sent by God to punish mankind for their failings. Any offensive taken to turn back the Turks was, in Luther's opinion, thwarting divine will.

Though he somewhat modified his position after the Battle of Mohács, Luther, along with the Protestant factions that he spawned, became an enduring enemy for the house of Austria. Indeed, as Protestants in both the local estates of the Habsburg lands in Germany made confessional privileges the price of aid against the Turks, the two enemies became one in Habsburg thinking. Protecting the Church of Rome was for Ferdinand I and for most of his successors a sincere profession of belief. But defending lands from heresy at home and the 'infidel' Muslim from abroad also gave Habsburg territorialism a religious rationale equivalent to the one that Süleyman the Magnificent had attached to his conquests.

However capably Ferdinand handled his other responsibilities, he was a mediocre commander-in-chief. He was in power when Süleyman failed to take Vienna in 1529, but the Western victory came not from Habsburg leadership but from the stubborn fortitude of the city's defenders. Some bad planning on the sultan's part helped matters along too. The Ottomans' heavy equipment bogged down repeatedly in the mud left by an unusually wet summer. Once an early autumn chill settled on Süleyman's elite troops, the Janissaries refused to fight.

Nevertheless, contemporary sources reported that both the city and the surrounding countryside had received a memorable introduction to Turkish practice. Murder, devastating fires and looting were the order of the day along with indiscriminate kidnapping. A flood of lamenting humanity made its way out of the city along roads, unbeaten paths and over the Danube in search of safety. Panic ruled. About a third of the city's adults, said one account, were wiped out by the sultan's troops. Others, thinking that Vienna's walls offered greater protection, fled from the countryside into the city, bringing horses and cattle along with them. Some, thinking that the Turks were not so close, remained at home in the countryside, only to be slaughtered by Ottoman soldiers as they passed through.[25]

Süleyman himself was bitterly disappointed; he had actually hoped to find Ferdinand in Buda and to capture him there. But Ferdinand would never get the better of the sultan either. Süleyman's formal takeover of Buda and Pest in 1541 was a particular humiliation for his Habsburg rival, as well as yet another alarm to all of European Christendom. Indeed, from a strategic point of view, the fall of the two settlements on either side of the Danube more than made up for Ottoman failure to take Vienna in 1529. The Turks and Islam were now positioned north of the Danube, as well as to the south, terrain that had for some time been considered their sphere of influence. Further advances into Hungary were also easier for them. On the other hand, Christians hoping to reconquer the kingdom along a north-to-south line of march now had a much more onerous task. Süleyman had also made it quite clear that faith and territoriality were inextricably linked in his thinking. Erecting a mosque and holding services in it marked lands as forever his. As the Ottomans saw it, their conquest of the entire kingdom of Hungary was legitimized by holding prayer services in Buda after they took over the city in 1541. Monies raised from prisoner-of-war exchanges were dedicated to construction of mosques. When Turks converted the Hungarian cathedrals in Esztergom, Pécs and Székesfehérvár to mosques, along with the church of the Holy Virgin in Buda, it was obvious that Christianity as well as Habsburg lands was under attack.

Ferdinand, however, had no realistic alternative beyond holding actions if he moved against the Turks at all. The few serious offensives undertaken by his immediate successors were at best compromised or at

Anonymous folk art depicting villagers fleeing Ottoman raiders, late seventeenth century, oil on wood.

worst outright failures. At the end of the sixteenth century Habsburg commanders admitted that they should defend local populations from Turkish marauding. They were reluctant, however, to do anything that invited Ottoman retaliation.[26] The forces at the sultan's disposal were never quite as massive as people of the time thought: a significant gap always existed between the number of troops called to duty and those who actually fought. Nevertheless, the forecast once made in Habsburg Carniola that the Turks were unstoppable was widely believed throughout central Europe. The house of Austria's lands, where a ruling dynasty was hard put militarily to defend its claims, were especially vulnerable.

The weakness of Habsburg armies did not wholly foreclose the possibility of curbing Ottoman expansion through diplomacy. Negotiating at the Porte, however, challenged fundamental European conventions of state relations. Decades went by before European rulers and their spokesmen recognized that they had no choice but to adapt to an enemy for whom duplicity was routine, at least to Western thinking. Past Christian rulers had often made armistices and peaces as matters of convenience. But other than payment of tribute, there seemed to be no way of striking long-term bargains with the sultans and his advisers. European monarchs had long used dynastic marriages to keep open lines of communication among themselves. The practice was known at the Ottoman court, but had fallen out of fashion there by the middle of the fifteenth century. Religious barriers made such arrangements even more unlikely. Emperor Frederick III might possibly have paired a daughter with Mehmet II if the latter would only become a Christian, but the latter was not interested. Nor when these matches came off did they generate much cordiality. For example, hoping to pacify Murad II in 1436, a Serbian prince arranged for one of his children to be a wife and servant to the sultan. A year later, his son-in-law was demanding more land.[27]

Tribute, moreover, was no long-term answer to conflicts, at least from the Habsburg perspective. Ferdinand I did acknowledge Süleyman's supremacy in Hungary in 1547 by promising to hand over 30,000 ducats annually. The arrangement implied the transfer from the sultan to the payer of some control over domestic affairs, and Ferdinand saw the use of such expedients in Hungary. The Habsburgs, however, chafed at making such demeaning concessions; what the sultan thought his due, the rulers in sixteenth-century Vienna called a 'donation'.[28]

Neither side was interested in permanently cutting off relations, if only because each of them wanted to anticipate the other's moves. The Habsburg government kept in near-constant contact with the sultan and those who spoke for him. Nevertheless, face-to-face contact between their spokesmen and their Ottoman counterparts did little to soften the negative stereotypes of Muslims in central Europe. If anything, such encounters gave these images greater profile.

Imperial ambassadors rarely had much formal knowledge of Muslim religion and society. European norms and values of their day ordinarily framed their experiences at the Porte. Even advisors to embassies who had studied Islam in some detail remained firmly persuaded of Christianity's unique rectitude and the superiority of most European customs. Stephan Gerlach, a personal chaplain to an imperial ambassador during the 1570s in Constantinople, was more sophisticated than most, but ever-ready to stand in judgment over Islam where it departed from Christian norms. On balance, Gerlach's opinion of Islam was very low. He found the Turks' religious behaviour laughable when 'priests' (*Pfafen*) regaled their audiences with marvellous tales about Muhammad: that the prophet threw huge stones into the water that rose again, that stones and mountains talked to him, and the like.[29] Christian moral scruples made it hard for him to take seriously the niceties of Muslim Paradise he had learned while attending a funeral:

> Two handsome kissing boys sit alongside every Muslim in eternal life. Standing around him are twenty, thirty, forty slaves to serve him – he only has to wish it [and] chicken, roasts, and rice will be there. And as soon as the Prophet Muhammad arrives, he is going to take four wives: the Virgin Mary, Pharaoh's daughter. I don't know who the two others will be other than that they will be the two noblest (*vornehm*) in the world.[30]

Though clearly interested in Muslim doctrine, ritual and institutions, Gerlach understood these through analogies to European practice: the Ottoman Mufti was a Muslim Pope, Turks at prayer repeated a kind of Pater Noster and the like.[31]

Less tutored envoys were even more direct and judgmental. Giacomo Maria Malvezzi, one of Ferdinand I's most trusted envoys, was typical. In 1551 he asked the Ottoman Grand Vizier Rüstem Pasha whether the giver or the receiver was more honoured in gift exchanges. The latter, answered the Grand Vizier, who then questioned the ambassador about Charles V's notion of honour. To honour and obey God, replied Malvezzi, to uphold the Christian faith and friendship, to administer justice fairly throughout his realms and to protect those lands against enemies.

Idealized though it was, the ambassador's answer was not wholly disingenuous; failure to reunite German Christendom added to the despair that would lead Charles to abdicate his imperial throne within the decade. The subtext to Malvezzi's answer, however, was his firm conviction that

Western moral standards and the behaviour he saw at the Ottoman court differed sharply. Writing on the subject for Christians, he was utterly straightforward. The Turks, he told Charles v, had no sense of benevolence at all; they did everything with an eye to the gifts they would receive.[32] Other Habsburg diplomatic personnel noticed the same thing. Several years later, a young Czech page to an imperial mission in Constantinople put it this way:

> as soon as [one] enters into their territories [one] must constantly be sowing money as a kind of seed, since for money he can procure himself favour, love, and everything that he wants . . . Should they [the Turks] fly into a rage, a common occurrence . . . they allow themselves to be calmed by money . . . otherwise it would be impossible to have any dealings or transact any business with them.[33]

Malvezzi was actually quite outspoken for a Habsburg ambassador. He frequently doubted what Ottoman spokesmen told him and sometimes called their bluff to their faces. In 1551, Rüstem Pasha put on display 45 captives whom he alleged were soldiers of Ferdinand, captured for marauding around Turkish territory. Recognizing a familiar tactic, Malvezzi did not believe the charge and forced Rüstem Pasha to admit that the prisoners before them were common thieves and bandits.[34]

Nevertheless, his opinions and official conduct, like that of other Habsburg spokesmen in Constantinople, was guided more by apprehension and simple fear than by peculiarly European notions of rectitude. Some ambassadors occasionally dared to circumvent the sultan's authority and smuggled captives out of his lands, a ruse that the Ottoman ruler expressly prohibited. But even when they stuck scrupulously to their official mission, imperial spokesmen and their staff were almost always at risk. The solid information about the Ottoman court that made an ambassador's memoranda valuable was hard to come by. Western envoys sometimes used both the dagger and poison to get what they wanted, but such tactics exposed them to retribution in kind. Simply pressing for such material from high officials often met with the same intimidating response. Tricking the sultan's officials was safer; a standard ploy was to coax them into drinking bouts in which they drank wine with Christians who downed non-alcoholic beverages that had been tinted to mimic the real thing.[35] Bribery, though ethically suspect to Westerners, was the safest ploy of all.

Even when they operated with great prudence, emissaries worked in an environment of constant danger. Vienna's spokesmen and their colleagues from throughout Europe were often jailed indefinitely because Süleyman or his Grand Vizier did not like or trust the messages they brought. They often sat out their sentences under guard in their homes rather than in famously awful Turkish prisons, which took no account of an inmate's age or physical condition and reeked so of excrement and vomit that Ottoman guards held their noses. But favourable conditions of confinement had many anxious moments too. Just where one's next meal would come from was often not clear. And all captives could become living martyrs. Galley slavery, for example, was gruelling enough without the physical mutilation that went with it. Victims' noses and ears were slit to mark their servile status. Their facial and skull hair were also removed, leaving them truly unrecognizable.[36] Emerging from such confinement in 1564, an ambassador noted that his limbs were torn, and though he feared the Turks might jail him once again, he was just too weak to travel home.[37]

The Ottomans were perfectly capable of negotiating effectively and reasonably in the sixteenth and seventeenth centuries. They had arranged mutually-respected spheres of economic interest in the Mediterranean with the Spanish and Portuguese. Even Malvezzi conceded that Ottoman officials had their thoughtful, good-humoured, even broad-minded moments, 'as these people go'. Rüstem Pasha, for example, once confessed to thinking now and again that, regardless of their faith, all morally good men would appear in the next world. Generally speaking, however, the negotiating style at the Porte was calculated to cow envoys and often did. One Habsburg emissary to Constantinople called his time spent at the sultan's court 'purgatory on earth'.[38] Rüstem Pasha, for one, normally shouted rather than discussed and interrupted his interlocutors in mid-sentence with frenzied gestures. Should the latter get a word in edgewise, he sometimes threatened them physically. Religion itself apparently meant little to him when he chose targets for his tirades: Jews, Christians, even his coreligionists were equally vulnerable. He reportedly upped his firepower even more for ambassadors, especially when they failed to pay him the honorarium he was expecting.[39]

Malvezzi occasionally responded in kind to these theatrical explosions. Having heard in 1550 that the Turks planned to invade Transylvania formally, he told the Grand Vizier that all of Christendom was obligated to defend Christian lands and might very well mobilize against the sultan. Flushing angrily, Rüstem declared that if he were the ambassador's ruler, he would have had the Italian killed for saying such things. Malvezzi swore that he was telling the truth; as far as killing him was concerned, his life and death were in the hands of God. 'Thereupon I left him with that bone in his mouth to chew on at his pleasure.'[40]

The ambassador had clearly overstepped himself, possibly because he may not quite have grasped the context in which his proposal would be judged. Malvezzi did, however, know when to keep his thoughts to himself. An audience with the Grand Vizier in 1550 in which the ambassador made known Ferdinand 1's desire to rule all of Hungary ended abruptly just as the translator began the Turkish version of what had been said. Rüstem stood up and ordered the emissary out of the room so vehemently that the Italian saved his opinions for a letter to his employer. 'Sire,' he wrote to Ferdinand, 'it would take a sizeable volume to tell you about the brainlessness, the idiocy, the arrogance, the triumphalism, the vapidness (*legerezza*), the total and crude ignorance of Rustan Pasha . . . He thinks that everyone is as blind as he is.'[41]

Malvezzi was even more circumspect during a heated rerun of the scene that took place a year later. According to him, he casually remarked to Rüstem Pasha that Ferdinand would never re-acquire Transylvania without giving consideration to Ottoman interests. The Pasha's eyebrows shot up and he said: 'So, the King of the Romans [Ferdinand 1] imagines that he has Transylvania?' Malvezzi replied that he was not sure, but that if Ferdinand did have such intentions, the Habsburg government would negotiate the matter amicably with the sultan. Rüstem stormed all the more; 'Vallaha, billaha', he swore, 'should anyone dare to demand Transylvania from the Ottoman ruler, I would cut out that person's tongue.' Malvezzi once again pleaded ignorance. 'Enough', shot back the Grand Vizier, 'you understood me'. With that, the official took his leave.[42]

Malvezzi may not have understood Ottoman notions of vassalage, generally a far more controlling status than it was in the West. An act of personal submission to the sultan, it did not give subordinate rulers the legal powers over land and labour force that Western feudal custom allowed.[43] But scenes such as these only confirmed Europeans' opinion that their Muslim enemy was incorrigibly domineering, bloodthirsty, ruthless and arrogantly corrupt. Dealing with them even formally took more than the normal human reserves of resolve, mental agility and tolerance for abuse. To be successful in their missions, sixteenth-century Habsburg ambassadors had to learn very quickly how to discriminate between simple rudeness and truly dangerous threats, all the while working to keep discussions between the two governments alive.

Technical conditions of Habsburg–Ottoman exchanges did not further mutual understanding either. Arguments and proposals on both sides were often buried or badly distorted in hit-and-miss translations. Until they learned what language officials in Vienna wanted to read, ambassadors at the Porte simply delayed forwarding dispatches and other written materials. Whole passages of important memoranda sent from the Habsburg court to its ambassadors at the Ottoman court also lay unread, especially if they were composed in the complicated and fast-changing ciphers of the time. Contacts in Constantinople between Turkish and imperial translators and interpreters sometimes descended into shouting matches.

Rendering documents from the Porte into central and western European tongues was normally the job of linguistically versatile people who may or may not have been locally available: Turks, Armenians, Jews, even Greeks. If most Habsburg emissaries to the Ottoman Empire learned Turkish at all, it was the result of on-the-job training or pure accident. Malvezzi even struggled with French. With King Henry II of France courting an alliance with the Ottomans in the 1550s, the language was crucial to Habsburg diplomacy. Yet, forwarding a copy he had done of a letter in French sent to the sultan from Henry, the ambassador warned Ferdinand I that he did not understand a word of what he had written. His handiwork, Malvezzi confessed, was 'somewhat haphazard' (*alquanto confuse*).[44]

But it was religion more than any other factor that set up intractable obstacles for negotiators on both sides. Though both Ottoman and Habsburg spokesmen were often curious about one another's beliefs and why they held them, their basic positions, along with the territorial arrangements linked to them, were ascribed to Divine Will and not to be changed. Nor was there much private interfaith exchange. When Rüstem Pasha once asked Malvezzi how Christians could revere an unknown God, the ambassador replied that the pope had forbidden Christians to talk about such questions with Muslims.[45]

Religious considerations could hold off resolution of even minor territorial disputes. The fluid borders between Habsburg and Ottoman Hungary in the sixteenth century were frequently crossed by raiders from both camps in search of prisoners who could be ransomed lucratively. Both sides profited from this enterprise, but they also inflicted injuries on local populations. Compensating these grievances could take years when Ottoman officials such as Rüstem Pasha refused to allow Christians to be heard in Muslim courts. The Prophet, he said, forbade it. Religion also complicated negotiations over issues of high territorial sovereignty in places like Transylvania. According to Muslim law, mosques and their land could not be turned over to female rulers. Ferdinand I, therefore, was unlikely to gain control of the region if only because internal dynastic rules of the house of Austria never explicitly ruled women out of its line of succession.[46]

The experience of sixteenth-century Habsburg diplomats with the Porte therefore substantially reinforced the already negative views of Muslims among central Europeans. Close contact with Ottoman armies did much more. Ottoman troops appeared to many as frighteningly superior to Christian forces. They were far better disciplined that most Christian armies from central Europe in the sixteenth century. They were renowned for personal simplicity and self-control, particularly in matters of food and drink, and a fatalistic willingness to risk their lives in combat that doubled as courage. For example, attempting to take Esztergom in 1595, Turkish soldiers strapped gunpowder sacks to themselves and tried to bring them into the fortress. Caught in a crossfire from the imperial forces, the men blew up with their cargo.[47]

But the peoples of the Habsburg lands, especially when they were on the receiving end of Ottoman attack, found little in their enemy's forces to admire. The Perchtoldsdorf massacre was just one among countless incidents that hardwired the European imagination with dark and unflattering stereotypes of Turks and their creed. Some of this imagery, both verbal and pictorial, was wildly distorted. It was, however, confirmed by contemporary Ottoman publicists themselves. Panegyric upon panegyric had Süleyman the Magnificent slashing his way through the infidels on his way to world domination and the imposition of Islam that would follow. The Ottoman ruler co-opted this language himself. Writing to King Henry II of France in 1550, he declared that Allah and Muhammad lay behind a recent triumph in Persia and future victories as well.[48]

Süleyman usually minced as few words as did Rüstem Pasha in describing what he would do to those who stood in his way. Negotiation was not invited. On the march in April of 1566 to block Habsburg efforts to capture Transylvania, he asked the Hungarian nobility to co-operate. Should they refuse, they would be responsible for what would follow. Not one of their fortresses, their lands and possessions, their families and all connected to them, would escape a miserable end. So-called 'conquest letters', issued by sultans when they were planning major campaigns, could sound even more savage. One such specimen, referring to a campaign in Hungary, promised that Turkish soldiers would make peasants drink the blood of nobles whose veins had been opened for the purpose. Should the latter die of such treatment, those same peasants could dine on their remains. Men would be forced to consume the entrails of disembowelled women as well. So impressive was this imagery that Habsburg officials may have used it for their own forged broadsheets that they sold publicly to make their case for defending the dynasty and Christendom.[49]

Even sophisticated intellectuals of the Renaissance such as Ogier de Busbecq, humanist, naturalist and an ambassador for both Ferdinand I and his successor Maximilian II, found the appearance of some Ottoman officials uncommonly bestial. On his way to Constantinople as a Habsburg emissary, he encountered the Ottoman commander Haly Pasha in Hungary. A thick-bodied eunuch with a sallow complexion, he had, said Busbecq, 'a sour look, scowling eyes, broad shoulders that stuck up, from which his head extruded as from a valley. With two teeth like boars' tusks dominating his mouth [and] his voice, hoarse . . . he was the Fourth Fury.' Equipped with great battle drums to fire up their troops on the attack, the sultan's armies could be aurally daunting as well.[50]

Ottoman troops, especially when they were in garrisons, often entered quite peaceably into the local economies that supplied them. If they had to live from the land, they behaved no more ruthlessly than their Christian counterparts who routinely foraged for food and supplies. Nevertheless, Ottoman military strategy itself tormented villages and rural communities in a distinctively systematic way. Great offensives were not the heart of the sultans' strategy; throughout the sixteenth and seventeenth centuries, entire seasons of major campaigning often had only one conclusive battle. The standard overture to Ottoman conquest was skirmishing and looting to soften up future targets. Raiders often captured peasants and sold them into slavery to supplement their pay. Trade in human chattel was not unique to the Turks or Muslims. The entire Mediterranean basin abounded in such tragic exchanges, especially in the sixteenth century. Italian mercantile cities such as Venice relied upon forced labour to row their cargo vessels; as non-Christians, Muslims could be held in bondage without any qualms of European conscience.[51] That the Ottomans ruthlessly seized those same Europeans for similar maritime and domestic purposes was in itself unremarkable. For Süleyman the Magnificent, however, such raiding was sometimes more a form of punishment than a commercial requirement. Anticipating a Habsburg offensive in Transylvania, he once ordered his forces to plunder, pillage and enslave inhabitants of the Vojvodina, then part of Hungary.[52] Populations scattered along the long and ill-defined border between the two empires were repeatedly targeted.

The core of this particular terror were a kind of light cavalry, largely made up of minimally armed but very mobile ethnic Turks who did not always wait for the sultan's orders before initiating these strikes. Turks, in fact, were only one of the several ethnic groups that made their livings in Ottoman raiding parties. One especially vicious group, the *Martolosan*, were Christians under Muslim commanders; Crimean Tartars were another. Even when they were formally under Ottoman command, they had a vandalizing and territorial agenda all their own. Tartars accompanying a Turkish army to Hungary in 1598 had visions of conquering Vienna, even Prague for their *khan*. Indeed, they behaved so abominably that local Turkish officials in Hungary complained. Their utter disregard for orders frightened even the Janissaries.[53]

Undisciplined though they were, these bands were too useful tactically for the sultans to downgrade them before the beginning of the seventeenth century. Even after the introduction of heavy artillery shortened the time needed to breach Hungarian redoubts and occupy the adjacent country-side, hit-and-run manouevres had a place in Ottoman battle plans. Impromptu strikes in the countryside or against towns added an element of unpredictability to Ottoman military operations that could confuse an enemy badly. Towards the end of the sixteenth century, Tartars used these sideline thrusts very effectively to draw off Christian forces that were pro-tecting fortifications in Hungary. Provisions seized in raids behind battle lines in Habsburg-imperial camps ended up in Ottoman camp kettles. Christian lines of supply were sometimes also broken in these episodes. Skirmishes were also a way of testing the Habsburg main forces and gath-ering intelligence. The possibility of capturing some major Christian fig-ure lurking behind the front in his own territory was always there. Advisors talked the seventeenth-century Emperor Leopold i out of joining his forces, not because he and his armies would fail to hold their own against the sultan, but because he might fall prey to Tartars in a rearguard action.[54]

The ever-present possibility of being kidnapped by Ottoman forces or being taken prisoner of war sobered spirits at all levels of society in the Habsburg lands. Many people would never return; their lives were left to folksong and tale to memorialize. A wistful young Hungarian writing a fictitious letter to his sweetheart in his homeland put it this way:

If she asks for me in fear, I am in prison here;
In chains, you should report, at the Great Turk's court.[55]

Prisoner exchange was frequent, but some captives were more likely can-didates than others. The rich and well connected were often able to buy their freedom outright. Military, tactical and financial considerations on both sides governed decisions about who was to be released, and the net worth of individuals varied immensely. Long-term or permanent incar-ceration, death or enslavement were the four remaining possibilities. Servitude itself, the most common lot of prisoners of war, may have been the most benevolent outcome. Muslim law required humane treatment of slaves, and many masters treated their subject labour kindly. Those con-demned to the galleys, Turkish or Venetians who often bought these men from the Turks, were, of course, less fortunate.[56] Imprisonment could be horrific too. Should the sultan lose a battle in Hungary, he ordered Christians jailed in Constantinople to be beaten. It respected class not at all. Captured nobles were as subject to arbitrary execution and mistreat-ment as common folk. Stories of such sufferings were legion; one followed the plot line of many. Taken by the Turks in Hungary around Győr in 1683, Claudio Martinelli, the imperial riding master, would be freed three years later. Nevertheless, his experiences were a stern test of human endurance. He was at first, he said, enchained prone on a wagon along with others who had suffered the same fate. Early the next day, they were 'led like dogs' and lined up in a row, to be beaten and whipped. One Hungarian captain, crippled by gout, could barely walk. A quick beheading spared him further misery.[57]

The destructiveness of Ottoman marauding and campaigning in eastern Austria and Hungary left long memories. It also complicated the lives of contemporaries immeasurably. A Turkish pamphlet estimated that, by 1683, 108,109 people in Hungary had fallen captive to the Ottomans. Among them were 204 young women from noble houses and 56,093 children. The Ottoman-Tartar presence in Lower Austria alone during the that year was devastating. Close to 8 per cent of the population of the region were either killed or carried off. Countless families were torn apart because spouses were separated. The local Catholic Church withheld sanctioning remarriages until it was satisfied that one or the other partner was dead. Missing wives and husbands turned up years afterward. And the Turkish wars cost the Habsburg regime dearly. More than 50 per cent of the Vienna government's outlays between 1670 and 1717 went towards military costs, primarily against France and the Ottomans.[58]

Townspeople and small farmers who remained under Ottoman rule were free to sell their property under certain conditions, but the terms of their ownership were often vague. What they knew very well, particularly in border areas, was that the sultan expected steep taxes for his protection, especially when he was at war. Payments also went to the immediate Ottoman landlord and provincial authorities. Property, moreover, was only one source of revenue for him; valuables, persons, even ceremonies such as weddings were taxed as well. Such levies were all the more onerous on the indeterminate frontiers of Hungary. Here both Christian and Muslim sovereigns believed they had fiscal rights, leaving the ordinary folk of the area no choice but to pay something to both regimes.[59]

Though nobles may have had an easier time of it buying their way out of Turkish jails, they lost much when Ottoman forces seized and occupied their land holdings. The sultan recognized no privileged orders of society. All of his peoples were his subjects, regardless of differences of wealth or class.[60] In the parts of Hungary under Ottoman occupation, roughly one-fifth of the land confiscated from proprietors went to the sultan as Allah's lieutenant on earth. Four-fifths of the territory went to Ottoman administrative and military personnel, who very much depended on these rewards since they received no official salaries. The majority of the noble proprietors fled to the Habsburg part of the kingdom to long for the day when their estates were theirs once again. And when the Ottoman regime repopulated vacated lands in Hungary, they often did it with Serbs, another people the sultan had conquered, rather than ethnic Magyars.[61]

Habsburg armies also looked distressingly impotent in the face of such an opponent. The targets and destructive potential of individual raids were so hard to forecast that planning any defence or counterattack was virtually impossible. Ferdinand I did establish a kind of frontier guard on his southern perimeter in Hungary that would later prove very useful. In his own day and during the reigns of his immediate successors, Christian forces in Hungary were ill-paid and ill-supplied, and Habsburg forces were almost always stretched too far apart to protect themselves and the civilian populations around them.

Worse yet, for those who had to live in these conditions, the behaviour of the government in Vienna often provoked Turkish raiding without a shot being fired on the Christian side. The sultans' tribute agreements generally proscribed plundering and capturing civilian populations, but Vienna often withheld payment because of truce violations, thereby leaving its peoples open to retaliatory strikes from Ottoman booty-hunters. Truces allowed small-scale incursions to continue. Some agreements specified that raiding parties of fewer than 200 men did not count as a breach of faith, a provision that virtually guaranteed that inhabitants of the exposed outer reaches of the Habsburg lands could expect dangerous and uncertain lives. Each of the belligerents had his own idea of where the Austrian dynasty's Hungary ended and the sultan's dominion began, and held to it tenaciously.

Even though the house of Austria had not always kept up its end of tributary relations, there were enough stories in central Europe of Ottoman treachery at the bargaining table to offset these lapses. Giving Turks money, it was said, only invited their leaders to change their prices. A late-sixteenth-century Czech account tells of the abbot of Sisak, a cloister in Croatia. Trying to negotiate his own safety along with that of other Christians in the complex, he was allegedly flayed alive. The abbey and surrounding fields were levelled for good measure. A Hungarian writer put it this way in 1581: what the Turks say today was 'as of nothing tomorrow'. Constantinople was conquered through Ottoman lies and betrayal; the greatest part of Hungary was lost to the same tactics. The sultan promised much to people, but once under his control, his Christian subjects were at the mercy of their Muslim overlord.[62]

Nor was the sultan's protection of Christian subjects as comprehensive as promised. Ottoman rulers allowed Christian religious practice in the parts of Hungary under their control, but they were far less likely to permit repairing and building of Christian schools and churches. And a ruler's policies did not always determine what Christians thought ordinary Turks might do to them. In 1551, Malvezzi wrote that should Süleyman's health fail, the populace seemed poised to turn on poor Christians and Jews and plunder them. Ottoman treatment of clergy, particularly who were associated both with Rome and the Habsburgs as a dynasty, could be appallingly brutal. Torture and even execution were common punishments, especially for priests suspected of being spies, rebels or simply enemies.[63]

Actual experience with Ottoman raiders, conquerors and officials, relentlessly negative accounts of their behaviour, the pronouncements of the sultans about their intentions in Europe and the world – all these factors gave the house of Austria's subjects little incentive to look evenhandedly at Ottoman rulers, their culture, their armies and religion. Devout Christians in sixteenth- and seventeenth-century central Europe recognized the imperfections of their kings and princes. Among them was the Jesuit, Georg Scherer, a cathedral and court preacher in Vienna and one of the most prolific Catholic publicists of his day. Nevertheless, the mere finger of the Turk, he declared, was more oppressive than the flaws of all Christendom's monarchs combined. What Western regimes enforced through lashes, the Turks exacted with scorpions. Should the Turk say, '"throw yourself into the sea", you do it'. Beheading, he pointed out, was routine procedure. So were patricide, fratricide and parricide. Nor did Ottoman leaders and their peoples think twice about wiping out their own families and friends. Fathers killed their own sons, sons murdered their fathers and one another, cousins did the same. The very survival of the regime at the Porte, he concluded, depended upon such tactics.[64]

MOBILIZING MINDS AND SPIRITS

Such were the notions of Turks and Muslims that the Habsburg government and its Church drilled into their peoples to persuade them that protecting themselves, their ruling dynasty and Roman Catholicism from such an attacker was a single process. Out of Vienna and Rome's chancellories and pulpits, printing firms, ateliers and workshops came relentlessly negative images of the Turks and Islamic culture to bring the faithful at all levels of society to the battlefield when required. Though the message was fundamentally defensive, it was as militant as anything that Süleyman the Magnificent's apologists had to offer. As in all propaganda, the simpler and clearer the image, the more effective it was. Racism, as such, would be an invention of a later age, but what Habsburg subjects heard about their enemy came close to it in significant respects. Turks and Muslims were inimical intruders into the culture of Christendom where they had no place. Alleged behavioural differences with Europeans were so ingrained that they might as well have been part of their biological makeup.[65] The possibility that Muslim and Christian could actually take one another's interests into account, even in hostile settings like the Hungarian borders, was left unmentioned; it was the polarity between the two faiths that audiences had to understand.

For the literate of central Europe, the Habsburg regime had a few ready-made texts to do its work. An array of travel accounts and captive narratives was already locally available to confirm dislike and mistrust of the Ottomans and their religion. The diary of Stephan Gerlach, the chaplain-advisor to embassies, was both widely read and typical. Turks were untrustworthy – 'This is what [they] call peace', he sneered in 1574 after watching a parade in Constantinople of females and children captured in Hungary. His text abounds in horror stories, some that the author probably learned at second hand, but which were nevertheless worthy of recounting. There was the unfortunate young woman captured in Cyprus who became a wet-nurse at the Ottoman court. Made pregnant by a Turk, she gave birth, baptized the infant herself, then killed it in order to keep it from growing up as a Turk. No matter where the Turks appeared, said Gerlach, even if they were only seeking shelter, they destroyed everything in sight. They chopped down trees and vineyards, carried off women, children, cattle, the young and the old indiscriminately. Nor, he reported, did they hesitate to hack up one another. Turkish sexual customs were particular and consistent objects of his scorn. The sultan, he noted, could forbid men to have women, but allowed them to take their pleasure with boys. The Koran was utterly worthless, a manual of Black Magic for the faithful. Muslims reportedly wrote down verses from it on slips of paper, then hung around their necks to ward off illness or to save their lives.[66]

Prohibitions on alcohol and efforts to circumvent them highlighted Muslim hypocrisy and foolishness at its worst in Gerlach's eyes. Among the greatest inconveniences Europeans suffered in Constantinople was supplying themselves with wine. Turks themselves were forbidden to sell or consume it. Nevertheless, local Greeks and Jews ran inns that were licensed upon payment to the sultan of a fee. Here infidels could drink more or less at will. For all their Muslim sobriety, noted Gerlach, the Turkish administrative elite, along with scholars who had successfully incorporated discreet consumption of wine and spirits to their creed, enjoyed such beverages in public establishments and at home. In the Macedonian regions of the Ottoman holdings, Turkish officials, peasants and Greeks routinely downed a local eye-opener as the work day began.[67]

Just where captive narrative breaks off and travel report begins in the work of the sixteenth century Croatian-Hungarian humanist Bartholomew Georgievicz is hard to say. Nevertheless, his several reworkings of his experiences supported Gerlach's stern indictment of Islam and Turkish rule. Captured at the battle of Mohács, Georgievicz spent approximately twenty years in the sultan's realms where his knowledge of Greek and Latin made him more useful at the court than less well-trained prisoners of war. Failing many times to escape, he was reduced to ever lower degrees of servitude as he was sold and resold to masters throughout the Ottoman lands. In his eyes, the 'War of Hungary' had landed him and others in a captivity and bondage far sterner than the Babylonian variant of biblical times.[68]

Georgievicz's changing domiciles brought him into contact with other Christian captive-slaves whose experiences he also recounted. Their lives, in his telling, were at the same time brutal and heart-rending. Families were often separated. Even if parents went free, unransomed children, especially sons, were kept behind to serve the sultan's regime. Slaves generally, of course, were at the mercy of their masters. Horrific punishments like mutilation of their feet or iron neck clamps that were never removed awaited those who were caught fleeing.[69] Such examples persuaded Georgievicz that Christendom had to do battle against the infidels. They also confirmed his certainty that Europeans surpassed Turks in faith, intelligence and valour. Like many of his time, he recommended a crusade to convert Muslims to Christian belief; to help the cause along, he added an Arabic version of the Lord's Prayer to one of his works.

Multiple versions of Georgievicz's grim saga – when he finally did escape and wrote both to support himself and to enlighten Christians about the government and army of their enemy – spread among the reading public exactly the negative images of the Turks that the Habsburg regimes were eager to circulate. Indeed, his little books were among the great literary successes of the sixteenth century. First published in Latin, they were quickly translated into several European tongues and reprinted for a market that lasted for more than 100 years after his death in 1556. When they appeared in England in 1570, the regime there made use of them to rally Christians of all stripes against Ottoman expansion.[70]

Such imagery and the attitudes that went along with it found its way even into the work of genuinely subtle and learned men. The most versatile of all the travellers from the court in Vienna to the sultan's lands was Ogier de Busbecq. His *Epistles*, like Georgievicz's accounts, were originally written in Latin, but translated many times for readers all over Europe who wished to know more about the Ottoman court. Thoughtful in many respects and charmingly written, his observations nevertheless echo conventional European opinions about the Turks. Busbecq chuckled when Muslims succumbed to the lure of strong drink. Indeed, he pointed out they overindulged quite readily on the theory that they might as well enjoy themselves if only one sip sent them irrevocably off to perdition. He deplored their venality, criticized by many who visited the Ottoman court. He pointed to the battle of Mohács and its aftermath in Hungary as an example of Ottoman destructiveness from which all of Europe had something to learn.

Islam was clearly in his eyes an enemy of Christendom. He was as moved as any of his contemporaries as he witnessed Christian children being transported to slavery. Busbecq had also seen Muslims jeering at Christians publicly, leading some of the latter to abandon properties in Constantinople for refuge in outlying districts where they were less likely to be harassed. And he had experienced at first hand the summary brutality of the Turks often reported by others. On a mission to the sultan's court in 1555 to reassert Ferdinand I's claim to Transylvania, Busbecq was told that his entire embassy would be thrown into prison for such a message. To make their displeasure even plainer, he said, the Turks threatened to sever his ears and nose from his head and forward the pieces to the government in Vienna. All in all, he concluded, the Turks were a 'Scourge from God', who would not be readily defeated. One did, however, have to resist them. A productive start would be to enlist and train local youths for the task rather than to rely on mercenaries.[71]

Busbecq's views of the Ottoman establishment, along with similar remarks in other travel reports, were worked and reworked in the Habsburg lands for a century or more. A close contemporary, the Czech writer Daniel Adam of Veleslavín, echoed both the Netherlander's opinions about the dangers of the Turks and his stratagems for defeating them. A threat to the 'Slavonic nation', they 'take the country, murder the rich and noble people because of their wealth, kidnap the youth to distant lands, destroy what embellishes life and drive out crafts and arts.'[72]

Busbecq's letters also served as a principal source for the so-called Turkish play *Ibrahim Sultan*. The work of Daniel Casper Lohenstein, one of the leading dramatists of the Baroque era in central Europe, it was written for the wedding in 1673 of the Habsburg emperor Leopold I and his niece Archduchess Claudia Felicitas. The 58-page explanatory introduction to the play rehearsed the negative perceptions of Ottoman culture that his contemporaries were in the process of absorbing. The pageboys of the sultans, said Lohenstein, and the sultans themselves routinely engage in homosexual acts, as do women in the harem who see one another naked all the time. The Turks are a superstitious lot as well: the tip of Muhammad's green banner is sometimes said to hold a heart containing hairs of the prophet's beard. They are mortal enemies of Christendom: the angel Gabriel is supposed to have promised Muhammad that Islam would be victorious in the contest between the two faiths.

The frontispiece of a seventeenth-century edition of the work makes its overall message even plainer. Leopold and his bride soar heavenward on a white cloud; a black cloud bears a potbellied Turk down to perdition. The dedication also pointedly announces that the author is contrasting the moral virtues of the Habsburg imperial couple with the familicidal 'counter world' in Constantinople where the tyrannical and mentally unstable Ibrahim I ruled. 'Crazy Ibrahim' was a problematic figure, who allowed himself to be drawn into a protracted and costly war with Venice and was violently deposed in 1648 – this is a matter of historical record, although Lohenstein expanded upon known fact considerably. Once impotent, according to the playwright, the sultan had been transformed into a hormonal Vesuvius by a powerful elixir. The plot turns around Ibrahim's infatuation with Ambre, the fourteen-year-old daughter of his chief judge, or *mufti*, who is already engaged to one of the sultan's high provincial officials. A central moment of the story is a rape scene in which the wildly impassioned Ibrahim struggles to make the girl yield to him. How, he asks, could she refuse kisses from her emperor, whom no woman has ever denied? When she rejects him, asking that he kill her instead, he orders that Ambre be thrown naked into his bed. Despairing over her lost virginity, Ambre stabs herself to death. The play ends with Ibrahim's dethronement, a botched effort to kill himself in prison (by ramming his head into a wall), and the spirit of Ambre dragging him to damnation where four mutes strangle him. Lohenstein ends the work with heaven conferring its blessings on the marriage of Leopold and his bride, a pointed contrast to the sexual animalism at the sultan's court.[73]

A yet quicker way for the literate and semi-literate in the Habsburg lands to remind themselves of the Turk was to scan one of the countless broadsheets available by the beginning of the sixteenth century. These were often illustrated as well. Writers read one another's screeds and rushed to publish any horror story that might pass as new. By 1600, publishers in the kingdom of Bohemia were gathering these reports into small books. The grislier the Ottoman atrocity, the more eager audiences were to read about it. A story of two miners, captured and fed to lions by the Turks around 1583, was typical. The impact of such reports intensified when such stories were bundled into the same issue with accounts of exceptionally bad weather, earthquakes, bestial crimes and other sensational events. A paper in 1597 coupled a battle with Ottoman forces in Transylvania and a woman who had murdered her husband. In 1611, an account of Turks nailing a cat to a cross in Constantinople and forcing

Christians to worship it appeared with the tale of a woman in Hungary who gave birth to an infant with three arms, three hands and three heads. For who needed their accounts of alleged Muslim savagery fed to them more gently, these publications, often no more than one or two pages, occasionally offered songs about flowers and love. Natural signs from higher powers that predicted Ottoman military prospects were also newsworthy. Christian Europeans, who could be as 'superstitious' as the Muslims they scorned, eagerly read about comets, which were thought to forecast victories over the sultan.[74]

Publishing *Türkenschriften* was a pan-imperial enterprise; stories of Ottoman behaviour in victory or defeat circulated very quickly in the Habsburg lands. Hungary was first to hear of a Turkish setback near Kanisza in 1587, an act of God, it was said, in view of the numerically superior Turkish forces. A printer in Graz, however, quickly picked up the happy news for publication. Reports of another military success in Croatia in 1593 came out in Prague. Reports of one more victory in 1594 in Croatia and in other parts of Hungary were published in the Moravian town of Znojmo. Pastors who needed a prayer 'to be used in today's troubled times against the Turks' and all other associated perils could consult the model provided in 1605 by the provost of the cathedral of Prague, who worked very closely with the resident emperor Rudolph II in generating these materials.[75]

For those who did not read at all, or who had never faced the Turks in person, the regime made it possible to learn about them vicariously. Indeed, one had to be deaf, blind, or both to miss the message. The Habsburg domains abounded in commemorative pictures and tablets thanking the Christian God for saving his people from Ottoman captivity. Contemporary folksong both informed people about faraway clashes with the Turks and set the emotional tone in which the often disheartening news was received. Some reports were printed in strophes to be sung to familiar tunes such as hymns.[76]

The number of such works multiplied swiftly following the Hungarian defeat at Mohács in 1526, a catastrophe that intensified images of Turkish savagery in popular consciousness for the next two centuries. Even in Bohemia, comparatively removed from the front lines of Turkish attack, the estates grew uneasy about a possible invasion and its consequences.[77] Though some of the most popular songs focused on Christian heroism rather than Turkish bestiality, the lyrics said more than enough about alleged Ottoman atrocities to make audiences shudder: amputated arms and legs left with dying live torsos were vivid but typical examples. Several of the worst Turkish offences, such as the murder of children and pregnant women, transgressed human taboos or came very close to it. These songs and the information in them often passed on to pamphleteers and newsletter scribblers who uncritically spread them even further. But, overly sensational or fictitious though many of these pieces were, the note of desperation that echoes through some of them was genuine. Neither prince nor the Almighty seemed able to drive this scourge away. All felt threatened in some way. Indeed, the fear of the Turks was perhaps the most widely shared feeling of all among the diverse Habsburg peoples. German and Hungarian fully agreed with the Czech who described the Ottomans as 'cruel and raging pagans', 'God's whip', 'the Devil's instrument', who slaughtered 'poor Christians against the laws of all nations'. Abandoned by the Christians elsewhere in Europe, they seemed to be saying, central Europe could only be helped by God.[78]

Visual proof of Turkish cruelty was everywhere too. From the sixteenth to the eighteenth centuries church walls, pilgrimage sites, public squares and buildings, even private homes turned some of their space over to reminders of the Muslim enemy. Turkish pillaging of Austrian and Hungarian towns remained a subject for artists long after such raids took place, even in regions where Turkish rule was lighter in practice than in theory. Hungary, for example, was exempt from raising fixed numbers of boys to serve the sultan in the Janissary corps or at the court. Privileged or not, Hungarians depicted Turkish savagery again and again.[79]

Representing the Ottomans as Christianity's anti-heroes was a favourite contrivance to underscore the evils of the enemy and his religion. Muslim Turks were shown performing the biblical Massacre of the Innocents. A turbaned Pontius Pilate festooned a decorative balcony in Lorch in Upper Austria and elsewhere. Jesus's tormenters on his way to Calvary, along with the Pharisees and their henchmen, wore Turkish headdress and brandished scimitars. Turks were coupled with the trials of this world as well. Sometime after 1480, the cathedral church of Graz commissioned a picture of God with three lances named 'Hunger, Sword and Pestilence'. Beneath them were three specific plagues – locusts, the Plague and the Turks.[80] In 1703, twenty years after the latter had been driven from Vienna for good, a public column of the Holy Trinity commemorated the survival of the city from dual torments: Ottoman attack and an epidemic. The Ottomans also became the measure of other enemies that the house of Habsburg faced. An eighteenth-century devotional picture in St Pölten, today the capital of Lower Austria, celebrates a Habsburg victory over yet another enemy, the King of Prussia, and compares this achievement with the triumph of 1683.[81]

Hungarian and Bohemian towns and churches also have their share of such mementos. One among several figures of Muslims on the Charles Bridge in Prague shows despairing Christians and their Turkish captors.

Battle scenes between Christians and the Turks decorated Bohemian churches. Hungarians produced woodcuts and etchings that commemorated real and imaginary encounters with the sultan's armies. Often these images appeared as illustrations for written materials; they also became models for frescos and figures on commemorative plaques and reliefs. Artists covered the walls and ceilings of Hungarian noble palaces with their versions of the conflict with the Turk. In Carniola, today part of Slovenia, the aristocratic Auerspergs apparently did not want future generations to forget that Muslim Turks had threatened their ancestors' lives. Having killed a Turkish soldier who had broken into their residence, they had the body flayed, stuffed, costumed and hung at the spot he had entered. Soldiers in the Habsburg armies wore ornaments and amulets fashioned from the bones and skin of dead Turks.[82]

Taken together, all of these artifacts show the Habsburg peoples to have been living experiments in the use of repetition to impress cultural attitudes on to a society.[83] The press of the Habsburg lands, its artists, composers and literarily-inclined travellers – all were instrumental in depicting the Turks and Islam in ways that inspired resisting them to the death. They also made their livings from it, especially when the money came from patrons in the government and the Roman Catholic hierarchy. Indeed, the Church may have had even better reason than the house of Austria to keep the anti-Muslim spirit in central Europe energized. Should Christian conviction falter and Muslim rule come to the Habsburg lands, the Catholic faith, along with its educational and clerical apparatus, would be at the mercy of the new regime rather than a central part of it.

Happily for the Church of the Habsburg lands, officials found that they needed only one style of rhetoric to combat two deadly foes, and they used it relentlessly. The Ottoman–Habsburg conflict took place in an age of deep belief. All classes of society routinely worried about the fate of their souls, even unprompted by the thoughts of imminent death that Turkish invasion brought with it. The success of the Protestant Reformation hung in part upon a critique of Catholic notions of salvation that had already pressed the Church of Rome into coming up with a competitive argument against forsaking traditional Western Christianity. Apostates, it was said, might be putting their spiritual welfare at risk. Catholic polemicists in the sixteenth and seventeenth centuries were quick to declare that Ottoman rule would have the same effect. Their armies often destroyed churches and cloisters, the sites of rituals that guided one in the quest for a blessed afterlife.

The more vigorously the Church denounced Islam and the Turks, the more plausible the case for supporting the Catholic establishment in the Habsburg lands became, especially when the state had good reason to co-operate with it. Indeed, the specific roles of Church and state, at least in the thinking of some polemicists, were all but lost. As the agents of God, high authorities were charged to defend Him and therefore deserved the greatest respect, said the late-sixteenth-century bishop of Vienna, Johann Casper Neubeck. Helping to finance the effort had redemptive offsets. The 'Turk Tax' (*Türkensteuer*) was usually hard to collect, in part because it came on top of local imposts for military campaigns. In the eyes of both Church and state, however, it was good for the soul. So also were special collections in the Austrian lands and Hungary to finance prisoner exchanges and ransoms.

Enforcing Christian moral norms in the name of protecting the faith also gave both throne and altar a chance to discipline a public that often tired of such burdens. Facing a massive onslaught from Constantinople in June of 1683, Emperor Leopold 1 exhorted his subjects in Austria above and below the Enns to give up the blasphemy, cursing and drinking that distracted them from otherwise hard lives. Bells at dawn and then again at dusk called for prayer. To give parishioners enough time to spiritually gird themselves for the worst, hours of preaching and the numbers of masses were extended on Sundays and holidays. Beer, wine and ale cellars and neighbourhood inns could not open before nine in the morning; dancing was allowed only at weddings. Provincial authorities were to punish infractions sternly. For its part the regime in Vienna did its best to show its subjects that both religious and political concerns lay behind these taxes and private sacrifices. Triumphal parades often followed victories over both Ottoman 'Tyranny' and the 'Infidel'.[84]

The Turks gave the Catholic clergy not only a way of using the state to serve its institutional purposes, but also a handy forensic ploy for undermining popular confidence in Reformation evangelicalism. Luther's first reaction to the Ottoman threat was to call it a scourge sent by God to chastise Christian sinners, rapacious German princes among them. The latter, he said, were responsible for defending their lands and peoples, but holy wars led by Habsburg rulers and the papacy falsely conflated the respective missions of Church and state. Catholic preachers in Austria and Hungary, on the other hand, declared that God approved of anyone who worked to drive the Turks from central Europe. Following a victory in 1581 over the Turks at the Transylvanian fortress of Koloszvár (today Cluj in Romania), one celebrant pointedly observed that his countrymen, unlike the 'German' Luther, asked God to bless their successful commanders. At St Stephen's in Vienna, Johann von Neubeck was even more reassuring. God, he proclaimed, had not sent the Turks to punish Christians but was helping Europeans to resist such an enemy. The Ottomans had succeeded only because of the many divisions the Church had suffered; first the Greeks, then, as he put it, the followers of Luther.[85] The Wittenberg reformer's statements, declared Georg Scherer, unmasked him as a client of Süleyman the Magnificent, enough to make anyone think twice before yielding to evangelical wiles. The enemy was anyone who was not a Catholic. 'What do Jews, Turks, Heretics and the Devil think of the Cross?', Scherer asked in his 1620 catechism. 'Jews hate it, heathens deride it, the Turks destroy it, heretics despise it and the devil runs from it for the pain that it brings'.[86]

Thus, Catholic preaching in the Habsburg lands piled on incident to underscore the dangers Islam posed to Christian belief. If audiences doubted Ottoman hostility to Christianity, Neubeck reminded them of the fate of Constantinople, for many Europeans the emblematic Muslim intrusion upon Christian institutions. Hagia Sophia had once had 900 priests and other clerical personnel attached to it, along with a rich store of vestments and other liturgical artifacts. The cross of the basilica was ripped from the top of the building and thrown to the ground. Turks threw manure on pictures of the Virgin Mary and Christ and the cross. One did not, Neubeck pointed out, need to be Christian or a 'righteous Jew' to treat conquered peoples magnanimously. Cyrus of Persia, Philip of Macedonia and Alexander the Great all did so; Mehmet II's far more violent occupation, or so Neubeck implied, was therefore out of step with fellow unbelievers.[87]

Equally eloquent, Georg Scherer rehearsed the same theme and many of its points. Turks had appropriated the best churches for themselves, Hagia Sophia for one. Should their modest facilities burn down, Christians could not rebuild them. Christians had to worship like thieves in hiding because the sultans' 'Muhammadan Superstition' proscribed appropriate settings for their liturgy. Living with Turks invited intermarriages that put especially heavy pressure on Christian belief. Those among the latter who accepted circumcision drew great respect, but the uncircumcised were far less fortunate: they were far more likely to meet with public scorn under Turkish rule than were Jews in Christian society. And the future, Scherer declared, did not look good. The sultan seemed unbeatable; the Habsburg lands, unless their military fortunes improved, promised to be 'breakfast for the Turks'.[88]

Battle sites between Christian and Muslim became distinctively Christian shrines. Islam does not recognize a triune deity, but a mountain outside the village of Amstetten in Lower Austria that the Ottomans failed to take was dedicated to the Holy Trinity. Catholic faithful were urged to visit it as pilgrims. The Church also made sure that the Habsburg armies themselves were fully aware of the spiritual side of their mission. In 1591 the sultan began a war in Hungary that lasted until 1606, once again over the issue of Transylvania. Preaching to Habsburg archdukes and their military officers before a major confrontation in 1595, Scherer reminded the men of St John of Capistrano, the erstwhile knight who spurred armies on with cross in one hand and sword in the other. His impassioned sermons played a key role in the one of the great victories in Hungarian history, John Hunyadi's successful defence of Belgrade in 1456. Indeed, almost 300 year after Scherer had left the scene, Capistrano lived on in the minds of Austrian Catholics.[89]

According to Scherer, all troops should go into battle with a good conscience. Should they be struck down in combat, or so he implied, Christian warriors might not have time to repent. For him, the very act of giving in to the Turks was the moral equivalent of yielding to Satan. The Habsburg armies, he declared, were waging a war of a living Christian faith; those among them who fled from battle might face divine punishment. Not to resist the Ottoman aggressor endangered the souls of imperial troops and commanders as much as the sultans' military prowess, formidable though he allowed the latter was. Scherer thought that cowardly officers were especially disgraceful. 'Proud lions, bears, hawks, eagles and the like are on your shields and coats of arms. How is it that you turn into little doves or sparrows?' Even the material interests of Christians would suffer. Nobles, he declared, actually had far more to lose by giving up to the Ottomans than commoners; the Turks did not recognize the titles that European aristocrats held. The enemy actually preferred townsmen, artisans, peasants and clergy to the landed highborn. Exemplars of pride and arrogance, the sultans and their armies richly deserved to be subdued. Both the Bible and secular histories demonstrate that God ultimately punished such pretensions. Sometimes, Scherer pointed out, He actually made use of female agents – the case of Judith and Holofernes, for example.[90]

Occasional Christian victories over the Turks in sixteenth-century central Europe did not soften the Church's hostile indictments of the Turks and their faith. Even after the death of Süleyman the Magnificent in 1566 when the Ottoman regime was preoccupied with the Persians, homilies in Vienna reminded audiences that their coreligionists still suffered under Muslim rule. Celebrating a defeat of Ottoman forces in Croatia during July of 1593, Neubeck declared that the widespread notion that the Turks do not force conversion was false. Christians, he said, endured far more mistreatment in Ottoman domains than did Muslims. Drawing upon Bartholomew Georgievicz, he pointed out that Christians were often unable to pay the tribute that bought their safety. Offering himself for circumcision eased a man's disadvantages considerably, but at the price of his religious identification. Christians on the borders sometimes received better treatment, but only when it suited Ottoman advantage. The Turks also forced their captured child slaves to accept what a newsletter correspondent of the day called 'the Muhammadan faith'. The biblical command to love one's neighbour, Neubeck said, did not apply to Turks and Muslims. They were 'godless' enemies of the Christian faith, Muhammad a 'satanic prophet', whose single passion was strangling and murdering Christians. War with such people was a holy cause, necessary in the sense that St Augustine had once explained, and the only way that true peace could prevail.[91]

Few though they were, Habsburg defeats of Ottoman forces gave the Church a splendid opportunity to sponsor common and often heartfelt celebrations that strengthened ties between parishioners and clergy. The week after Easter in 1598, Habsburg troops retook the fortress of Győr (Germ.: Raab) from the Turks. Close to the borders of the Austrian lands, it was regarded as the key to preserving the integrity of Christian central Europe generally. Preaching triumphantly from biblical and historical examples, Georg Scherer declared that 'ours, ours is not the glory Lord, but yours'. God, he said, enabled his Christian peoples to penetrate a fortress thought to be impenetrable. It was God who helped attackers to fashion a key that gave them access to the redoubt, just as the risen Jesus penetrated the door of a room where his disciples had gathered. God also sent the wind that made it difficult for the Turks who were inside the fortress to hear the dogs barking as Christian army began penetrating a side wall of the structure.[92]

The entire population of Vienna echoed his mood. News of the event came about eight in the evening; clergy and laity ran through the streets telling their neighbours and urging them to join a procession the following day to St Stephen's Cathedral in the centre of the city. A celebration with gunfire would take place, but not until the service had ended. The palpable spontaneity of religious feeling amazed even the devout Scherer. The next morning found virtually everyone outdoors; knotted together in groups on public squares, markets and streets, people alternately talked about the event and offered prayers of thanks. Drums sounded, trumpets and trombones blew, organs and other instruments joined in, and church bells rang. So many in the throng piled into the cathedral – several thousand it was said – that the building could not hold them all. The overflow heard the mass and the choral music that accompanied it in the cathedral courtyard. After that, the whole city celebrated. Scherer had never seen the inhabitants of Vienna so excited and happy. Indeed, he himself had already anticipated not only the spiritual but the material benefits of Christian success against the Ottomans. Three years before, he had predicted that a major military victory was a step to a peace that would secure 'your vineyard, your meadows and fields, [your] barns and haystacks', rising real estate values, more sources of credit, and opportunities for employment and education. It was, as far as he was concerned, the Christian peace that Jesus and the apostles would recognize.[93]

The war itself ended in 1606 in more or less a stalemate, the result of bad judgement and overestimation of strength on both sides. Ottoman finances and military infrastructure had never altogether recovered from Süleyman the Magnificent's Persian campaigns in the sixteenth century. Nor were his successors conscientious and effective rulers. Indeed, Emperor Rudolph II, Ferdinand I's grandson, had actually expected to gain something from going to war with the 'hereditary enemy'. He even tried to bring other east European polities in a coalition – Poland and Transylvania, along with Moldavia and Wallachia, today regions of Romania. The imperial army, however was shamefully undisciplined. It provoked more hatred than support in Hungary, and Rudolph never could exploit the advances that his troops finally made.

Nevertheless, the military and political exchanges of Ottoman and Habsburg governments changed subtly but significantly. The peace of Zsitva-Torok, which ended the conflict in 1606, had the elements of a working compromise, with each side open to serious negotiation. The Habsburg regime persuaded Constantinople to accept a one-time payout of 200,000 ducats in exchange for cancelling the humiliating annual tribute. The sultan recognized the emperor and his successors as his equal. The agreement also bound both signatories and their successors for twenty years.

AN ENEMY IN RETREAT

Hungary would be reunified and the Ottoman empire driven safely to the European south-east only at the end of the seventeenth century. Emperor Rudolph II had no legitimate offspring, and the family members who took his place were embroiled in religious and territorial warfare with virtually every polity on the continent throughout much of the seventeenth century. The sultans were equally distracted by troubles in their own lands – the erosion of feudal landholding arrangements upon which local administration of the Ottoman empire depended, fiscal shortfalls, overall economic stagnation, mediocre political and military leadership and social unrest throughout the empire, especially in its Christian outposts and among non-Turkish Muslims in Asia Minor. Boys once torn from their families and trained for the civil service had matured into a cohort of young males ready to put pressure on their Turkish overlords, however modestly.

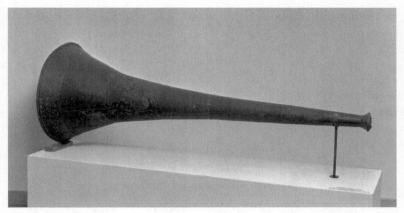

Megaphone used from the Tower of St Stephen's Cathedral, Vienna, to announce movement of nearby Ottoman armies.

With neither Constantinople nor Vienna positioned to resume their contest immediately, propaganda in the Habsburg lands ebbed markedly. No one, however, thought that they had seen the last of the sultans' armies, nor did anyone, even the highly educated, substantially revise the picture of Turkish behaviour embedded in contemporary culture. The pre-eminent Czech thinker and writer of the seventeenth century, Jan Amos Comenius, admired Muslim religious fervour, the spotless upkeep of their mosques and their commitment to charity. Once they left their places of worship, however, all of these virtues were forgotten, replaced, according to Comenius, by brutal disregard for human life and violent sectarian quarrelling. Georg Scherer had never thought that Ottoman aggression was at an end. Overjoyed though he had been by the recapture of Győr and by the popular religious fervour that it sparked, he was convinced that the Turks would 'neither slumber nor sleep'. They had suffered a great insult in 1606 and would eventually avenge themselves. Nor had their armies totally collapsed. The sultan's armies had fought very bravely if desperately at Győr, wounding 700 men in the Christian force and cutting or blowing to pieces 200 more.[94]

Scherer, therefore, saw no reason to jettison his programme of Christian moral armament against prospective Muslim challenge. The introduction to his catechism of 1620, while basically a polemic against the Lutheran reform, weighed in heavily on the alleged falsities of the 'scandalous Muhammad the Prophet' and the Jews.[95] By 1660, his forebodings were confirmed. Energized by an ambitious Grand Vizier, Muhammad Kupruli, the sultan began serious military campaigning in central and south-eastern Europe.

Ottoman manners had not changed in the slightest, at least as Christians had come to read them. In August of 1663, the Grand Vizier laid siege to Ujvár (Germ.: Neuhäusl, Slov.: Nové Zámky), today on the border between Hungary and Slovakia. His terms sent to Count Adam Forgács, the commander of the fortress, sounded as arrogant as ever:

> Through the mercy of God and the miracle of our prophet, who is the Sun of the World, blessed and famous, I, first councillor and general of the mighty, invincible, richly famous Turkish emperor, the king of all kings on this earth [do] make known to you Adam Forgács, highest among the Hungarian nobility, and general of the fortress of Neuhäusl, that upon the command of my merciful ruler, we have arrived by the will of God with countless forces to take Neuhäusl. Thus, by the command of our merciful Lord and the prophet, should you surrender the fortress, everyone, great and humble will be peacefully released, with all their possessions; should you not surrender the fortress, we will conquer it with blood and arms, and none of you, great or small, regardless of rank, will be spared, and in accordance with the will of the illustrious will and mercy of God, to whom no one is equal, will be killed – for this is what the law requires. Should the Hungarians experience and come to know with what good will our powerful, invincible Turkish Emperor bears toward this city, they would surrender themselves, their progeny, even God to him.

Forgács replied somewhat more respectfully, but unconditionally. Declaring that divine law proscribed the wasting of countless poor people whose 'innocent blood cries out to Heaven', he promised that any Turks who got through the walls of the fortress would find men ready to meet them.[96] However brave they may have been, the Hungarians were no match for the sultan's forces. The siege that the latter laid around the fortress showed off Ottoman military tactics to best advantage. Their entrenchments were well thought out and constructed, their ordnance needs fully met. Though the Habsburgs had upgraded the complex considerably, it fell to the Turks, though with less savage consequences than either side had promised the other: Forgács surrendered in September, and his men were allowed to leave freely.[97]

The Hungarians, however, kept up the rhetorical fire as the enemy continued to move at will around the increasingly wasted kingdom. The poet and military commander, Count Miklós Zrínyi, who had lost a substantial part of his family lands to the Ottomans, turned what for him was a personal enemy into the most loathsome creature he could imagine, calling them 'madly enraged people who had emerged from Caspian caves', whose destructiveness reminded him of the effects of a rampaging wild boar on a well-tended vineyard. The Habsburg government was no less pointed in showing what it hoped to bestow upon the sultan and his forces. On a mission to Vienna in 1667 the Turkish governor of Buda was treated to an exhibition of *Türkenrennen* complete with mounted Europeans striking, spearing and firing at turbaned heads.[98]

By the summer of 1683, more was required of the house of Austria's armies than mock combat. A terrified Vienna watched an Ottoman offensive edge towards it from the south and south-west. The Turks, in truth, were less prepared for war than they had been in Süleyman the Magnificent's day, but that is a conclusion of more recent scholars and not of the city's seventeenth-century defenders.[99] And the sultan's forces certainly appeared to mean harm to Christian belief. Earlier in the spring Ottoman raiders had chosen Easter Sunday to invade a church near Nové Zámky and carried off a number of worshippers.[100]

The Roman Catholic establishment in Habsburg central Europe had been for some time in verbal overdrive, haranguing audiences with some of the most envenomed images of the Turks ever heard. Though not the only clergyman committed to these efforts, the popular Viennese homilist Abraham a Sancta Clara was arguably the most gifted. A Swabian – his real name was Ulrich Megerlin (Megerle) – he was born in 1644, the eighth of nine children of a serf from around Meßkirch. Schooled locally, then at Jesuit and Benedictine universities and seminaries in Ingolstadt and Salzburg, he became a Decalced (Barefooted) Augustinian and started to call himself Abraham a Sancta Clara. He arrived in Vienna in 1662, where his powerful sermons eventually brought him to the attention of Emperor Leopold I, who made him court preacher in 1677. A professor of theology at the University of Graz as well, Abraham died in the Vienna St Loretto cloister, near the imperial *Hofburg*, in 1709.[101]

High station in no way compromised Abraham's power to sway both commoner and courtier. People from all walks of society revelled in his white-hot invectives against the Turks, even when he also took the opportunity to remind Christians of their own moral failings. War against the sultan was religious war: Christian versus Islam and its infidel followers. The full title of one of Abraham's most powerful homilies was entitled 'Arise, Arise, O Christians to Fight Against Muhammadan Error and [the] Turkish Hereditary Enemy'.

What is the Turk? You Christians, don't answer before you are informed! He is a replica of the antichrist; he is a piece of a tyrant; he is an insatiable tiger; he is the damned assailant on the world; his

Anonymous portrait of Abraham a Sancta Clara, late seventeenth century, oil on wood.

cruelty is unlimited; he steals crowns without conscience; he is a murderous falcon, a dissatisfied, condemned bag of a wretch; he is oriental dragon poison; he is the hound of hell unchained; he is an epicurean piece of excrement; he is a tyrannic monster.[102]

Abraham's resume of Muhammad's background and sexual preferences was shamelessly fictitious, culled from sources that had been discredited long before he used them. The father of 'the accursed snake's spawn' – Muhammad that is – was a wizard who protected witches; the mother was Jewish. The Prophet's lusts were those of a 'smelly goat', he had 40 wives and even more concubines in his thrall, 'like some beast'. As for Islam:

> The Muslims believe that their Muhammad on Judgment Day will be changed into a ram, and they themselves all into fleas. After they have settled down in his soft wool, he will take them to heaven, where they will change back into their former appearance . . . Muhammad is a devil's cook of Old and New Testaments, Arianism and Nestorianism, [he] cut off some slices from various religions and roasted them in a pan so that the Turks lick their finger for that mixed dish.[103]

With such outrageous but evocative caricatures as moral inspiration, Vienna's defenders and residents dug in to await the arrival of its enemy. At the beginning of July, observers on the outskirts of the city reported skies lit up with fire – some thought it was as far to the east as Győr; others thought it might be much nearer in Lower Austria. Ruthless Tartars were allegedly in the neighbourhood too – as many as 20,000 of them. Scores of people streamed to the countryside for safety, among them the imperial family and a very pregnant empress. The armed peasants whom they encountered along the way were not at all sympathetic; they scorned the panicky crowd for abandoning perfectly usable property.

The Christian defenders put fire to use as well. To get a better advance view of what was coming, defenders burned down part of the Vienna Woods, an outcropping of the Alps that was not far from the city. The tactic worked, but those who climbed the tower of St Stephen's Cathedral on 12 July hardly liked what they saw: two nearby country villages of Fischamend and Schwechat in flames. Adding to the fears of the remaining residents was the discovery that disguised Turks had slipped into their midst. Two were captured and executed as brutally as the Ottomans supposedly slaughtered Christians. One was drawn and quartered, the other 'violated', in ways a witness, Count Ferdinand Bonaventura von Harrach, the imperial stable master, left to the reader's imagination. By 20 July, the sultan's army had settled down for a siege outside of the city walls that had been considerably enlarged since Vienna's initial face-to-face confrontation with the Turks in 1529. One report said that after the Turks had vanquished the city, they would move north to Prague, normally beyond their line of march in past offensives.[104]

For the soldiers whom the emperor had left to protect his capital, the situation looked truly desperate. Enemy forays in settlements around the city were as savage as ever. Perchtoldsdorf was perhaps the most unfortunate example, but the Turks gave other towns equally good reason to fear for their survival. The burghers of Wiener Neustadt were promised that if they yielded gifts in cash and kind, not even 'their chickens would suffer harm'. Should they refuse, however, they would be 'crushed (*überziehen*) with a total might that is unsupportable on earth, and . . . destroyed down to the ground'.[105]

Ultimately, however, both personal and tactical flaws in the Ottoman camp spared Vienna from Muslim conquest once again. Hoping to cover as much ground as they could in a short time, the Turks had left behind much of the heavy cannon needed to bombard the city effectively. The morale of the army weakened along the way when the Grand Vizier, Kara Mustafa, failed to distribute special favours and bounty as generously as his troops had expected.[106] The timorous emperor Leopold, on the other hand, had managed at the last minute to cobble together a large European coalition in aid of his beleaguered capital. The Turks mistakenly read the hasty recruitment and organization of the Christian forces as a sign of weakness. In fact, both in terms of military cunning and weaponry, the latter were far superior to their Ottoman foe. In September 1683, the Turkish armies were as far to the West on the European continent as they would ever be. The following day they began a humiliating and precipitous retreat.

Ottoman military weakness certainly helped to make possible this victory and those that followed. Troop quality had generally declined as armies grew larger to meet European challengers. Though their materiel did not lag too far behind technological advances in the West since the fifteenth century, the logistical infrastructure that delivered it was altogether inadequate. Manufacturing sites were generally very far from battle lines, leaving expeditions like the 1683 campaign under-equipped. The Habsburgs had also steadily re-fortified key locations in Hungary when they could. And the imperial armies had also learned how to countermine the enemy's camp, long an Ottoman speciality.[107]

Nevertheless, the defeat of the Turks before Vienna also owed much to raw human endurance and local commitment. Emperor Ferdinand I had said 150 years earlier that all his subjects, regardless of social station, were needed to rid themselves of the Turks; sixteenth-century preachers had

A print showing the front and back of the Celebratory Cross placed on the tower of St Stephen's Cathedral, Vienna, in 1684.

echoed his call. Contemporary observers saw just such efforts. The bravery of the citizenry, students and hand-workers in the city under the command of Count Rüdiger von Starhemberg, an Austrian high aristocrat, was the key to the scattering of 'the crazed and frightful Turkish Bloodhound'.[108] And while God and Emperor Leopold, 'our anointed Joshua', had spearheaded the triumph, more prosaic mortals had played significant roles too. One well-to-do burgher, Johann van Ghelen, a printer and the university of Vienna's publisher, a job that carried with it faculty status, was not on the walls defending the city. He did, however, underwrite the costs of four men in a university company that did fight actively. He also was quick to celebrate publicly the flight of the Turks, delivering an oration on the apparent victory on 12 September, the day the retreat began. He then went on the road to Italy where he gave similar addresses and continued to publish on the theme too. In 1701, Leopold I cited him for his singular services.[109]

Neither the house of Habsburg nor the Roman Catholic hierarchy wanted their faithful subjects to forget that high authority had been the driving force in the great victory. Religious motifs had abounded on the battlefield; soldiers for the emperor who came out of Moldavia and Wallachia, identified themselves with flags bearing crosses and images of the Virgin. The retrospective literature that began pouring out almost as soon as the Turks had taken flight reemphasized these notions. A typical short narrative of the victory in 1683 underscored the doctrinal convictions at stake. The struggle to save Vienna had pitted Christian against Turk; with the help of God, the Christians won. God's very Law had been respected in the process. The Turks had retreated on a Sunday, but the troops, on pain of capital punishment, had to wait until the next day to plunder the enemy's camp.

> Rush, brave Germans, rush to repair the empire's tear,
> Support, as you can support, use your heroic fist,
> To cut generously into the real enemy of Christians.
> For this the great God will help you.
> Be mindful of only strangling and blood baths,
> And do not spare those who did these things.
> Good fortune to the war of the Lord! Victory will never be his!
> [the Turk's]
> Long live Leopold: His hero's sword will triumph.[110]

Nor did Leopold's military successes end in 1683. Pushed hard by Pope Innocent XI, who backed up his exhortations with substantial funding, the emperor tried his luck with a coalition again. The self-baptized Holy League of the Habsburg lands, Poland and Venice, came together in the Upper Austrian city of Linz in 1684. They quickly launched what has been called the fourteenth Crusade to rid central Europe of the Turks and Islam. Several German princes from the empire along with a few Italian rulers soon joined the effort. The pan-European army liberated Hungary in short order. Esztergom, the seat of the kingdom's episcopal primate, returned to Christian hands in August of 1685.[111] Buda, under Ottoman occupation for nearly 150 years, was freed from Muslim control in 1686. Its elderly pasha, the 99th man to serve in the office, died with his sword in his hand in defence of a redoubt with far greater military and symbolic meaning to the Porte than Vienna. The celebrations were as exultant as they had been in the Austrian lands three years earlier, and not only in Buda itself. All of Europe rejoiced in songs, verse and picture.[112] A year later, the Turks were defeated at Mohács, the scene of their great Hungarian triumph in 1526.

On 11 September 1697, the emperor's forces delivered a catastrophic blow to the badly outmanouevred Ottoman army at Zenta in southern Hungary. Around 25,000 of the enemy were lost, including the Grand Vizier. Many simply drowned in the nearby Danube. The European coalition's losses, on the other hand, were exceedingly light. Their success had symbolic weight too; Christian troops came away with such emblems of high Ottoman authority as a venerated seal with which the Vizier travelled on campaigns and seven horsetails that designated rank and power. The victorious Habsburg general was Eugene of Savoy, himself the embodiment of the multinational force that he led. A princely Italian younger son and soldier of fortune, who first tried to make his way at the court of Louis XIV, he had joined Leopold's service and risen very quickly. A treaty signed at Karlowitz (Srb.: Karlovac) in 1699 formalized the complete withdrawal of the Turks from Hungary, with the exception of the Banat of Temesvár (Rom.: Timisoar). Both sides agreed to respect the integrity of the border between them for the next 25 years; the Ottomans also promised to put Tartar raiding to an end. The Catholic Church benefitted from the treaty as well, having won a guarantee of the sultan's protection of Roman Catholics, their priests and their pilgrims not only from Muslims but from Ottoman subjects who followed the Orthodox or Armenian rites. For its part, the regime in Constantinople had reason to treat its non-Muslim populations with more consideration, regardless of any agreements with their Habsburg opponents. Centuries of warfare had played havoc with agricultural production in the sultans' European holdings. One way of encouraging Christians to remain on the land and to cultivate it was to ease the conditions under which they could restore or build their churches.[113]

Nor was this the last of Eugene's triumphs over central and east-central Europe's once-invincible foes. Pushing Habsburg forces into areas where the dynasty had no territorial claims, he wrested Belgrade from the Turks in 1717. Casualties among the Ottoman forces were once again enormous – estimates run between 9,000 and 13,000. The treaty of Passarowitz (Srb.: Pozarvac) in 1718 returned the Banat of Temesvár to the kingdom of Hungary; for a short time, Habsburg forces occupied Belgrade as well. Vast quantities of ordnance, petty trophies and this time nine horsetails fell into the Christian army's hands; much of this booty soon resurfaced in the private salons of Vienna and Munich. Christian superiority to Islam had been confirmed: unbelieving Muslims had received a well-deserved drubbing. A contemporary orator in Vienna compared them to the Indians of the New World who had taken flight after their first glance at Columbus's forces.[114]

The regime in Vienna and the Church it defended celebrated victory after victory lavishly and publicly. The court of Emperor Leopold I staged and restaged versions of a struggle that would become the foundational epic of the Habsburg monarchy. The monarch himself was no mere bystander. A talented and serious amateur composer, he wrote part of the music for a court opera, *The Paladin in Rome* (*Il Palladio in Roma*) two years after the Turks had abandoned the siege of his capital. The libretto extolled his dynasty as the 'shield of Christendom', always understood in Vienna to be the Church of Rome. The audience was reminded again and

Bernard Vogel, *Prince Eugene of Savoy, c.* 1735, print after an oil by Johannes Kupetzky.

again that the Turks were defeated. To underscore the point, 120 elephants and camels, beasts conventionally associated with Turks, along with slaves, captives in chains and references to the destruction of Carthage were trotted out for all present to see and think about.

Through vanquishing the Ottoman armies the Habsburg monarch, at least in the minds of his supporters and clients, was now the master of both Orient and Occident. Many of the emperor's nobles, as relieved as he and often far richer, commissioned even more grandiose renderings of the conquest of the Turks. Vienna and Prague virtually exploded in triumphal buildings. Though a measure of self-interested political calculation lay behind these projects – the greater Bohemian nobles were eager to win favour at court by shows of enthusiasm for their rulers' victories – the visual results clearly declared that the Turkish menace had largely passed, thanks to the efforts of Church and state. The victory of God-willed order and peace through such co-operation at the battle of Zenta dominates the brilliant decoration of walls and ceiling of Wenzel Adalbert Count Sternberg's 'Imperial Ballroom' in the Troja Palace near Prague.[115]

The imperial house, the nobles of their lands, even some people of the middling sort with money for good causes, also had a more practical way of spreading the triumphant Christian message. Many sponsored the conversion of captured Turks to Christianity. The prototype of this ceremony had been in place long before 1683 and its aftermath; in 1624 Emperor Ferdinand II and his wife stood in the Church of St Augustine, directly adjacent to the Vienna *Hofburg*, as godparents to a Turk who had himself baptized Ignatius Ferdinandus in deference to the emperor and the first head of the Jesuit order, which many Habsburg rulers had supported generously. Leopold I and the empress appeared as patrons at the baptism in 1696 of a leader of the Turkish resistance in the fortress of Buda. Following the lead of the court once again, noblemen, high military officials and the great clergy, even the monied bourgeoisie sought out Muslims for Christian candidacy. Some of the latter even came straight from the battlefield. Social calculation played a role in these moves, to be sure, but so did religious conviction. Standing as a godparent was in itself a meritorious act that might smooth one's way to heaven; that one's protégé had abandoned Islam, Christendom's arch-enemy, might make the gesture doubly effective. Yet it was easy for Europeans, whose environment was awash in anti-Muslim fervour, to congratulate themselves for saving souls from what they knew to be a false religion. Children were simply 'removed from the Turkish superstition', according to Anna Apollonia, Countess Sinzendorf, who brought a little girl into the Catholic faith. These affairs were even more compelling when one-time Muslims renounced their original faith vehemently and voluntarily, as did a young Turk in 1629. Having fled a diplomatic mission sent by the sultan to Vienna, he asked to be baptized. As a sign of his sincerity, he, like many other apostates from his faith, tore his turban from his head, threw it to the floor and cursed the 'sect of Muhammad'. The last of these ceremonies in the Church took place only in 1746, with members of the imperial family sponsoring fourteen former Muslims.[116]

Christian antipathy to the Turks and Islam certainly endured, even as it became ever clearer that the sultan's power to expand had passed its zenith. The extent of time during which the dynasty's subjects had been exposed to the threat of Islamic expansion through the Ottoman sultans and the countless horrific encounters, actual or vicarious, of Turkish untrustworthiness and cruelty virtually guaranteed that negative visions of the Muslim enemy would remain for centuries to come. As late as 1817, the date that the forces of Islam captured Constantinople was memorialized in the Habsburg empire.[117]

The Ottoman empire may have been far less dangerous in 1683 than scholars today will allow, but the Porte itself had no inkling of the string of defeats it was about to suffer. The powerful forces of fear and self-interest had organized the defence of Vienna and the liberation of Hungary, creating in the process a vivid and unforgettable assortment of stereotypes with which Habsburg rulers and their subjects described and evaluated their foe. The title of a pamphlet describing the battle of Zenta makes clear that it was a victory over Muslims.[118] Even as the reconquest of Hungary was well underway, a captured Turk dispatched from the Ottoman camp to round up aid for his army was beheaded on the order

The decorated interior of the Grand Hall of the Troja Palace, Prague, 1690s.

of Count Stephen Zichy, a Hungarian commander. The man's severed skull was then strung up in front of the fortress Zichy was defending. Apparently thinking that he had not made his point, Zichy then had an inscription added to the display: 'You, Aga, sent me out to get help for the imperilled (*bedrängt*) fortress. Because there is no such thing on this earth, I have gone to the underworld to seek it out.'[119]

It was hard, however, not to look somewhat differently at the dreaded and demonized arch-enemy of central Europe once the stubborn, if rarely brilliant, leadership of the house of Habsburg had driven him from central Europe. Public triumphalism over the Ottomans' withdrawal from Vienna in 1683 and Habsburg follow-up victories subsided remarkably soon. Contemporary authors paid relatively little attention to the theme; where it did crop up was largely in popular songs and stories, and then only for a brief time A change in attitude about Islam and the Ottomans was apparent in some quarters of the Habsburg empire as soon as Vienna and Buda were safe. The contemporary diary of Johann Sutter (Johannis Sutor), who served the Habsburg army either as a military physician or some sort of clerk, revealed the swiftness with which people can change their perceptions of an opponent once he is decisively beaten. The brutal invader who beheaded people routinely had become for Sutter the 'very polite' Turkish commanders who travelled to Vienna in 1688 to surrender the fortified city of Székesfehérvár to Leopold. The emperor had once expressed his preference for soldiers who were partially humiliated rather than in total despair. The Habsburg, along with his officers of state, was as good as his word. The visitors, along with Sutter, were invited to a meal with the imperial translator, Marc-Antonio Mammucea de la Forre, an invitation that the Turks happily took. Once at the table, they did not shrink from some festive alcohol – they had a large glass of a good Vienna wine with which they toasted the emperor who had accepted the provisions of the turnover. Shortly after the signing of the peace of Karlowitz, Abraham a Sancta Clara had a plaque placed in front of his cloister. Rather than celebrate one more defeat of the Turks, the man who had turned anti-Muslim invective into an art form showed a Christian soldier and his Muslim-Turkish counterpart having coffee together.[120] Did this improbable icon reflect sincere Christian charity or the magnanimity of the much-relieved victor? Or was it a sign that the hostile stereotyping of the Turks in the Habsburg lands had been constructed within certain limitations all along? For those who wish at all times to communicate productively with dangerous, persistent and abidingly distasteful enemies, the background of Vienna's sudden change of heart, its causes and consequences merit examination.

East-central Europe *circa* 1721.

CHAPTER 2

Conciliation, Coffee and Comedy

AN ENEMY QUALIFIED AND ACCOMMODATED

Strident and persuasive though it was, anti-Muslim rhetoric in the Habsburg lands had been delivered in a cultural and political context well stocked with modifiers. Christian doctrine advised humility, even in the face of the great victory at Vienna in 1683. Rather than celebrate the Turkish defeat too ostentatiously, John Sobieski forwarded the great battle flag that he captured to Pope Innocent XI. What was achieved at the Habsburg capital, according to the Polish king, was the result of a collective Christian effort rather than his leadership alone. The faithful, at least if they chose to follow his model, were well advised to celebrate modestly and with due deference to the Almighty. After Eugene of Savoy's capture of Belgrade in 1717, Franz Peikhardt, a Vienna Jesuit whose forte was elaborate ceremonial oratory, predicted that the house of Austria would rule the known world. He insisted, however, that it was not the ingenuity of the dynasty's commanders, but Divine grace and the Virgin Mary's intercession that thwarted a Turkish scheme to block access to the fortress with a chain stretched across the Sava river. There was always the possibility that if the Almighty had once brought the Turks to Europe to punish the continent for its sins, He might do so again. One anxious, if anonymous, writer observed in 1684 that unflattering and untrue comments about the Ottoman forces were in themselves enough to provoke the sultan's retaliation.[1]

In fact, neither Church nor state had ever made anti-Turkish propaganda an end in itself. Officially-sponsored denunciations of Islam were political manouevres, not critical theology. Welcome though Turkish conversions were, the house of Austria's overriding duty was to save the regime and the faith from Ottoman aggression, not to wipe out Muslims collectively, or their faith. Christians in Central Europe may have worried about their chances for salvation should they not be able to worship properly, but the government in Vienna was as concerned about the territorial consequences of Ottoman imperialism as about being locked out of heaven.[2] 'We wage war in order to bring peace', said George Scherer, giving St Augustine as his source. Once people and property were secure, armed conflict would cease.[3]

Dynasty and the Church of Rome, and not chastised sultans, were therefore the centre of attention in illustrations of Turkish defeats or theatrical performances with Turkish elements. The dominant theme of Eugene of Savoy's victory at Zenta, as depicted in Prague's Troja Palace, is the service of pious rulers from the house of Austria to their faith. A contemporary tapestry now on display in the Hungarian National Museum shows Emperor Charles VI (King Charles III to Hungarians) proceeding into Budapest amid a throng of adoring classical figures. Only a couple of horsetails scattered at the bottom and a discreetly cowering Turk at the back of the carriage remind viewers that overwhelming victories and abject defeats lay behind the story.[4] A Jesuit school drama performed during festivities that accompanied the distribution of academic prizes in 1652 dwelled not on the Muslim enemy but on the contribution of the imperial dynasty to the defence of Christendom. Less literate audiences received the same message in more prosaic settings. Joseph Anton Stranitzky, who produced, acted and directed wildly popular plays at Vienna's Theatre at the Carinthian Gate put on only one production with a Turkish theme, but it ended with a stirring 'May the august house of Austria live and flourish'. Singular though it was in Stranitzky's total *oeuvre*, the piece spawned many imitations through the eighteenth century.[5]

The many political and military problems of the house of Austria also encouraged it to relativize the Ottoman threat. A late-seventeenth-century copper etching by Christian Dittmas does its best to render the droopy-jawed Leopold I as Constantine and Hercules in triumph over 'Turks, heretics, rebels, etc. etc.' Heretics were the Protestants, largely re-catholicized or driven altogether from most of the Habsburg empire by the beginning of the eighteenth century. Even in the grim year of 1683, a Hungarian pamphlet in rhymed couplets called for people to beseech the help of God, but not when they were praying in lands where the Reformation had taken hold. Only if Sweden, Denmark, England or Holland were to decide of their own free will to help would their assistance be welcomed.[6] Rebels were members of the Hungarian nobility who had resisted the imposition of dynastic absolutism in their kingdom.

As for 'etc.', there were any number of candidates. Jews, for example, had been seen heckling Christian public rituals. They were known to make fun of Christians who prayed at the sound of the Turkish church bells. In 1575 they allegedly mocked the Christ figure during a Good Friday procession in Vienna. Once suspecting a tavern owner of watering his wares, Jews were supposed to have called upon Christendom's saviour to turn water into wine once again.[7] Indeed, Leopold expelled Jews from the city altogether in 1669–70 for their supposed connections with the wars and outbreaks of plague that were afflicting his realms. Equating the 'Turk' with apostate Christian or the often despised Jews was no certainly no compliment to Islam and the Ottomans. Nevertheless, thinking in these terms reduced the specificity of the Turks as enemies of the Church and the dynasty fighting for it.

Catholic Christendom itself produced enemies to plague Leopold throughout his reign. His contemporary, Louis xiv, the allegedly 'Most Christian' king of France, commanded as much attention in Vienna as the Turks, if not more. Beginning in the sixteenth century, French monarchs had occasionally joined with the sultans to thwart the hegemony of the house of Habsburg. An imperial ambassador warned Leopold i in 1677 that Louis xiv aspired to the role of Europe's universal monarch, even if he had to call upon the sultan for help. The emperor's war council advised in 1682 that yielding a province or so in Hungary was preferable to losing the west to the Sun King, who surely had his eyes on both Germany and the Habsburg dynastic lands in it. No one would miss a province or two in Hungary, but many would lament the removal of the Habsburgs from Germany and their Austrian family patrimony. The lands in the east, argued the memo, could be recovered at some time or other. Indeed, the Turks were more likely to keep negotiated agreements than the king of France. Seventeenth-century broadsheets coming out of Habsburg governments and the Church declared that the morals of the Ottoman army differed only in degree from their Christian, meaning French, counterparts.[8]

The diverse peoples of the Habsburg empire probably disliked one another almost as much as they did their Ottoman formal enemy. They were quick to spot territorial inequities in support of the war effort. The kingdom of Bohemia contributed taxes, substantial contingents of troops and materiel along with tactical thinking to the anti-Ottoman resistance. Their artillery and manouevres, especially their practice of circling wagons against onrushing forces, helped John Hunyadi against the Turks at Belgrade in 1456. Yet they mistrusted their fellow Christian Hungarians profoundly. It took anti-Ottoman propaganda in Bohemia three-quarters of a century after the disaster of Mohács to generate the emotional intensity that such appeals provoked in other Habsburg lands. Even at the end of the eighteenth century, the Czech historian František Pelcl blamed much of the disaster at Mohács on an overly-proud Hungarian nobility who wanted sole credit for whatever victories over the Turks there were.

If only these men had accepted foreign, meaning Bohemian, aid, the out-come might have been different. The quality of Hungarian leadership left something to be desired as well. Pelcl was particularly scornful of Archbishop Pál Tomori, who, in clerical garb and with sword in hand, took a contingent into battle.[9] At the outset of the Thirty Years War in 1618, the Bohemian estates had briefly hoped to combine forces with the Porte against a then common enemy, the Habsburgs.[10]

Christian society in central Europe, especially in Hungary, also had always had reason to believe that Turkish behaviour was less oppressive and destructive than Vienna's official propaganda had it. Hungarians suc-cessfully resisted the taxes and compulsory military duty that Ottoman rule exacted elsewhere. On the way to Constantinople in 1591, the ambas-sadorial page Wenceslaus of Mitrowitz noted that the cathedral of Esztergom still held a marble statue of the Annunciation scene when he stopped there. Pictures of saints were to be found in at least one private chapel as well. Upon arriving at the Porte, he reported that while some-one had shot an arrow into the mosaic of the Trinity in the dome of Hagia Sophia, the image was still there.[11] His agonizing imprisonment turned decisively for the better when his guard reminded the higher Ottoman authorities that the Koran proscribed brutal treatment of embassies. Lohenstein's portrayal of Sultan Ibrahim's sexual animality also presented Islam's self-correcting side. It is Islamic law and Koranic checks upon forced marriage and mistreatment of parents that persuade Ibrahim's opponents to abort his reign. It is the divan, the highest law court of the Ottoman empire, that declares that anyone who flouts its judgements is neither 'a sultan or a Muslim'. None other than the violated Ambre urges her conflicted but loving father to flee for safety with her to the holy city of Medina. In general, Lohenstein seems to have been quite certain that virtue deserved God's respect, even when the exemplars were Muslims. According to the Janissaries at the end of the play, the Almighty also blesses the killing of rapists. Indeed, for all of Lohenstein's extolling of the house of Habsburg and its Christian mission, his God is a quite neutral presence in the drama, more the dispenser of Providence than an irascible Old Testament patriarch.[12]

Long before 1683, central Europeans and Muslim Turks could meet in Constantinople on friendly terms. Not every ambassador from Vienna expected to waste away in one of the sultan's dungeons. Preparing to leave for the Porte in 1644, Count Hermann Czernin von und zu Chudenitz advised that outfits being tailored for himself and his party should not be cut too small. While they could always be taken in, not much could be done to enlarge them. Christians also had a few unofficial spokesmen at the Porte. These were Hungarians, often Protestants, who had become Muslims and joined the sultans' courts as translators. Conversant with both faiths, they sometimes interceded on behalf of their erstwhile countrymen who had been captured by the Turks. They also encouraged cultural exchanges by bringing translated Christian literature to Constantinople as well as Muslim books to Hungary.

By the beginning of the seventeenth century, Christian travellers to Buda were cordially received at the local Turkish baths. Room was made for them in the bubbling waters; knowledgeable patrons even advised the visitors against sitting near the drains that carried off impurities. Contacts between embassies from Vienna and Ottoman officials in Constantinople could be relaxed even when the two powers were on the brink of war. As early as the 1590s, the Habsburg resident at the Porte, Frederick von Kregwitz, held open houses for Turkish administrators almost every evening. Young Mitrowitz and Ottoman equestrians raced horses together; the Bohemian page and some of his colleagues also took up Turkish archery for amusement. Regardless of their private feelings about the Turks, ambassadors and their staffs soon took up shopping in Constantinople for trinkets, manuscripts, fabrics and other artifacts. Von Kregwitz bought six horses and two sets of equipment for each of the animals.

Not every Turkish prison was like the dreaded Black Tower where Mitrowitz was eventually incarcerated. Christians held in the Csonka Tower of Buda were free to stroll in adjacent gardens, have clergy to minister to their spiritual needs and keep servants if they could afford them. In the process of trying to proselytize each other, a considerable exchange of religious views took place between Catholics and Protestants and occasionally with the Turks, apparently without rancour. Turkish public manners distressed some, but one could put up with them. An Ottoman shipboard crew that escorted a Habsburg embassy down the Danube from Vienna on the way to Constantinople in 1584 was too boisterous for European tastes. Nevertheless, they reportedly calmed down quickly when necessary.[13]

For its part, the Habsburg government had never thought that it could manage the Turkish challenge through polemics and invincible Catholicism alone. Officials in Vienna were always on the lookout for solid information about the sultan and his court. In 1559, Ferdinand I quickly ordered a translation of a history of the Ottoman Empire that his treasury director, Hieronymous Beck, had brought back from Constantinople. Commentary from Habsburg field commanders on the Ottoman armies' potential, mobilization and tactics was noticeably cool, dispassionate, even complimentary when the facts called for it.[14]

Diplomatic dispatches were equally crucial sources of information for their governments. Their usefulness was directly proportionate to the regularity with which they came, the objectivity of the writer and the detail they contained. After the middle of the sixteenth century, the imperial envoys to Constantinople paid noticeably more attention to the concrete minutiae of their activities and contacts with Ottoman officials. They also had to analyse what they saw objectively. Antal Verancsics, sent on an important mission by Ferdinand I to Constantinople in 1552, understood this perfectly. To him, Süleyman the Magnificent's problems with the Persians were comparable to Ferdinand's difficulties in Transylvania, for all that the two rulers were of different religions. The more educated the men whom Ferdinand I sent to Constantinople, the more likely they were to be consistently factual reporters and especially predisposed to cool thinking. Ogier de Busbecq stood out for his intellectual versatility. The archaeological remains in the Ottoman lands fascinated him, as did their languages, topography, natural world and culture. However, he was not the only emissary from Vienna who could stand back from cultural and emotional prejudgements in assessing policy in Constantinople. Even the excitable Malvezzi could be very sober when discussing the relationship of Grand Vizier Rüstem Pasha and Süleyman within the Ottoman court and the possibilities of new offensives in central Europe.[15]

By the middle of the seventeenth century, religion was just one of several factors considered by a Habsburg ambassador, Johann Rudolph Schmidt, in weighing up what inclined the sultan and his Grand Vizier Mustafa Pasha towards war or peace. Important for him were the Ottoman ruler's deeply flawed character and the crude ways of his chief official. Schmidt laid out the ruler's physical and psychological flaws with no mention of his faith at all. The Albanian Grand Vizier was the real power behind the throne, even though, Schmidt reported, he was ill-tempered, impatient, gluttonous and illiterate. Nevertheless, the ambassador also pointed to the official's energy, dedication and quick-wittedness. That he governed such a vast empire said something for the man's talents too. In estimating the probability of a renewed Ottoman offensive in central Europe, Schmidt weighed up reasons for and against such a move without editorial comment.[16]

At the same time as they profited from sensationalist *Türkenschriften*, publishers were also making it possible to see the Turks in a more positive light. The most critical commentaries on captivity, enslavement and distasteful Ottoman political customs are artlessly interspersed with remarks about more admirable features of Turkish behaviour and institutions. In part these writers were only observing contemporary canons of style and intellectual purpose: Renaissance writers presented empirical data in discrete segments rather than consecutive arguments. Information was to be classified and compared rather than linked analytically in support of some synthetic hypothesis. That the evidence and opinions offered in one part of a book might be altogether inconsistent with another does not seem to have troubled them. Nevertheless, it was possible for readers to learn something about the Ottomans from them.

Those same central Europeans who scorned the slavery, the subordination of women, the tyranny and unnatural sexual practices in the sultan's empire were just as likely to report on similarities and differences between Ottoman society and their own with clinical calm. One of the earliest and most enduringly popular central European accounts of Turkish imprisonment, servitude and liberation, George of Hungary's *Treatise on the customs, state and worthlessness of the Turks* (*Tractates de moribus, condictionibus et nequicia Turcorum*), written in the last third of the fifteenth century, made plain that the author thought the Turks to be the embodiment of evil, bent on destroying human freedom and leading Christians astray at the expense of their souls. Sultanic rule was clearly a tyranny. The tract explicitly sees no possibility for the co-existence of Christians and Muslims. Yet, the latter culture had admirable features too: its army was disciplined; its leaders good; and all were characterized by personal cleanliness and simplicity. The much-tortured Bartholomew Georgievics detested the Turks as the enemy of Christendom and of human liberty as viscerally as did his contemporaries. Nevertheless, he preferred some Muslim practices to Christian ones, the absence of ecclesiastical benefices, for example. He even spotted some practices in which 'Musulmans' – that is, Turks – and Europeans were substantively identical. They cultivated many of the same grains and animals and they both kept vineyards, albeit for different purposes. Christians made wines, the Turks a kind of unfermented extract that they took for its allegedly medicinal effect.[17] Half a century later, the young Mitrowitz described impeccably maintained mosques in the same painstaking detail that marks his account of his filth-strewn prison sites.[18]

Many of Ogier de Busbecq's analogies between Christian and Muslim came down solidly on the side of the latter. Rejecting the view of contemporary Europeans that aristocracies kept kings from becoming despots, he argued that the Ottoman regime worked more efficiently because it did not have to factor noble privilege into its policy decisions. Even as he was advising the government in Vienna on how to defeat the sultan's forces decisively, Busbecq not only approved of some features of his enemy's culture, but even relativized practices that Christendom all but universally deplored. Though no champion of slavery, he had seen that its application in the Ottoman lands could be humane. Freedom, he argued, meant little to people who did not have the means to enjoy it. All human beings, he said, required some authority over them.[19] On some distinctly un-Christian behaviour, he passed no judgement at all. Lesbianism, he said tersely, was common among women in Constantinople because they viewed each other so frequently in public baths.[20]

Reliable armies, declared Busbecq, were obedient armies, something Turkish leaders seemed able to command at will. Even the much-feared Janissaries had, as Busbecq saw them, a distinctively positive side. Their garrisons in Hungary shielded local Jews and Christians from the popular 'rabble'. They lived more like monks than like soldiers; their chief vice was a craving for 'cash' which they happily took at any time. Other Turkish practices were sensible enough to be adopted much more easily; soaking bread in sour milk to quench one's thirst in hot weather was one. Like other Western observers, Busbecq was much taken with Turkish personal cleanliness and general sobriety. Unlike practices in Christian military camps, Ottoman forces buried their excrement in pits that they opened up before defecating. Nor did they drink or gamble. And though he found the architecture in Ottoman cities mediocre, Busbecq approvingly noted that major functionaries at the Ottoman court and other officials throughout the empire retained their essential simplicity even when dressed at their most splendid.[21]

Most important of all, the Ottoman realms both provoked his deep curiosity about the natural world and his resolve to describe it as accurately and as fully as he could. Religious passions had little place in such endeavours, and Busbecq was not alone in keeping them out of many of his more scientific passages. His near contemporary in France, Pierre Belon, who travelled throughout the Middle East between 1546 and 1549, had similar academic interests and wrote a strikingly reportorial account of the Turks, quite free of theological considerations.[22] Busbecq, moreover, was not alone among Habsburg diplomatic personnel to turn postings to Constantinople into learning experiences and to draw positive conclusions from them. On a mission to Constantinople as early as 1577, Václav of Budov, an important Czech advisor to Emperor Rudolph II on Ottoman affairs, looked forward to informing himself more fully about the East. The government he found there had positive and negative features. A tyranny it certainly was, but the system had a certain amount of toleration built into it, something altogether praiseworthy for a Protestant such as himself. Though little more than animals in the eyes of his sovereign's armies, Ottoman subjects were not burdened with the disadvantages of hereditary property that Budov knew in the West.[23]

A shift from inflammatory stereotyping to factual reporting, even in the sixteenth century when the Turks were at their most dangerous, often occurred in authentically popular settings as well. Folk songs and homilies in the Habsburg lands contained bits of solid information that told parishioners about the structure of the Ottoman government, its legal and military systems and the personnel that administered these institutions. Embedded in the text of Abraham of Sancta Clara's malicious account of the prophet Muhammad's parentage and sexual inclinations was some straightforward biographical data. There was, in short, a growing curiosity throughout early modern Europe about the world beyond the conventional frontiers of the continent both to the east and the west, and the Ottoman lands were a prime target of interest.[24]

A few took the opportunity to learn about the Turks and to take away something from their culture, even in the most extreme settings. Hungary's greatest poet of the Renaissance, Bálint Balassa, fought in several major battles against Ottoman forces. Nevertheless, he not only knew Turkish, but even worked Turkish motifs and musical elements into his verse and prose. Bartholomew Georgievicz put his linguistic training and gifts to good use during his captivity and enslavement by adding Greek, Turkish, Arabic and Hebrew to languages he already knew well – Latin, Croatian and Hungarian.[25] Fearful and deprived, Frederick Seidel, apothecary to an imperial mission from Emperor Rudolph II, broke the monotony of his confinement by learning to read and write Turkish. His colleagues joined him, among them Wenceslaus Wratislaw of Mitrowitz, who hoped some day that these skills would make him a better servant of his state. Indeed, he became so fluent that Ottoman officials insisted that he become a Muslim, at which point the young page abandoned his studies altogether. He and his colleagues also put to use another skill that they had learned from the Turks, knitting gloves, hats, purses and stockings which they either sold or bartered for food, water and cooking utensils. Under a form of house arrest in Constantinople, Busbecq assembled a menagerie of local animals that turned his house, he said, into Noah's Ark. The six female camels he kept were allegedly to carry his baggage when he was released; his real purpose, however, was to breed them in the West for their enormous utility. Some of the aesthetic features of Ottoman culture worked their way into central European literature very early as well, regardless of ongoing hostilities between Christian and Muslim.[26]

Through these accounts and the legion of others like them, Europeans in the sixteenth and seventeenth century therefore were better acquainted with practical details of Islamic culture in its Ottoman form than any medieval crusader ever had been, at least before they got to the Middle East itself.[27] Such books were at first directed to merchants, governments and their armies, rather than, as in Georgievicz's case, to wider audiences.[28] By the end of the seventeenth century, however, Vienna's publishers knew that they had a sizeable market for the literature of Turkish exotica and for fact-based descriptions of life in the Ottoman empire, especially when these came with the promise of novelty. A history of the Ottoman empire translated from Turkish into Italian and published in 1649 offered information 'never before available'. It also carried the imprimatur of both the '*superiori*', presumably the clergy and Emperor Ferdinand III, who apparently asked that the work be available in a Western language. Though it ended in a short prayer, a 1662 travelogue contains descriptions of the 'Turkish faith', commercial practice and culture along with a glossary of Arabic and Turkish terms. Yet another history of the Ottoman empire supplemented a celebration of a Polish victory over the Turks published in 1674.[29] Folkways generally, eating customs prominent among them, interested readers regardless of the horrific material that they had to wade through to find these passages.[30]

This juxtaposition of information and unbridled polemic was not unique to authors in central and east-central Europe. British theologians and writers, members of a polity that was unable to reduce the Turks to semi-colonial status in the early modern era, demonized the Ottomans, their subjects and their religion, as routinely as did Christians up and down the Danube. Turks were harsh, despotic, untrustworthy, given to lust and unable to discipline themselves. On the other hand, official documents, the stories of prisoners and especially the reports of commercial agents to the British Isles discussed those same people in perceptibly calmer tones. Indeed, racial, sexual, even ethical pejoratives are comparatively rare in these accounts.[31] Moderation perhaps came more easily to those who did not share borders with an enemy. But even in the Habsburg lands, decades before the Turks were brought decisively to heel, it was possible to find people whose views about the Muslim Turk were more thoughtful and complex than the dominant themes of official propaganda.

Even the Church and the state that had tirelessly promoted anti-Turkish polemic and censored religious views contributed modestly to these developments. Catholic polemicists were willing to acknowledge good qualities in the enemy, at least when he was defeated. Following the imperial victory at Győr in 1598, Georg Scherer had commented on the brave and manly defence of the fortress that the Turks had made for more than four or five hours. He described at some length and approvingly the resistance of the commanding Pasha of the fortress, who refused to become a captive and fought with a sabre in one hand and a second weapon in the other until two shots brought him down.[32]

Thus, long before the Turks were rolled back from central Europe, something akin to 'the feelings of but' that the American philosopher William James detected in the make-up of the unprejudiced person, was emerging.[33] Turks and Muslims were 'bad', but not all the time and in some ways no worse than other identifiable enemies. Even as it generated vast amounts of incendiary propaganda, the Habsburg government knew that it had to look at its foes through other than confessional lenses. Not every subject of the Habsburgs shared this attitude, to be sure, but enough of them were crucially positioned to persuade others to judge the Turks and Islam in a more nuanced way should conditions be favourable. Once the Turkish threat truly subsided, it was easier to spread the habit of looking at the Ottoman empire more coolly, even generously. But it had not required military victory in and of itself to set such thinking in motion.

THE INTERPLAY OF POWER AND OPENNESS

History is an ongoing interplay of change and continuity. None of these attitudinal shifts took place in the Habsburg lands without cultural and diplomatic bumps. Memories of a once-belligerent relationship between Christian and Muslim endured. Church rhetoric continued to exploit a rich assortment of traditional pejoratives for the 'hereditary enemy'. A revised edition of Georg Scherer's catechism published in 1752 continued to conflate Ottoman brutality and destructiveness with Reformation evangelicalism. Protestants who mutilated crucifixes were behaving like 'real Turks' (*gutt* [sic] *Türkisch*). Well into the eighteenth century, victories that Habsburg forces rang up against the Turks were celebrated as defeats of unbelievers, and not simply of an enemy army.[34]

Some self-declared victims of Ottoman abuse in central Europe put such recollections to quite practical use. In Hungary, the battle of Mohács and the death of the inept King Louis II had become a staple of the national consciousness by the seventeenth century. The kingdom's aristocracy, particularly in its lower ranks, had specific material motives for keeping records of alleged Turkish savagery at hand. Royal letters granting titles and the property attached to them had often vanished in the melee of Ottoman raids. To reclaim their status, noble families had to demonstrate the loyalty and valour at arms of their ancestors. The Turkish wars were likely to have created such evidence; Hungarian country gentlemen stretched their research and rhetorical skills to the utmost in digging up stories of their progenitors' battlefield performances and describing them. The more gruesome the narrative, the more effective the case, or so the strategy seemed to be. In 1733, one elderly lord testified at an ancestry hearing for one of his peers that the Turks had impaled the head of the claimant's uncle on a castle wall.[35]

Perceived cultural differences continued to keep Christian and Muslim far apart, especially in settings where they had to co-operate directly. Efforts at the end of the seventeenth century to resolve Ottoman claims against the injury to Muslim merchants in central Hungary done by a Hungarian force on the look-out for bandits, were a farrago of accusations and counter-accusations. All of these were further embittered by different government procedures in dealing with these matters. To the great annoyance of the Turks, who were prepared to settle issues on the spot, Habsburg negotiators had to refer everything back to their home government, which took decisions at a glacial pace. Disputes about missing possessions, along with religious antagonisms that dogged a great Ottoman embassy and its imperial escorts on the way to Vienna in 1719, only reinforced familiar stereotypes of Turks as duplicitous and Christians as their potential victims. When a couple of Muslims in the Turkish party declared that they wanted to become Christians, the imperial officer whose help they enlisted, a Marquis de Botta, felt obligated to help. He then, however, had to pacify the Turks who were doubly furious because the converts-to-be were their servants.[36]

Traditional suspicions extended to higher levels of the Habsburg government as well. The sultan's officials were not yet trusted as negotiating partners. As late as 1738, in working out a complicated treaty to end Emperor Charles VI's war in the Balkans, the Habsburg councillor Johann Christoph Bartenstein said that both the Russian Tsarina Anna and Charles should be on the lookout for 'customary' Turkish bad faith and artifices. Two weeks later, reading another comment of Bartenstein's about Turkish cunning and slipperiness, Charles put his concurring 'hoc-placet' in the margin of the memorandum.[37]

The environment of Constantinople left much to be desired for Christians too. The city could be dangerous for non-Muslims who were often assaulted because they had looked at things that they were not supposed to see – the Holy Flag of the Prophet in a parade, for example. Only during the eighteenth century did the Ottomans stop imprisoning residents routinely should hostilities break out between the sultan and an ambassador's government. Not the least of a Western emissary's trials was the fear of the bubonic plague that was endemic in the Turkish lands. The Habsburg regime would actually establish and enforce a border quarantine to keep the disease from spreading westward.[38]

Nevertheless, for all of these deeply difficult moments, both on the battlefield and in formal diplomatic exchanges, the atmospherics of Austro-Turkish relations relaxed markedly and quickly in the final two decades of the seventeenth century. The Turks evacuated the fortress and one-time bishopric of Hungary at Esztergom in 1683 with a minimum of bloodshed – even though, as contemporaries noted, it was the first time in 80 years that imperial troops had taken a city with a mosque in it. The terms of surrender were also notably humane. The victors took over all the ordnance, but they granted the defeated Ottomans two days to vacate the redoubt. They could also remove their clothes and furniture, their coffee and their *serbet*, a syrupy concoction of water, fruit juice and sugar that delighted Westerners who tasted it in Constantinople. The enemy property left behind could be stored in guarded houses. The Christian commander even offered his Turkish counterpart space on a ship for himself and his belongings and to move his remaining troops to a friendlier location. Though fleeing adults and children created some disorder, the imperial coalition forces policed Christian and Turk alike who tried to turn the confusion to their advantage. Several Poles were shot when they tried to plunder or to capture Turkish women. The behaviour of officers on both sides at the exchange of prisoners was positively courtly.

Six years after humiliating their enemy before Vienna, the Habsburg government treated a major embassy from the Porte with exquisite sensitivity. Since the visitors did not eat pork, its by-products or beef, none was served to them at common meals that in themselves were a novelty. Coffee and *serbet* were available for Muslim guests, though some among them took a glass of wine. Negotiations that kept the mission in the Habsburg capital for several months led some local hosts to complain that the erstwhile enemy was enjoying himself too much to leave. A certain amount of goodwill characterized the 1699 treaty of Karlowitz, humiliating to the Ottomans though it generally was. Provision was made for a generous exchange of war prisoners on humanitarian grounds alone. In 1700, another embassy led by Grand Vizier Ibrahim Pasha himself was entertained with a significantly amended version of *Türckenrennen*. The targeted heads were not turbaned Muslims, but figures from the pantheon of classical mythology.[39] Minor controversies, such as the grievances of the Muslim merchants in 1709, were eventually settled by back-channel negotiations between the two sides, that enabled both parties to work without ritual posturing.[40]

All of the courtesies imaginable could not disguise the hollowing-out of the Ottoman regime and the ascendancy of the house of Austria. Following the treaty of Karlowitz, the Porte launched a brief offensive again, but got nowhere. Sensing that it might lose Belgrade, one of its remaining strongholds in Europe, the sultan's government did its abject best to cut losses. A manifesto from Constantinople to all of Europe in 1716 spoke for itself. God's will, it declared, was at work; what was done was done. The Ottomans begged the emperor, Eugene of Savoy, and all of European Christendom, to forgive their breach of the Karlowitz provisions. This time, said the Turks, they were beaten and they knew it. Peace was to be their legacy to their own children; they would never take arms against a Europe that in any case had enough money and arms at

Anonymous print of 'Abdu Bassa', Abdur Rahman, the last Ottoman Pasha of Buda, end of the seventeenth century.

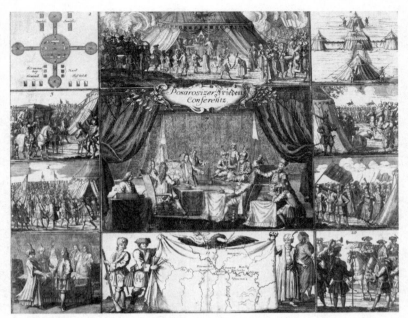

Print showing the negotiators at the Peace of Passarowitz, 1718.

its disposal to wipe out the Ottoman state forever. Eugene, nevertheless, pressed on; he took Belgrade in 1717. Imperial representatives summarily handed Ottoman officials their options and gave them an hour to think them over.[41] The Turks regained the Serbian redoubt in the eighteenth century, but without driving further westwards.

Sultans had good reason to expect that their remaining territorial holdings in the Balkans would continue to attract Christian predators. With their military strength visibly weakened, they had no choice but to follow the model of Emperor Ferdinand I that was to preserve their realm through careful negotiation. Even here, however, diplomats from the Porte were not at first working with their European counterparts on a level playing field. As comparatively late participants in the international state system, Ottoman spokesmen were not immediately privy to its social conventions. Isolated from the informal gatherings of resident ambassadors, who talked frequently among themselves about the military infrastructure of their home governments, Ottoman officials were deprived of potentially crucial information. Linguistic barriers also persisted, as did many of the more exasperating customs that annoyed foreigners at the Ottoman court. Most European monarchs could and did make themselves accessible, even unofficially. Resident envoys in

Constantinople encountered the sultan in person only twice: once at the outset of their mission, again when they introduced their successors. Until 1719, Western envoys had to pull caftans over everyday wear when they met with Ottoman rulers to avoid insulting them by wearing European clothes. The sultans' officials could be quite ignorant, even illiterate, and it was difficult to develop close relations with them: they lost their positions frequently and at the slightest notice, often for what Westerners thought trivial reasons; street mobs sometimes drove them from office.

By the second half of the eighteenth century, however, both the Habsburg and the Ottoman governments were learning that they faced a common enemy. Russian rulers and their armies had designs on lands and harbours to their south and west; they also hoped to play a role in the Balkans as protectors of native Orthodox Christians. The Treaty of Kuchuk Kainardji in 1774 gave the Romanovs a toehold in the Crimea, along with broad rights to intervene on behalf of their coreligionists in Bulgaria and the Danubian Principalities of Moldavia and Wallachia. In 1783 Russia annexed the Crimea outright, giving them control of a substantial number of Muslims whose native tongue was Turkish – 'Old' Muslim land as distinguished from the European conquests of sultans from the fourteenth through to the seventeenth centuries. Like it or not, the Turks had to court actively the goodwill of Vienna and European governments generally to preserve what they had left of their holdings. Diplomatic communiqués from the sultan and his officials gradually dropped referring to European Christians as infidels or thieves worthy of hell. For their part, makers of Habsburg foreign policy, though not averse to joining in a partition of the sultan's holdings, were ready to help Ottoman rulers keep their lands together if doing so would frustrate the designs of a new and potentially very dangerous challenger.[42]

The continued ebbing of religious concerns in Europe's conduct of foreign relations also made it easier for Vienna and Constantinople to talk to one another more civilly. The Treaty of Utrecht of 1714, which aborted Louis xiv's drive for European hegemony, was the last international peace to refer to the continent as the Republic of Christendom. Pacts that followed referred simply to 'Europe', particularly in agreements struck with the Porte. Not surprisingly, the usage hung on longer in Vienna than elsewhere, but Emperor Charles vi had abandoned it by the time he died in 1740. Religious passion was utterly absent in the diplomatic calculations of Prince Wenceslaus Kaunitz, the chancellor of Charles vi's daughter, Maria Theresa, and her son, Joseph ii. It was the usefulness of the Ottoman regime in the latter's Russian, Prussian and Polish concerns that drove his policies towards the Porte, and not the faith of the sultan and the majority of his peoples.[43] Even Maria Theresa herself, whose devout Catholicism often verged on crude bigotry, had scruples about forsaking the Ottomans during the Russian-Turkish War of 1768–74. They had been her allies in the recent past, and she did not want to undercut them so cold-bloodedly.[44]

Commercial contacts had also smoothed the relations of Christian England with the Islamic and Ottoman world in the sixteenth and seventeenth centuries. Self-interested mercantile contacts between central Europe and the south-eastern regions of the continent had also been known to make people forget their religious differences, at least temporarily. As early as 1589, one Habsburg commander reported that the Ottomans did not molest Hungarian villages in which Turks and Christians conducted business side by side. The Balkan borders of the sultan's lands were an especially lively point of contact for traders of many faiths. Long before the Ottoman armies were driven from Hungary, an exceedingly lively trade in livestock and agricultural products was taking place on Habsburg–Ottoman frontiers in Hungary.[45] The Porte itself was keenly aware of the revenues that commercial tariffs and similar imposts generated and treated their conquered populations accordingly. After taking the fortress of Nové Zámky in 1663, the Ottomans allowed Christians to remain in the emplacement and in the surrounding villages and employed them in the local work force. The Turks also quickly exploited the area's position on a tributary of the Danube by turning it into a small trading and manufacturing centre. Purveyors were brought in from the Balkans, and natives of the region sold their own livestock and produce in the markets too. Cloth, timber and various finished goods were brought down various rivers from the north and west; millstones, salt and hides went back on the return trip. Though most Muslim business activities were exempt from some taxes and tithes, they were not disproportionately privileged over their Christian counterparts. Here and there, Christian and Muslim married.[46]

Like the Muslim rulers in Constantinople, European monarchs were eager to exploit all forms of trade and commerce to increase their revenue flow throughout the heavily militarized seventeenth and eighteenth centuries. Extraterritorial trade was a favoured way of replenishing empty treasuries. Among Europe's most needy rulers was Emperor Leopold I. Two centuries of war with Constantinople alone cost the house of Austria vast sums of money – more than 50 per cent of its total expenditures between 1670 and 1717 went towards military costs, primarily against France and the Turks.

Leopold did not have a seacoast worthy of the name, but south-eastern Europe was a natural point of exchange for the goods and commodities of the Habsburg lands. Commerce of scale, however, had been gravely suppressed by the belligerent standoff between Vienna and the Porte. Although the peace of Vasvár of 1664 had called for free trade between the two states, Christian merchants from the Habsburg lands were not always welcome in Constantinople and for good reason. The tense relations of the two realms had turned central European businessmen into informal agents of Habsburg policy. To circumvent enemy inspection of diplomatic communiques and other correspondence, the Vienna regime often co-opted merchants into shipping these dispatches along with business papers to Vienna or other European capitals. Merchants also coached and supported Christian prisoners who were trying to buy their freedom, sometimes to the great financial disadvantage of their Muslim captors. Individuals from the lands of the house of Austria who were doing business in Constantinople up to the beginning of the eighteenth century thus lived as precariously as did resident ambassadors. Their movements were often restricted as well.[47]

Traders from the Ottoman lands had not been fully at home in Vienna either. Though baptized Turks were familiar parts of the city street scene at the end of the seventeenth century, along with the Greeks and Armenians from the Ottoman lands, the government watched for spies among them. Vienna had a 'Rumour Captain' (*Rumorhauptmann*) to whom suspects were to be reported. The latter were released, however, if nothing could be proven against them. Muslim Turkish traders in the city apparently performed their religious rites in their homes as surreptitiously as Protestants until the end of the eighteenth century. They did, however, enjoy one advantage – they could always flee to the Ottoman Empire if they decided to skip out on their Christian creditors.[48]

Vienna, however, had good reason to persist in establishing economic relations with south-eastern Europe and the Porte. Nor were the Ottomans altogether hostile to Western imports and skills. Throughout the sixteenth century, the Turks had studied European armaments and reconfigured them to their needs with great ingenuity. Repeated military setbacks made adaptation to new technologies more crucial than ever in the Porte, and Western manufacturers happily filled their orders. More peaceful applications of mechanics attracted the sultan himself. In October of 1668 Mehmet IV asked the resident imperial ambassador whether it was possible to send a costly watch, perhaps a gift from the king of Poland, to Vienna for repair. No one in Constantinople could handle the work, nor, as it turned out, in Vienna. The ambassador advised sending it on to Augsburg where there were craftsmen acquainted with such timepieces. By the eighteenth century, European decorative arts began to attract Ottoman subjects too.[49]

Hoping to capitalize on at least some of these possibilities, Leopold's government moved ahead. An Oriental Company to foster commerce between the two realms was set up in Vienna in 1667, but did not outlast the hostilities of 1683. Once the Turks seemed to be thrust back from Vienna forever, trade with the Ottoman lands became more economically appealing. Having captured Belgrade in 1717, Prince Eugene of Savoy thought that his emperor, Charles VI, now had both a defensible forward line for all of the Habsburg holdings and real prospects for stable commercial ties in the region.

Unfortunately for the house of Austria, military advantage and economic improvement of government finance did not go hand in hand. France and England quickly monopolized trade relations with merchants in Constantinople and in the Aegean generally; the European lands of the sultan were too underdeveloped in the seventeenth and eighteenth centuries to throw off high profit commercial relations with them. They also lay relatively far from the centres of production in the Habsburg holdings.[50]

Nevertheless, half-realized though they turned out to be, such measures suggested that Muslim-Christian relations were changing in the marketplace as much as they were in foreign policy decisions. Indeed, these were the kinds of changes that were reshaping public sensibilities about Turks and Muslims in the Habsburg empire at large. For all the suspicions that surrounded tradesmen from Constantinople and the Ottoman lands, everyday commercial experiences were doing much to enlarge a cultural comfort zone shared by Christians of central Europe and their erstwhile enemies.

Individual merchants from Constantinople, though not necessarily Turks, had long sold their wares in Vienna; it was their presence there and their commercial connections in the Ottoman lands that led the Habsburg government to think that its first Oriental Company might succeed. Even though the venture failed, the tradesmen themselves did rather well, if only because the Habsburg regime feared that enforcing import duties on their merchandise would trigger a violent response from the Porte.[51] For their part, their Viennese customers, along with other city dwellers in the Habsburg lands, welcomed several commodities and manufactures brought and sold to them by people linked to the 'hereditary enemy'.

The runaway success among these products was coffee, which, having made its way from Yemen over Egypt to the Porte, had been lubricating formal encounters between the Ottoman and Habsburg spokesmen for some time. Coffee-drinking replaced the ceremonial glass of wine in representational functions at the sultans' courts when some form of toasting between Christian and Muslim took place. At the departure of the Grand Embassy from Constantinople to Vienna in 1719, representatives of Habsburg and Ottoman sides saluted each other with coffee and confections, shook hands, then went to their horses. There they stood, one facing east, the other west, and invoked the name of God.[52] Westerners liked the beverage so much that they complained when the sultan's officials failed to serve it. The Viennese themselves had apparently tasted 'black water', sweetened and sometimes perfumed as the Turks prepared it, when Ottoman embassies were visiting.[53]

Coffee brewers and traders from the Ottoman lands, often Armenians carrying messages from the East to Habsburg governments, were in Vienna and probably other cities of the empire even before 1683. The most notable among them was John Diadato, who had spent part of his childhood in German lands where his father was a jeweller and merchant. Having become a Roman Catholic while in Constantinople, Diadato was well-positioned to act as a commercial emissary to the Austrian public at large. He was still more than a little suspect. His ongoing contacts with Ottoman emissaries to Vienna troubled the war ministry, and local merchants resented successful foreign competitors. Nevertheless, Leopold I's court found him very useful. He was an ever-ready source of credit, and his contacts with the sultan's regime were good. Most important of all, from the standpoint of the general public, he performed welcome commercial services. He sold things that they wanted: rugs, perfumes and eventually, coffee, so unimportant at first that it was imported toll-free.

It was, however, Diadato's greatest mercantile triumph, especially after 1685, when he became the first person, as far as we know, to be licensed and exclusively privileged by the court to sell the beverage from a fixed place of business. He offered other 'Turkish drinks' such as tea and syrupy fruit concoctions, but coffee was the mainstay of his trade. By 1734, a contemporary observer remarked that once peace had been made with the 'hereditary enemy', Turks were to be found throughout the city and the German world generally, setting up shops with little stoves to cook and sell the brew, an 'Asian' import, said one commentator, that either eased overly full stomachs or made them feel worse.[54]

Ottoman material culture altered Hungary's gardens and fields as well. Roses, almonds and figs in the kingdom grew from Turkish plantings around the Buda mountains well into the early part of the twentieth century. The Turks brought sweet corn and melons into Pannonian agriculture and saffron into local recipes. The stuffed peppers and cabbage that the world associates with Hungarian cooking came from Turkish cuisine, along with the use of squash and tomatoes. Craftsmen incorporated Turkish motifs into leather and metal products as well.[55]

The Porte was not always eager to rush things with its erstwhile enemy. The growing presence of Europeans in Constantinople during the eighteenth century encouraged the Ottoman government to allow Christian visitors more personal freedom and legal safeguards, but only gradually.[56] Only in the 1760s did the sultan grant traders from the Habsburg lands the privileges that Christian merchants from elsewhere in Europe enjoyed.[57] The same reservations about foreigners were heard in Vienna. However much Habsburg subjects accommodated themselves to the signature commodities, horticulture and handicrafts of the Ottoman, they remained in some way alien. One hundred years after the second siege of Vienna, coffee still could be called a 'foreign' drink with such nasty side effects as 'overexciting the blood'. Native substitutes were available. In 1783, a Josef Polliger let the public know that he had an official license to sell 'health coffee'. Concocted from the roots of unnamed plants, it allegedly improved circulation by thinning the blood. It helped the gastrointestinal system along too. Milk and cream could be added, but if the end product left people coughing, as it apparently did now and again, it could be doctored with some of the real thing. Curiously enough, the issue of the quasi-official *Wiener Zeitung* that published Pollinger's announcement also ran a pathetic commemoration of the Perchtoldsdorf massacre on its front page. Few readers, however, seemed to take the alien origins of coffee amiss, and Polliger's formula never took off in his native land. Coffee, caffeine and all, would remain both lastingly popular and part of Vienna's historic identity.[58]

The Turks were not forgiven their religion and the brutal customs that the peoples of the Habsburg lands associated with it. From the standpoint of the latter, the sultan and his subjects remained a 'barbaric nation' whose religion predisposed them to fatal obscurantism. Commenting on persisting outbreaks of plague in Constantinople and in the provinces of the Ottoman empire, the *Wiener Zeitung* deplored the passivity in the face of death that Islam impressed upon its believers.[59] But such feelings did not crowd out other considerations in everyday contact with Muslims, particularly in the higher levels of society. By 1783, the centennial year of Ottoman retreat from Vienna, a Moroccan ambassador's appearance in the city to inspect the infrastructure of porcelain manufacture in the Habsburg capital was reported as calmly as a visit from Christian Europe itself, a measure of just how comfortable with Islam and its believers many residents of the city had become. The *Wiener Zeitung* of 22 February 1783 casually noted that he had delayed his arrival, in part to observe the Prophet's birthday. Once present, he was conveyed in a state carriage accompanied by servants in gala dress to meet with Prince Kaunitz. He enjoyed the same treatment at the hands of Rudolph Colloredo, the imperial vice-chancellor. He was taken to performances at the court theatre and invited to state balls – one with 500 nobles in attendance where he and some members of his retinue partook of the supper. Whether the repast took account of Muslim dietary prescriptions went unmentioned, suggesting that such courtesies were routine or that they were not important. When the ambassador became ill during the course of his stay, Joseph II saw solicitously to his medical care.[60]

The general fashion for 'Oriental' exotica that took hold in Europe in the seventeenth and eighteenth century eventually came to Vienna too, though, once again, more slowly. A lottery sale of porcelain manufactured in the city in 1735 listed no items with specifically Turkish figures. What Eastern motifs there were took the form of 'Indian' and 'Japanese' flowers and figures. But in the end, the interest in the Habsburg lands in food, drink and ornament of the Turks and Islam, became the central European equivalent of the fascination that drew the Spanish conquistadores to the fabrics, jewellery and buildings of the natives of the New World. It was fashionable throughout the eighteenth century to have to have people of 'exotic' origins in one's household; as late as 1796, the Emperor Francis I had the body of a 'Moorish' slave, who had worked for the noble Lobkowitz and Liechtenstein families, stuffed and put on display in the imperial court museum. Even the remote countryside was touched. A minaret stood in the garden of the Liechtenstein oriental chateau on the border of Upper Austria and Moravia. Muslim garb and design were no strangers to Habsburg rulers themselves. A state portrait of Maria Theresa and her husband, Francis of Lorraine, both in Turkish dress, was done around 1776. The empress also commissioned drawings of herself and her daughters in Turkish costume.[61]

Contemporary perceptions of Turkish and Muslim culture in the eighteenth century also found their way into the most intensively cultivated of all Austrian art forms – music and musical theatre. Central Europeans had many unpleasant associations with the sounds of authentic Turkish musical instruments. The tones of huge bass drums, cymbals, triangles, zithers, cornets and pipes had once fired up Ottoman armies on the march and the attack. For some, one of the most memorable elements in an early Turkish assault on Vienna in the summer of 1683 was 'the warlike Musick, such as Flutes, Cymbals, and brass Trumpets, which gave a shrill Sound, to play with their highest Notes, to encourage their Soldiers to make the Onset'. Popularly, the environment for 'Turkish' music remained decidedly aggressive. A suburb of eighteenth-century Vienna had an animal-bating ring, a *Hetz-Theater*, where dogs and wild beasts set upon oxen to the accompaniment of 'Turkish' music. People from all walks of life showed up at these spectacles.

Anonymous print showing a stage design for Josef Starzer's ballet *Le Turc Généreux* (1759).

More sophisticated composers folded these elements into their work to underscore violence and crude behaviour too. Mozart added a 'Turkish' march to one of his widely-republished dance scores, this one inspired by Joseph II's declaration of war against the Ottoman Empire in 1788. Antonio Salieri's calculated use of 'Turkish' music, with the absence of the piccolo which he could not stand, was to signal to his audiences the 'barbarousness' of oriental settings. For Joseph Haydn these harmonies and rhythms never lost their belligerent resonance. His symphony 100, the 'Military', scores the clashing of armies *alla Turca*. Joseph Starzer, who scored the ballet *Le turc généreux*, reserved his lyric and sweeter music for Christians; the more menacing Janissary strains for his Turks. Beethoven called for the noisiest instruments in the orchestra when he wrote in the Turkish mode. The intrusion of a species of 'Turkish' instrumentation in the final movement of the Ninth Symphony has puzzled many commentators. One suggestion is that the straightforward and simple tune is a march of all humanity towards a universal brotherhood that challenged the fundamental premises of contemporary aristocracy.[62]

Nevertheless, music *alla Turca* was also to be heard in settings virtually free of political and military connotations. Haydn's younger brother, Michael, and the popular and prolific Karl Ditters von Dittersdorf worked for a times in Hungary where they heard and experimented with 'Turkish' instrumental combinations used by local gypsy orchestras rather than

Ottoman armies on the offensive. By the latter third of the eighteenth century, one could enjoy 'Janissary' music, as it came to be known, as pure and simple entertainment. In 1784, Mozart's father, Leopold, encountered a monk in Salzburg who was on his way from his Tyrolean cloister to a new post in Linz. As the elder Mozart and other onlookers asked one another how someone sworn to poverty had the money to travel by coach, the cleric alighted with two chests filled with Turkish instruments. These he set up on the ground or strapped to his body, enabling him to act as a one-man band that played 'altogether naturally' (*ganz natürlich*), at least to Mozart's ears.[63] Even the invincibly Catholic Francis I, Emperor of Austria during the Napoleonic period, reportedly hired an excellent 'Turkish' choir for the court opera. Rebuilding Europe's boundaries after Napoleon's defeat and exile in 1814–15, negotiators at the Congress of Vienna looked forward to 'Turkish' music as a cordial diversion. Janissary music became a staple of not only of military bands in the Habsburg empire, but in Europe generally, and went beyond conjuring up the glories of war. In Vienna and elsewhere in the house of Austria's territories, army ensembles played such scores for an assortment of more civic functions: coronations, dynastic marriages and funerals, even religious processions on Corpus Christi procession. A recent suggestion that the mysterious 'Turkish' strains in Beethoven's Ninth symphony might also be a 'metaphorical wedding march', may be more probable, though less 'metaphorical', than it seems. Muslims themselves did not take offense at the reworking of the 'Turkish' musical tradition. The Moroccan ambassador who visited Vienna in 1783 was serenaded with some 'Turkish' music by a little band drawn from an orphanage where he was a guest for an afternoon. He professed to have enjoyed himself thoroughly.[64]

REINVENTING THE MUSLIM

The 'Terrible Turk' retained his presence in all forms of entertainment in the Habsburg empire. His threatening embodiments continued to perform decapitations, fly into seismic rages, gratify his promiscuous lusts and capture and enslave women and children. Theatrical renderings of licentiousness in the seraglio continued to titillate Western imaginations, though under an increasing cloud of guilt. Far more self-consciously monogamous than before, the middle classes of eighteenth-century Europeans were offended and disgusted by such goings-on. Trying to forestall such reactions from his public in 1788, Anton Vigano, a ballet master in the Austrian lands, warned that his *Muhammad and Irene: a Heroic-Tragic Ballet* of 1788, was not for the delicate classes. Set in the amoral harem of Mehmet II, the conqueror of Constantinople, its climax has the sultan stabbing his submissive inamorata to death because the law forbids him to marry anyone.[65]

Nevertheless, the erosion of Ottoman military discipline and administrative willpower also made representations of Turks and Muslims as power figures less plausible. Ottoman amorality and murderousness were no longer routine metaphors for a state whose political and military power had once terrorized Europe. Though Europeans had long deplored the sexual conduct of the Turks and, by extension, Muslims collectively, it was only after the sultan and his coreligionists ceased to menace Christendom that they became synonyms for undisciplined debauchery.[66] The contrast between what the fictional Turk said he would do, and what his state could enforce, made his threats and hyper-physicality more than a little ridiculous. Public jesting in the Habsburg empire at Ottoman enfeeblement after the treaty of Karlowitz moved one commentator to warn that good relations with the sultan would follow only if Christians respected their enemy's positive qualities. Succeeding generations largely ignored him.[67]

The great victory over Belgrade of Eugene of Savoy's army in 1717 shifted the emphasis in Catholic homilies from Christian failings to Christian prowess. Once scolded for their rowdy and licentious behaviour, soldiers came in for especially high praise. Three decades into the eighteenth century, sermons were reassuring Christians that they were superior to the very foe God had once visited upon them for their lapses.[68] Folk songs turned the enemy into an object of contempt and scorn and satirized his weaknesses. Some lyrics artlessly bragged about the booty that the imperial army had taken in encounters with the Ottomans. Dramas with explicitly Turkish themes marginalized the story of military conflict itself. *Die Befreyte Wien*, a preachy drama about the second Turkish siege of Vienna, written around 1775, is full of local patriotism. Though there are references to Turkish and Tartar brutality and rapaciousness, audiences do not see any of them. Social and marital problems dominate the work. A noble father, thinking his first son dead in Tartar and Ottoman captivity, makes his second son his heir, only to have the elder sibling reappear to reclaim not only his inheritance but his fiancée, who has fallen in love with the younger brother too.[69] A play of 1783, *The Loyalty of Vienna's Citizens Rewarded, or September 12, 1683*, portrayed Ottoman officials as murderous careerists whose courage crumbled quickly in encounters with lippy Viennese who fought them or stole into their camps. During a Habsburg campaign in 1788 to recapture Belgrade, soldiers' songs promised to teach the Turks a much-needed lesson and mocked the sultan's forces for preferring slash-and-burn tactics to a real fight.[70]

The stereotype of the Turk as the bloodthirsty and barbarian Muslim conqueror in central Europe and elsewhere morphed into the less daunting image of the Turk as a trivial, ignorant and hapless fool. Europeans, including some from the Habsburg lands, had always enjoyed bits of private mischief at the expense of Islam. Ogier de Busbecq imported a pig into Constantinople after his stablemen told him that its odour benefitted horses. Local Muslims, while they were horrified, had never seen such an animal and came to his house to view it. Tired of having his dispatches

Anonymous print showing the strangling of Grand Vizier Kara Mustafa, 1684.

opened by the guards who supervised his house arrest, the scholar-ambassador warned them that roast pork was enclosed. Thunderstruck, the Turks handed over the packages instantly, still sealed.[71]

But by the eighteenth century, such jesting, implicit and overt, was widespread in the Habsburg lands. A Turk-like *putto* struggling to hold up a wine barrel perched above him, might provoke Christians chuckling at the vapidness of Muslim pretension and the hypocrisy of their clandestine tippling. If Muslims were clever at all, they were hardly admirable. Voltaire's *Le Fanatisme ou Mohamet le Prophète*, performed for Viennese audiences in German many times, presented its antihero as a fraudulent trickster. The Koran did not have Voltaire's respect either. Appropriate to its own time, it was an empty babble for a French *philosophe*.[72]

This new reading of the Turk came to the Habsburg lands from various Italian stages and France. The prototype of the genre, *Soliman*, was first performed in Italy in 1619. Its theme was a familiar one – the palace intrigues of a mother to elevate her son to the sultanate – and treated quite seriously. Lighter elements, however, slipped into these pieces very quickly from the *Commedia dell' Arte* which had its own Turkish stock figures. In the German lands beyond the Habsburg holdings, there were so-called Soliman operas performed before they appeared in Vienna, complete with Janissary music when identifiable Muslims came on stage. A standard plot – a captured and enslaved Christian girl rescued by a lover whose constancy withstands all challenges – first cropped up in Italy then jumped quickly to France along with the doltish and often dangerous Muslim figure who becomes ever more laughable as the story unfolds. When these scenarios finally reached theatres in Vienna, they quickly took hold, in part because they were packaged in exotic productions that gave curious audiences some idea of the furniture, fabrics, jewellery and gardens of the East.[73] It was probably more than coincidental that the greatest number of these productions in central Europe came between 1768 and 1774, when Russian forces were campaigning successfully against the Ottoman army.[74]

It was the comic Turk and/or Muslim, however, who was the immediate hit once he arrived. So-called 'Turkish operas' were rarely without him, and the greatest composers made sure to include some variant of the figure in their work. Christoph Willibald Gluck set off the fad in Vienna and provided future models for his musical successors. Of Czech parents, though born in the Rhenish Upper Palatinate, he had wandered for several years throughout the Habsburg lands in various musical capacities. In the 1740s he was working for Italian theatres on projects that often had Turkish themes. In Vienna, his comic opera of 1762, *The Duped Magistrate* (*Le Cadi dupé*), featured a Muslim judge hoodwinked into accepting a grossly ugly woman as a bride; it also involved some Turkish instrumental effects that Gluck had never used before. Enormously popular throughout the German-speaking world, it had two revivals in the Habsburg capital in 1764 and 1768. More successful yet was Gluck's *The Unexpected Encounter* (*La Rencontre imprévue*) adapted in 1764 from a venerable staple of French vaudeville theatres, *The Pilgrims of Mecca*. The Muslim turned comic by his own religion and culture appears in the first scene of *La Rencontre* as a dervish in Cairo babbling nonsense syllables. He claims to be singing a chant for working beggars composed by the Prophet 'in the obscure style of the Koran'. The obligatory drinking scene, embedded in almost all of these spoofs, centres on a rapacious Calendar, the spiritual leader of a band of Muslim mendicants and a caravan driver whom the orchestra serenades into woozy oblivion with Janissary music. There is also a slow-witted servant named Osmin.[75] Emperor Joseph II ordered a German translation, *Die Pilger von Mekka*, that played widely throughout the German lands.

Turks were an unlikely source of amusement for Joseph Haydn, the first of the great Viennese classical composers. He recalled many times throughout his life that Ottoman troops had killed his great-grandparents during a raid in 1683 in Hainburg, close to Austria's modern borders with Hungary and Slovakia. One of their sons, a brother of Haydn's grandfather, was captured and never heard from again. Haydn's birthplace, Rohrau in Lower Austria, had also been plundered by bands of Crimean Tartars on the way to Vienna.

Nevertheless, the composer whipped out several operatic works with comic Turkish themes. He was especially proud of *L'incontro improvviso* (a sprightly version in Italian of *Die Pilger*) that he contributed to lavish festivities for Archduke Ferdinand and his wife in 1775 on their visit to the composer's patron and employer, Count Nicholas Esterházy. The nobleman's family itself had experienced problems with the Turks; the Esterházy Palace in which *L'incontro* was put on had been occupied by Ottoman troops in 1683. Very well received by that audience, Haydn thought the piece noteworthy enough to single it out in a brief autobiographical sketch he turned out a year later. Of the 60 symphonies he had written by that time, he mentioned not one.

Revived in 1780, Haydn's *L'incontro* was a forerunner to the greatest of all operas to rehearse 'Turkish' themes. This was Mozart's *The Abduction from the Seraglio* of 1782, an effervescent mix of every stereotype of Turks, Islam and the East that the eighteenth century invented.[76] It was wildly popular in Vienna, far more so than the composer's subsequent masterpieces, *The Marriage of Figaro* and *Don Giovanni*. The *dramatis personae* include young Christian ladies in Muslim captivity and young Christian men clever enough to figure out how to save them and brave enough to do it. There is also the conventional comic foil, a Turkish palace guard and overseer Osmin whose name was becoming synonymous with his stereotype. With a super-size body and a temperament to match, his appetite for food, drink and sexual pleasure is unbounded. The exaggerated gesticulation that pumps up his already larger-than-life personality makes Osmin even funnier.

He does have a vicious side: in their first encounter, he threatens to torture Pedrillo, the servant of the hero-lover Belmonte. Nevertheless, stupidity and greed, along with Western craftiness, reduce the Turk to ridiculous impotence. His childish emotional transparency makes him even more laughable. It is clear that he is a Muslim – he repeatedly swears 'by the beard of the Prophet', or 'by Allah'. He is not, however, a role model for his faith. Indeed, he lashes out against what he calls its absurdities during a drinking scene in the second act. Mozart himself regarded him as an archetypical brute. Though he did not want to overly offend the ears of 'the Viennese gentlemen' with rough sounding harmonies, he stepped up the tempos of Osmin's music to make the man frightening but funny to listeners.[77]

Both as a type and a name, Osmin triggered laughter and mockery for generations of Viennese and European audiences. His virtual reincarnation on the Viennese stage appeared in 1805 in the form of Omar, the palace gardener in Joseph Alois Gleich's *The Moor of Semegonda*.[78] When two European young men on yet another quest in an imaginary Islamic land encounter Omar for the first time, all three of them expect that their religious opposite number will eat them the spot. But the elderly gardener's long-standing fondness for the bottle has considerably mellowed his natural roughness. First insisting that what he is drinking is sherbet, he finally admits that it is wine. To the question what the Prophet would think, Omar replies 'He's a good man; he'll close an eye. Long live Muhammad!' Having gulped down the first toast, Omar offers a second to 'The Virgins in Paradise'. All drink to that raucously.[79]

Islam as portrayed in Austrian theatres comes off without much moral substance either. Preparing to flee in Friedrich Gensike's *Die Belohnte Treue*, set during the siege of Vienna in 1683, Grand Vizier Kara Mustafa debates what would be more useful on the trip, his wives or his treasures. He finally opts for the latter, on the ground that burning his wives would please the Prophet more. The cardinal good works of his faith become urgent personal priorities – pilgrimages, endowing mosques, abundant charity – any gesture to promote divine intervention on his behalf. That his current chief adviser is a wry but fawning Jewish quack named Herzschmul makes the Turk even more laughable, especially when audiences learn that the defenders of Vienna came across the doctor in the Grand Vizier's abandoned baggage.[80]

The Turk as a comic ignoramus was not the only unflattering and unrealistic stereotype drawn from his culture to amuse the much-relaxed Viennese theatregoer in the eighteenth century. The term 'Moor' (Germ. *Mohr*), generally associated with black skin tones, evil and sexual excess was conceptually interchangeable with Turk and Muslim in early modern Europe. Mozart's other great orientalizing opera, *The Magic Flute*, first performed in 1791, made telling use of this image in the figure of the slave Monastatos. His first appearance on stage has him pawing at the heroine Pamina who is repelled both by his dark skin and his advances.[81]

Hungarians continued to write in more heroic terms about their struggles with the Turks than did their Austrian counterparts. Nevertheless, the painters in the recently liberated kingdom turned away from depicting the Ottomans in combat to associating them with religious and patriotic subjects. Turkish motifs in the plastic arts and decorative fashion took on the playful, but trivializing, character brought to Turkish figures on the stages of the Habsburg lands. Images of Turks stared back from tobacco boxes and other forms of everyday packaging. Hungarian authors also became far more comfortable with their former arch-enemy. One of the great writers and advocates for his native tongue, Ferenc Kazinczy, was being complimentary in the eighteenth century when he described a fellow author's wide reading, styles of behaviour and thinking as half-French, half-Turkish.[82]

The Osmin figure was, however, was not the only Eastern stereotype to find an enduring place on the stages of eighteenth-century Vienna. 'Turkish' stage pieces often paired him with a kind of moral and intellectual corrective. This was the noble Muslim, embodied by Pasha Selim in the *Abduction*, an avatar of benevolence for all of the world's rulers. Though he once suffered great injury at the hands of Belmonte's father and now loves Constanza genuinely, Selim releases her to her lover. Vengeance, he announces, should not poison human relations indefinitely. Like Osmin, the magnanimous Pasha had several immediate forebears – Sultan Soliman in Mozart's operetta *Zaide* of 1780 is one – along with clones who showed up on stages throughout the Habsburg empire for years to come.[83]

Unlike his loutish underling, Selim has a genuinely humanitarian side. Nevertheless, such behaviour belittled Turks or Muslims as much as did Osmin's excesses. Stereotyping often expresses a perverse kind of admiration and respect, even when it is wildly negative. Lohenstein's Sultan Ibrahim was a repellant beast, who exploited human life rather than honouring it. His lusts epitomized the sexual perversions and inversions that Christians had long associated with Ottoman culture generally. And he probably did more harm than good to his domains. Nevertheless, he was a believable spokesman for the raw military and political power that the Porte imposed upon a good part of Europe and the Eastern world through much of the early modern era.[84] Though Pasha Selim himself often could not discriminate between self-indulgence and interests of state, he now stood before audiences who knew that Ottoman decline was a fact. His personification of the softer side of identifiably Muslim rulers and their officers was credible only in the context of their proven military and political weakness. Nor is Muslim benevolence rewarded. Gracious though he is, Mozart's Selim also loses the woman whom he very much wants.

Sultan figures come across as mediocre ditherers in other theatrical productions of the day. The eponymous hero of *Soliman der Zweyte*, a 1799 musical play (*Singspiel*) by Franz Xaver Süßmayer, Mozart's student and assistant, is so personally torn among three different, but attractive, women that the possibility of having more than one wife apparently escapes him. It takes an Osmin figure in the story to remind the sultan of his rights as a Muslim to polygamy. It is a female captive – a spunky German named Marianne – who at the end of the piece convinces Soliman to exercise political powers that are unequivocally his. Indeed, it is women, prominently identified as Europeans from the western reaches of the continent and British Isles whose nerve and candour make Turkish rulers and their underlings look especially ineffectual. Blondchen, Constanza's spitfire maid in the *Abduction*, and the impudent Marianne, who has upended decorum in the harem, brush off the domineering males of Muslim establishments regardless of the possible consequences. If Turkish women are foolish enough to submit to men like him, says Blondchen as she resists Osmin's advances, so much the worse for them. Europeans, she declares, understand these things differently. To the bedazzled Soliman's question of whether all German women are like her, Marianne snaps back 'almost'.[85]

Far less familiar in Europe than Marianne thought, the dominant role of such women was all but unknown in contemporary Ottoman society. Young ladies such as Blondchen and Marianne therefore underscore the weakness of Ottoman officers as authority figures in a grossly provocative way. Moreover, when Selim, and occasionally Süßmayer's Soliman, extol the values of human dignity and just rule, they are mouthing phrases more closely associated with contemporary Western culture than in the Ottoman East. In fact these figures are giving lip service to the ideals of the eighteenth-century Enlightenment, the radical reorientation of thought that had touched almost all areas of Europe by the late 1790s.

Compared to France, England and some of the German principalities such as Hanover, the Habsburg lands were late participants in this great intellectual sea change. The close link between the government in Vienna and responsibility for defending Catholic Christendom against Protestantism and the Turks stifled any impulses towards religious toleration. No sooner did ideas prompted by the Scientific Revolution and philosophical empiricism of the seventeenth century gain some traction in the regime than they were compromised by other interests and policies of the dynasty. Activists though they were for some of the Enlightenment's core programmes, especially those that curbed Church influence in public affairs, Emperors Joseph ii and his very progressive brother and successor Leopold ii were not ready to transform themselves into constitutional monarchs. Though they longed to trim down local noble privilege, they did not plan to revamp the hierarchical order of their society from the bottom up.[86] 'Light ruled the highest intellectual circles, twilight the middle range, and deep darkness precisely where people lived their everyday existence', said Karl Leonhard Reinhold, an influential Kantian philosopher and a supporter of Joseph's early religious reforms that stressed the intellectual and humanitarian side of Christianity over its redemptive message. Indeed, when faced with unrest caused by his policies late in his reign, the Habsburg ruler cracked down sharply on public expression of opinion. Reinhold took refuge elsewhere in Germany.[87]

Open-mindedness, however, and the unity of mankind regardless of religious creed were ideals of the Enlightenment that the regime could put to good use. The often opportunistic Maria Theresa led the way, even on the cultural front. To persuade an Ottoman ambassador in 1758 that an Austro–French alliance her government had concluded was not directed against the sultan, she invited the envoy to Starzer's ballet *Le Turc généreux*. Specifically created for the occasion, the piece's central motif was Muslim magnanimity to Christian lovers. The tactic apparently worked, at least theatrically: the Turkish guest was much impressed by the authenticity of the stage set and the music. The public also gave the piece unusually warm acclaim, even in an era when Turkish ballets were growing in popularity.

Decidedly mixed motives drove the Patent of Religious Toleration issued by her son, Joseph, in 1781. One of his most influential and lasting edicts, it was grounded both in his belief that conscience could not be compelled and his even deeper concern for the interests of state. Allowing confessionally marginalized subjects, in this case Protestants, into the mainstream of the productive economy benefitted everyone. Joseph later followed through with a series of measures that lifted restrictions on Jews throughout the empire; both he and Leopold held to the spirit of these policies quite consistently.[88] At the very least, they maintained, abandoning traditional religious restrictions and the prejudices that reinforced them promoted sound thinking. As Joseph's often influential adviser, Josef von Sonnenfels, himself of Jewish extraction, put it on the title pages of one of his publications, *The Unprejudiced Man* (*Der Mann ohne Vorurtheile*):

Just as when a brilliant sun shines through tinted glass,
And makes all that it touches a single-coloured mass;
Bias does the same; it only lets us see,
Things not as they are, but as we would have them be.

Nor did these ideas gather dust in the state chambers of the Habsburg empire. They were central to the agenda of contemporary Freemasons, whose lodges brought together Catholics, Protestants and Jewish converts to Christianity. Very active in the first few years of Joseph II's reign, several government figures were members, including Sonnenfels himself. One of his pet enterprises, a periodical called the *Journal für Freimaurer*, was specifically intended to free mankind from all of its prejudices. Though the Viennese lodge *Zur wahren Eintracht* (True Harmony) edited and published it, the *Journal* was to circulate throughout the Habsburg lands as a whole.[89] The first issue carried an essay by the lodge's master of ceremonies, Baron Augustin Veit von Schlittersberg, which pointed out how prejudice against people of foreign birth divided humanity.

Such thoughts found their way into theatres too. A lodge brother himself, Mozart built them into *The Magic Flute*, the composer's masonic paean to the virtues of toleration, particularly in its final act. Supported by the mystic trappings of 'Eastern' wisdom, the character of Sarastro, a less culturally specific and more philosophically refined Pasha Selim, celebrates wisdom and reason as antidotes to 'evil prejudice' represented by his enemy, the Queen of the Night, who gets her way through trickery and superstition. Even the Catholic establishment of the Habsburg lands began to see advantages in coexisting with other faiths. Concerned about their own survival in a secularizing polity, Church officials took the position that the aims of Christianity were best served through reasoned argument and a living creed of charity. Toleration of other religions in one's own land would, they suggested, encourage reciprocation abroad.[90]

Muslims benefitted to some extent from this official and public change of heart even during the reign of Joseph II's resolutely Catholic mother. The title page to the 1752 revision of Scherer's catechism hints that the Catholic Church in the Habsburg lands was ready to soften the rhetoric of religious discourse generally. The 1620 product had proclaimed itself 'An Easy-to-Read (*deutliche*) Description and Defence (*Beschirmung*) of Catholic Belief and Ceremonies and a Clear Counterargument of Non-Catholic Doctrine'. A little more than 130 years later, it had become the far less contentious 'Catechism or Christian Teaching on the true Catholic Apostolic Faith for the General Good (*zum allgemeinen Besten*)'. Muslim Turks still were no better or worse than Jews, heathens and heretics, meaning Protestants: all refused to make the sign of the cross. Nevertheless, many of the most serious distinctions in the original version between Christians and non-Christians, such as Muslims, had vanished. But a passage in the 1620 catechism that categorically forbids Christians to bear false witness against Jews, heathens, friends or neighbours, strangers and enemies remained in the new text. Jesus, Scherer noted, had been convicted on such grounds.[91] As for the educated layman, the more illogical the Christian prejudice against Islam, the more ludicrous it was. A travesty of the Spanish Inquisition that Sonnenfels published in the *Journal* in 1784 poked fun at the notion that reading one line of the Koran was enough to condemn anyone to the *auto-da-fé*.[92]

Not every secularized intellectual saw all faiths converging towards a common core, especially where matters of ritual and ritual phrasing were concerned. Johann Pezzl, one of eighteenth-century Vienna's shrewder and busier commentators, continued to think that Islam and Christianity would not readily understand one another. He questioned how any Muslim at the Porte would react to communiqués from the Habsburg chancellory that opened with invocations to the Christian Trinity. Looking at religions comparatively, as he professed to do, could also prompt critical conclusions that only the most broad-minded could accept. To him the common features of Christianity, Judaism and Islam were ridiculousness and enforced obscurantism. 'Screaming' imams, rabbis, popes, bishops, Protestant superintendents – all used their authority to oppress their followers and insult their intellects.[93]

In rejecting theological religious absolutism, however, Pezzl accorded Muslims the full power of reason both within and outside of their own religious context, a concession that Christians of the sixteenth and seventeenth century had rarely made. In his *Marokkanische Briefe. Aus dem Arabischen*, the fictitious commentary of someone in the entourage of the Moroccan ambassador who came to Vienna in 1783, the writer declares that he had undertaken his trip in order to learn something. He had therefore purged his mind of preformed ideas. Natural human understanding, not prejudice, would be his only guide. Though he had some serious reservations about Islam, even before he came to Europe, he could not blame Catholics for laughing about the story of the Angel Gabriel's appearance before the Prophet. And he far preferred educated feminine company in the West to the submissively sheltered women of his own culture. On the other hand, he marvelled that Europeans could poke fun at various Eastern faiths and not realize that Christianity had equally improbable practices. Islam, furthermore, had many insights that Christianity might well consider, particularly its conventional rejection of celibacy as counter to nature. How Catholic clergy could speak with authority on marital morals was beyond him. Polygamy actually had social advantages. Limiting men to a fixed number of sexual partners curbed the spread of venereal disease and guaranteed generation upon generation of servants to the sultan's government.[94]

Thus for the real or self-described enlightened such as Pezzl, it was possible to compare Christian and Muslim societies and to respect important distinctions between them. This outlook, however, was exceptional. For many, the shift in power relations between the house of Austria and the Porte had only reversed the roles of the two states in the interaction of dominance and subordination, not the fundamental nature of the discourse itself. The victor could think as he pleased, particularly when amusing himself. The imagery that emerged out of this change was as negatively simplistic as was the reflexive demonization of Muslims in the sixteenth and seventeenth century.[95] By portraying Turks as 'dull and backward people', buffoons and downright fools, sultans and servants alike, the artists and entertainers of the Habsburg lands and their audiences, as in Europe as a whole after the middle of the eighteenth century, merely substituted one set of stereotypes for another.[96] Turbaned Eastern rulers prattling the boilerplate of the eighteenth century Enlightenment were no less figments of the Western imagination than were the incorrigibly oafish Osmin, or the invincible Blondchen and Marianne. In their own way, all of them underscored Ottoman moral and political weakness and the general superiority of western values. Selim is wise because he is a Westerner at heart, not because his culture has educated him to it. Mozart himself confessed that his 'Janissary' chorus in *The Abduction* was 'short, lively and written to please the Viennese' and not to replicate authentic Turkish sounds. Sarastro in *The Magic Flute*, his name itself a reworking from Persian, was modelled on the very western Count Ignaz von Born, the Bohemian nobleman who was the guiding spirit of *Zur Wahren Eintracht* and something of a cult figure in his day. His lectures on Egyptian Mysteries were one of the sources for the opera's libretto.[97]

At the same time the replacement of Lohenstein's repellent Sultan Ibrahim with Pasha Selim, Osmin and their innumerable stand-ins on the stages of the eighteenth-century Habsburg empire made it easier to think that the culture of the East was to be enjoyed and not feared. Patronizing though the motives of their creators may have been, these figures humanized the Turk. Both the dimwit servant and the pseudo-Eastern *philosophe* in a turban who ruled him were at least approachable, raising the possibility that greater communication with them was possible. Earlier images of the Muslim enemy given to Habsburg subjects were so grossly subhuman that one could kill him without regret. Now one could deal with him if need be without putting one's life on the line.[98] Something of the same could be said about Islam as well. Even as it lost singularity by being incorporated into the generality of human belief systems, it also shed the overtly menacing character that Ottoman conquest had brought to it.

It was within the context of these revised perceptions of the Turks and their religion that the Habsburg empire approached 1783, the centenary of the second siege of Vienna. Extended public celebration seemed clearly the order of the day. For the government it was especially convenient. Joseph II and his advisors were working overtime to break down the ethnic and historical differences among the polyglot peoples that he governed; reminding them of a period of collective suffering would have been a useful and uncontested tactic to advance his programme.

Habsburg officials, however, let the opportunity pass. The one authentically spectacular event in Vienna itself was a massive fireworks display in a new amusement park, the Prater. Its designer, Johann Georg Seuwer, the 'imperial royal licensed fireworks man', promised to detonate sounds and sights of the siege and the subsequent Christian victory that would recall to the general public the fortitude of their ancestors.[99] Formal observances themselves were quite subdued, focusing on the benevolent intervention of the Virgin and the courage of Vienna's one-time defenders and residents rather than on the misdeeds of the hereditary enemy and Islam. There was a procession to St Stephen's Cathedral that included many Church dignitaries and private citizens, but Joseph II was not among them. The *Wiener Zeitung* soberly published some suggested readings for those who wanted to pursue the topic further.[100]

The court had let this particular benchmark occasion slip by before; prior festivities had not always taken place in Vienna. One should not, therefore, read too much into this behaviour, even though 1783 was a hard date to pass up. On the other hand, public reminders of the fearful 'Turk' and his image were fading quickly from the city. Turks were there, of course, but only as one of any number of foreigners in native dress who were coming to the Habsburg capital in the eighteenth century. Souvenirs of Ottoman defeats such as horsetails, drums and Turkish weaponry, once displayed in the church of St Augustine near the imperial *Hofburg*, were gone. The extensive fortifications around the Inner District of Vienna had become a favourite place to sit or stroll; in the summer there was a coffee house on the parade grounds below with light refreshments. Aside from the seventeenth-century graphics illustrating some quasi-historical fiction, fewer and fewer pictures of the Turks and the terror associated with them were to be found.[101] Nor was there much public interest in the Turks and their state. By 1783 the few mentions of the sultan and his forces in the newspapers of the day were usually in reports about Ottoman decline. For court-sponsored journals, the 'Turk' was no longer a big story. Coverage of the sultan's establishment in Constantinople for the *Wiener Zeitung* between 1782 and 1783 was noticeably thin: far more space was given to reports from London, Madrid and Paris and their overseas colonies than from Constantinople. Looking at wars of liberation going on in the British North American colonies and elsewhere in August of 1782, an anonymous writer observed that 'brave Albanians' were following the same path in the Ottoman empire. Aside from occasional laconic reports of personnel changes in the government in Constantinople and provincial centres and reports of disastrous fires and natural catastrophes, the picture of the sultans' realm was of a state beset by internal challenges such as reigning in greedy pashas. Indeed, the journal occasionally ran accounts of Muslim–Christian co-operation. After a great fire in Constantinople itself in 1783 some of its Turkish residents were reported to be on the way to Slavonia where they could buy potatoes, butter and other provisions from German merchants. These they took back to their homeland for resale.[102]

There was also a new kind of relativism to be found in the Habsburg lands to tamp down exaggerated self-congratulation in the 1783 anniversary. Just as the Turks and Muslims of earlier centuries were one of the house of Austria's several religious enemies, the Turks were fast becoming, in the opinion of Johann Pezzl, one of several invaders that the city of Vienna had withstood even more recently. The troops of the dissident Hungarian nobleman Francis Rákoczi had attacked it at the beginning of the eighteenth century and so had the combined French and Bavarian armies who were contesting Maria Theresa's succession in 1741. And the Turks, though individually brave and disciplined, were simply no match for the Habsburg forces, at least as an increasingly self-confident Viennese public saw it in 1783. Indeed, so secure had many become that the government could not exploit religious appeals to raise troops and money as it once could. Widespread middle-class prosperity in the

Habsburg capital had secularized their outlook on Muslims considerably. Military victories over the Ottomans were primarily the works of man and not God. Wild celebrations erupted among Habsburg subjects after the temporary recapture of Belgrade in 1789, but in thanks to an army, and not a Christian deity.[103] Indeed, before that, the regime's efforts to whip up its peoples into a new war against the Turks by recalling the hostility between Christian and Muslim fizzled badly. The Viennese public was even making sour jokes about Joseph II's alliance with Catherine the Great of Russia. 'Where are you taking me, Cathy?' asks the Habsburg ruler. 'Into an awful mess,' replies the Tsarina. Some found it hard to believe that two powerful states needed to fight the Turks at all.[104] Indeed, after a promising start, the offensive fell apart. The inflation that the conflict brought on caused far more anxiety and unrest in the general populace than did a possible reappearance of the Ottoman forces and their religion in the land.

The public seemingly could take the Turks or leave them, in international relations or on the stage. Of all Salieri's operas, Joseph II most admired *Axur, Re d'Ormus* (*Axur, King of Ormus*) first presented in 1788. A conventional portrayal of the downfall of an Oriental despot, it echoed the spirit of the emperor's military goal of the year. Performed 100 times before 1805, it was very popular. Nevertheless, composers no longer had to embellish operas on Eastern themes with 'Turkish' music, contrived orientalisms or venerable stereotypes to win over audiences. Clearly set in the Muslim orbit, Salieri's *Palmira, Queen of Persia*, made little use of these artifices. The work however, was put on a respectable 39 times in the court-sponsored theatres of Vienna between 1795 and 1798.[105]

THE TURK AS HISTORY

The growing sense of security once an enemy is truly vanquished, the conversion of a feared figure into an object of laughter and scorn, the turning of public attention to personal pursuits – all are familiar signs of a culture no longer under threat. So is the inclination to relativize. But below the surface of conventional relaxation in the Habsburg lands *vis-à-vis* the Ottoman Empire in 1783, a more radical shift in thinking about the Turks and their religion was afoot, one that combined the long-standing Western curiosity about the East and the Enlightenment pursuit of open-mindedness in a way that made each a precondition of the other. The need to be critical of information about Ottoman culture had been recognized by earlier travel reporters. Stephan Gerlach had admitted that some of his most negative comments about the Turks were not always based on his own experience. He could also distinguish between fact and fancy, a capacity that allowed him to make the Turks somewhat less formidable than his contemporaries believed. He mistrusted the Turks as much as did any imperial emissary to Constantinople in the early modern era. Ottoman body counts of enemy armies, he said, could be shameless lies. But he was equally suspicious of Western tall tales about the Turks. He had heard a story that some Ottoman cavalry troops, the Spahis, could ride on their heads with their horses at a full gallop, all the while picking up objects such as hats and lances from the ground. The pastor refused to believe it, as well as other 'dubious things' (*ungläubige Sachen*).[106] He could compare Christianity and Islam without editorializing. The Turks, he noted, recognized all of the biblical prophets before Muhammad; they rejected the New Testament because it had overlooked Islam's visionary. Gerlach's derivation of the term Muslim (*Musulman*) was purely philological; it came, he said, from the Arabic word for Islam which means 'the one true faith'. A *Musulman* is someone who has cast out false belief for truth.[107] Bartholomew Georgievicz apparently sensed that he could look at his Muslim captors from multiple perspectives and make money while doing so. He brought out his sufferings in one book and his account of the manners and institutions of the Turks and the Ottoman lands in nineteen chapters of a second, and larger, volume.[108]

None of this writing was based on a discernible intellectual programme. An anonymous *Soldiers' Jubilee* (*Soldatenjubiläum*) that came out in 1783 to commemorate the victory over the Ottomans one hundred years before was strikingly different. It opened with the bold declaration that not much was known about the second siege of Vienna, crucial though the event was in the history of central Europe. What Habsburg subjects knew came from deplorably one-sided (i.e. Christian) documentation. Readers of these works, said the author of the slender volume, had little information about the strategic and political thinking of the Ottomans and what their own historians and commentators had said about the episode. His remedy was to develop the habits of scepticism, factuality and wide reading in sources, both European and Ottoman.

He dutifully followed his own prescription. To explore the plans and reasoning of the sultan's commanders, he consulted Ottoman historians themselves. He described the debates among officials at the Porte, who disagreed sharply among themselves about the goals of their campaign as they moved up the Danube through Hungary. Some thought that they were too far away from Constantinople to stay in Vienna for very long. Grand Vizier Kara Mustafa, in this text, comes across as a humanly complex figure: very intelligent and experienced in some ways, he is a victim of his overweening pride, the power he arrogated to himself, and the inexperience and indecision of his generals. In a flourish of authenticity, the writer dated the siege with the Muslim year (1014) and month (*rabio lakhir*). He was also sure that many more of such accounts would come out as part of the centenary observances.[109]

He was right. The *Wiener Zeitung* of 30 August 1783 carried a book notice of a history of the siege of 1683. The author, Gottfried Uhlich, was a Piarist, a Catholic order known in Europe for promoting the scientific educational agenda of the Enlightenment. He was a numismaticist, dramatist and moralist as well as an historian. Like the journalist Pezzl, he looked at the Turks as only one of several enemies to have besieged Vienna in the Middle Ages. But, eager to raise his work far above the level of common journalism, Uhlich assured his readers that he had outdone all of his predecessors in the number of sources he had consulted, particularly on conditions at the Turkish court. He had also explored archives to supplement diaries used time and again in conventional accounts. His efforts apparently paid off: the quality of the documentation persuaded even a twentieth-century historian to call the book one of the best on the subject to have appeared up to that time.[110]

Critical reserve and preference for the factual over inherited legend and polemic made its way into the popular theatre as well. Friedrich Gensike was a good example. Director of the well-patronized Theatre at the Carinthian Gate and author of *Die Belohnte Treue*, a play that memorialized the centenary of the second siege, he admitted openly that he had intended to do more historical research on his topic but never got around to it. He was confident, however, that he had fully documented Kara Mustafa's cowardice (*Kleinmütigkeit*).[111] Like the author of the *Soldatenjubiläum*, Gensike relied more heavily on recorded human error than the hand of God in explaining the Ottoman defeat. Kara Mustafa's pride, therefore, is not a sin, as Catholic dogma would have it, but simply a failure of character that distorts his strategic judgement and persuades him to go ahead with the siege. Only as the piece ends does Rüdiger Starhemberg, the commander of the Vienna militia to whom the play was dedicated, urge people to thank God for the victory. Though worshipped at an altar, this divinity has no further Christian attributes.[112]

Such mixtures of sacred and worldly causality were not wholly absent from earlier accounts of Ottoman–Habsburg conflicts. Even when the fate of Christendom seemed to be most in the hands of Divine Providence – in 1529 and 1683 at Vienna, for example – some thought that quite mundane circumstances were crucial factors in the outcome. The annals of the monastery of Melk in Lower Austria left open the possibility that God had intervened on the behalf the city in 1529, but also reported that the Turks abandoned the field upon hearing that reinforcements were on the way from Bohemia and other Austrian lands. Defending Nové Zámky in 1663, Adam Forgács had little to say about his Christian mission as he refused to yield to the Turks. Beyond a routine 'God forbid', when he raised the possibility of defeat, the commander saw himself as simply obeying his king's orders to defend royal holdings. An anonymous account that followed the second Turkish defeat before Vienna in 1683 respectfully acknowledged the blessings God had conferred upon imperial weapons. It also, however, laid great stress on the surprise factor of John Sobieski's advance from the mountains outside of the city.[113]

By the end of the eighteenth century, however, the secular side of human affairs was becoming the centre of historical narratives, even in works where religion figured prominently. In the literature of Bohemia and Moravia in the eighteenth century, for example, military figures rather than a Christian divinity became responsible for great victories. If truth was accessible at all, increasingly it was through the data of this world. Both notions were on the way to becoming foundational building blocks for serious scholarship of any kind, in the Habsburg empire and the Western world generally.

The house of Austria itself had something to lose in this resetting of intellectual values in its lands. Stripped of their confessional nimbus, Habsburg rulers were in danger of becoming one among many in the human cast of characters who drove the Turks and Islam from central Europe. Eugene of Savoy remained in a category by himself, but none of Vienna's other commanders nor members of the ruling dynasty itself had that larger-than-life quality. New heroes closer to regional sensibilities than the interests of the ruling dynasty entered the story of victory over the Ottomans. Czechs discovered Jan Spork, a seventeenth-century cavalry leader in the Turkish wars. As early as the eighteenth century, František Pelcl demonstrated how Czech historians would treat the house of Habsburg's victory over the Turks in 1683. His two-volume history devotes little more than a page to the defence of Vienna in 1683; the Czech religious revolt of the Hussites in the late fourteenth and fifteenth centuries is presented in blow-by-blow detail.[114]

Should localist passion in the Habsburg empire find help in the weakened but still adjacent Ottoman state, the integrity of the house of Austria's lands could be seriously jeopardized. The first of the dynasty's realms to do so in the first half of the nineteenth century was Hungary. Struggling with national and social revolution throughout his holdings in 1848 and 1849, the new emperor, Franz Joseph, called upon Russia to help him put down a separatist movement in the kingdom. With the tsar's forces bearing down upon him, the leader of the rebellion, Louis Kossuth, realized that patriotic Hungarians and Turks faced oppressors in both St

Petersburg and Vienna. Hungary's once-mortal foe was now benign compared to the regime in Vienna.[115]

Kossuth made quick use of his newfound ally. Indeed, he owed his life to the sultan. Fleeing before the combined Russo-Austrian forces, he took asylum at a camp in Ottoman territory where he hoped to regroup his supporters. The Turks would not extradite him to Vienna, even after he refused to become a Muslim. Only if he changed his religious allegiance could he join the Ottoman army, a step that would have released him from Habsburg control. Guarding him vigilantly, the Ottoman government foiled several Austrian attempts to assassinate or to kidnap him, but eventually interned the rebel and his family in Anatolia. Though he escaped in 1851 for the United States and then permanent European exile, the Ottoman interlude gave Kossuth the chance to build the case for Hungarian independence that he would preach to anyone who would listen until his death in 1894.[116]

Another signal to Habsburg monarchs that Hungary's revision of its historical relationship with the Ottomans could be dangerous was the publication in 1853 of the memoirs of János Szalárdi. An archivist in seventeenth-century Transylvania, the author gave a glowing account of the regime of Gabriel Bethlen, a Calvinist ruling prince of the region, who found the Turks more tolerant than most rulers of the day, and enjoyed their trust and respect in return. Best of all, Szalárdi observed, Bethlen had kept his peoples out of the imperial armies, letting the Habsburgs to fend for themselves.[117]

But even as Habsburg rulers would lose some preeminence among their peoples as the latter substituted one history of relations with the Turks for another, the government in Vienna had more to gain from the broadening of its perspectives on the Ottoman empire than by resurrecting the stereotypes of the past. Distorted images told one little about the tastes and behaviour of a realm that Vienna was eager to exploit economically. Nor did such cliches help diplomats in the give and take of international relations. Even though the Porte no longer threatened central Europe directly, Vienna could not write off alliances with anyone. Habsburg forces had pushed the Ottomans back to the Balkans, but both states still had an extensive common border. The cross-cultural analogies of men like Busbecq and Gerlach, even stereotypes themselves, may have opened up a virtually inaccessible world to Europeans who thought readily in these terms. One had to move beyond such devices to come to a clear and productive understanding of others. Such work, however, was not for amateurs. By the eighteenth century Vienna was coming to realize that it had no alternative but to support serious scholarship in the study of the East if it hoped to protect its perceived interests in the region. The results of the policy, however, reached far beyond the conduct of foreign affairs. They contributed to and reflected a reshaping of the intellectual and cultural life in the Habsburg empire as a whole. They also remain significant today both to scholars and to the authorities who need their expertise.

East-central Europe *circa* 1815.

CHAPTER 3

Servants to Government and Learning

PUTTING SCHOLARS TO WORK

The cosmopolitan side of Renaissance humanism lived on in the Habsburg empire, though outside of its cultural mainstream until the eighteenth century. Learned arguments for the moral solidarity of humankind were irrelevant to the sectarian polemics of the Reformation in central Europe and pressures on both government and Church to indoctrinate an entire population against the Muslim Turks.[1] Rulers in Vienna certainly needed information about the non-European world, but they routinely satisfied themselves with what came to them through occasional commercial reports and more often the memoranda of commanders and ambassadors.

Original and illuminating though these accounts often were, they were almost always reflections of the author's personal interests, professional orientation and serendipitous experience. All European governments with political and economic interests in the Ottoman empire needed more consistently reliable information about the Ottoman regime. Some states got to the problem very quickly. France and England, interested in both trade relations and military alliances with the Porte from the sixteenth century on, were among the first to address a basic problem of communication. Arabic had been taught at the Collège de France from 1538. Oxford and Cambridge established chairs for the language by 1630s, in part to strengthen Christian biblical scholarship and theological learning, but also because the sheer size of the Islamic world, including the Ottoman empire, called for greater knowledge of it.[2] The kings of Poland had their own translators' institute in Constantinople after 1621; John Sobieski himself had studied Oriental languages. France's Louis XIV set up a school in 1669/70 to train boys as translators and interpreters for service in the East. Reorganized in 1796, it put the French capital on the way to becoming Europe's centre of Arabic and Turkish studies.[3]

The government in Vienna took more time, even though by the middle of the sixteenth century imperial ambassadors were reporting that the Turks negotiated far more willingly with people who spoke their language. The Habsburgs initially relied upon local help from the Levant to translate and interpret Turkish materials for ambassadors and special missions sent to Constantinople. The work of such people often fell short, in part because they often put a text from Turkish into European languages familiar to Ottoman officials, then retranslated them into something that Vienna's emissaries understood. Italian or Croatian were the most common intermediate tongues. Finding people who not only knew Turkish well enough to serve effectively in Constantinople but were also politically trustworthy was a constant and sometimes crucial problem. Some likely choices talked more than they should, others were too old or too infirm. Important documents that were sent to the Habsburg government in the sixteenth century lay unread in its chancellories because no one who could read them was immediately available.[4]

By the middle of the seventeenth century, imperial envoys to the Porte were growing increasingly uncomfortable with these arrangements. Off to the sultan's lands in 1644, Count Czernin asked that four 'poor' boys be assigned to him who could pick up the fundamentals of Arabic, in his view the basis of Turkish. Though his philology was faulty, his reasoning was sound: the emperor, he said, could use young people with such training. Officials in Vienna had been thinking along these lines, but had yet to move. Four years earlier, their resident ambassador at the Porte, Johann Rudolf Schmidt, ran across a lad whom he dispatched to the emperor's court in Vienna to be trained as a translator. Of German extraction, but now a slave and a Muslim, the youth was sent back to Constantinople immediately. The Habsburg government feared that he might be a spy; it also instructed Schmidt not to send such persons to the Habsburg capital again. Soon after, however, youngsters from the various regions of the Habsburg empire were being assigned to the Porte to study language and translation skills in a government school of sorts, the *Sprachknaben Institut* under the supervision of the ambassador, or *Internuntius*, himself.[5]

As in England and France, the Vienna regime quickly saw that higher levels of linguistic scholarship had their uses too. In 1665, Johannes Baptista Podestà, an Italian from Istria who had studied Eastern languages, arrived in Vienna as a translator in Leopold I's chancellories. The emperor ordered him off to Rome where he could further polish his skills under the tutelage of Ludovico Marracci, whose translation of the Koran, while it took issue with Islam where it ran counter to Christian belief, far outclassed earlier efforts.[6] Leopold's government thought enough of

Maracci to ask him in 1683 to decipher the text on the captured Turkish flag that Sobieski sent to the papacy.

In 1674 Podestà became the first professor of Oriental languages and of Koranic law at the University of Vienna. Here he not only lectured publicly but privately used his position to argue before both state and provincial officials for money to found an Institute for Oriental Languages modelled after one at the University of Heidelberg in the Rhenish Palatinate. Such studies, he argued, would not only be useful to the 'fatherland but enhance its honour and reputation as well'. He also urged the estates of Lower Austria to pressure Leopold I to take over some of the expenses for a print shop with Eastern type fonts that he was running out of his own pocket. For a short time, he also headed a school in Vienna to train students in Turkish. Though this endeavour collapsed quickly for lack of enrolment, he accompanied some of the boys sent for language training in Constantinople. There he applied himself to preparing texts for teaching purposes.[7]

Podestá was not alone, either in his professional interests or in the lengths to which he would go to bring his discipline to public attention. A comparative grammar of Arabic, Turkish and Persian that he put together carried an introduction written by another (and eventually far more influential) orientalist then in Vienna, Franz von Mesquien Meninski. Born in Lorraine – the noble name Meninski was given to him in Poland where he had tutored the son of the Polish-Lithuanian grandee Alexander Radziwiłł – he was largely self-trained in Eastern languages. He served in several Polish embassies to Constantinople before joining the court of Leopold I as High Translator in 1671. The regime called upon him for other services as well. Meninski both gathered intelligence and acted as a state informant: in January of 1684, he reported to the Imperial War Council that two suspicious Armenians clad as Germans were in Vienna.[8]

Like legions of scholars before and after him, Meninski was an unabashed prima donna. John Diadato, the first (and very prickly), licensed coffee house proprietor in Vienna, bitterly resented him for not acknowledging the merchant's help with Turkish words in the massive comparative study of Turkish, Arabic and Persian that would be the linguist's enduring achievement. He would have been very happy to know that the size of his publication list dwarfed that of his likeliest contemporary competitor in the Habsburg lands, Jacob Nagy von Harsányi, a Hungarian who had compiled an excellent collection of Turkish expressions with their Latin equivalents.[9]

Pettiness, however, did not compromise Meninski's scholarship or his commitment to the well-being of his discipline. After 1675, he also had a small print shop in his own home in the Rossau, which at the time was one of the outlying areas of Vienna. Though he had the imperial privilege to publish books, his own prominent among them, he most certainly was not in the business for profit. He was his own printer, proofreader and salesperson, even filling in letters by hand in his publications when his type fonts failed him. Compiling exhaustive studies of oriental languages was for him a sincere passion. When a band of Turks burned his house, his shop and some of his manuscripts in 1683, Meninski set right back to reconstituting his work and completing it.[10]

Thus, though the victory of 1683 may have marked a serious turning point for German scholarship generally in the peaceful study of Islam and the East, it had been underway several years before that in central Europe. The working relationship between research in oriental languages and interests of state that Meninski established with the Habsburg government furthered these studies incrementally. He was long since dead when his completed *Institutiones Linguae Turcicae cum Rudimentis Paralellis Arabicae & Persicae* came out in 1756 in Vienna under government sponsorship. But he would have been thoroughly gratified to see that Kaunitz and Maria Theresa had discovered that meticulous learning helped them to deal effectively with the Porte. Indeed, the empress herself, whose formal education was sketchy to say the least, could sound quite professorial when it came to Eastern languages. Commissioning a later edition of Meninski's work for use both at home and abroad, she ordered consultations with translators/interpreters in Constantinople on new words and current usages. Once verified and explained in a Western language, this information was also to be added to two other lexicons compiled by Eastern scholars and to be used in the revision process. The appearance of the finished product in three volumes in 1780 could not have been better timed from the standpoint of the Habsburg government and sales generally. A Russo–Turkish War was in the offing, and the work was enthusiastically received throughout Europe. With the empress sending gift copies to learned institutions abroad, the first printing quickly sold out.[11]

Supporting the study of Eastern languages even conveyed intellectual prestige in the Habsburg lands. A memorandum to the court in 1780 requesting the appointment of a professor of Arabic at the University of Vienna emphasized budgetary advantages: such a person could work part-time on the Meninski project and do odd jobs for the government in the Orient and in the imperial library. The paper also pointed out, however, that the presence of such a man on the faculty would make the institution itself more competitive with its counterparts in Paris, Rome and Göttingen.[12] Joseph von Sonnenfels knew better than most how rewarding the study of Eastern languages could be for even the humblest of Habsburg subjects. His father, born Perlin Lipman but baptized Aloysius Wienner in 1735, was expert in several tongues: Hebrew, Chaldean and Aramaic among them. These he taught at the University of Vienna while he also provided language services for both the Habsburg court and the government. A coat of arms from Maria Theresa and a new name – Aloys von Sonnenfels – brought him high rewards for his labours, and also the respect of his son. In sketching a plan for an Academy of Arts and Sciences in 1784, Joseph made sure to include Oriental languages among the disciplines represented.[13]

The introduction to the 1756 edition of the Meninski dictionary also implied that the work would have a broader audience than scholars and government officials who occasionally consulted them. Written by Adam Francis Kollár, the first historian to direct the imperial court library, it declared that Arabic, Turkish and Persian literature was in itself worthy of study, especially by 'wellborn boys'.[14] Though aesthetic niceties were not their first concern, Maria Theresia and her advisors were indeed revisiting the problem of schooling young men in Eastern languages at that very moment. Sending future Habsburg translators to Constantinople for systematic job training had been a major advance over the improvised hiring in earlier times. By the middle of the eighteenth century, however, it had outlived its uses. The *Internuntius* had too much to do to instruct his charges properly. Prince Kaunitz, who steered many aspects of the Empress's government, thought that the programme cost far too much. Having students leave Vienna for Constantinople at a point where their Turkish language skills required only a final polishing would cut budgets for their education by half. A longer period spent in their homeland would allow state and Church to ground the youngsters more thoroughly in Christian-Catholic morals – a hint that some earlier trainees, who had virtually grown up at the Porte, had adjusted all too well to local custom and religious belief.[15]

In 1754, the Habsburg regime opened the 'Imperial Royal Academy of Oriental Languages'. The first director was a sensitive and intelligent Jesuit, Father Joseph Franz. The order both housed the school in its college, at the time attached to the University of Vienna, and subsidized it directly for twenty years. With two prefects to assist him, Franz now had the opportunity to realize a professional agenda that was all his own: he was the author of a Turkish grammar that his fellow clergy had used successfully, and he was eager to try it out on students. But even a thoroughgoing anti-clerical like Johann Pezzl believed that Franz was linguistically up to this new responsibility.[16] He had, in fact, spent several years in the Ottoman lands as secretary to a Habsburg resident ambassador and had applied himself not only to learning Turkish, but to studying the political structure of the Ottoman empire. He was therefore quite sympathetic to the utilitarian motives that prompted the empress and Kaunitz to found the Academy. Imperfect knowledge of Turkish in negotiating with the Ottomans encouraged slips of the tongue that deeply offended the sultan's officials; fluency in local tongues also improved trade relations in the East.[17]

From its outset, the goals and curriculum of the Oriental Academy shifted according to the administrative needs of the day. Kaunitz intended at first to prepare only translators. By 1774, he realized, as had Louis XIV much earlier, that his government needed well-trained interpreters as well. Students from Vienna were being posted not only to Constantinople but along the far reaching Habsburg–Ottoman borders where oral communication often took place between peoples whose native languages were mutually unintelligible. The Habsburg institute, however, broadened its mission significantly over the years. Whereas the French counterpart continued to turn out only translators and interpreters, the most gifted students in Vienna were treated as candidates for the higher grades of the consular and diplomatic corps.[18]

Political and military pressures throughout Europe also shaped the programmes of the Academy. Russia's emergence as a contender for influence in eastern and south-eastern Europe made the government in Vienna all the more eager to have politically trustworthy linguists. Habsburg subjects rather than foreigners quickly became preferred students. Franz's successor, Johann Negress, would argue for a two-year intensive language course at the Academy as a way of training a larger number of native sons more quickly. In fact, he did not want to accept foreigners at all. 'Greeks', he said, were especially suspect when they were dealing with the Russians, probably because they shared Eastern Orthodox faiths. Military commanders also required loyal translators and interpreters. Growing contacts with the Porte and with Ottoman subjects in south-eastern Europe and the Middle East also created a demand for instruction in demotic Greek, Armenian, even Georgian, languages other than Turkish. By 1786, the academy would be teaching all of these languages.[19]

In 1785, the Habsburg government was dispatching graduates of the Oriental Academy to a wide variety of regions in the Ottoman empire. Twenty-one graduates were deployed abroad from the European borderlands to Morocco. Ten were in Constantinople itself, including four *Sprachknaben* honing their speaking and writing skills.[20] The Academy had also received some public recognition as a scholarly institution. Johann Pezzl, who also wrote a popular guidebook to the city of Vienna – it went through five editions by 1820 – praised not only the school but its library. Eastern manuscripts there and in the Imperial Library, he said, received the same careful attention as Greek and Latin materials.

The Academy's policies also reinforced other causes that confirmed Josephinists like Pezzl endorsed. Minimizing class distinctions among the personnel in Habsburg administrations and government service was one. Father Franz recommended that students wear the same colour of clothes without gold and silver ornaments, a way of keeping the high nobility from signalling its presence in the student body. Reporting the socioeconomic makeup of the first class he admitted to the institute in 1754, Franz stressed his efforts to find pupils who were talented, industrious and more or less socially equal as 'Landeskinder'. These he apparently took to be the offspring of men who had served the Habsburg government well as mid-level bureaucrats. Those who sired large numbers of children also deserved preferential admissions for their sons. The seven civil servants whose sons entered the academy in 1754 had produced an average of seven offspring. Professing the right confession helped too. Among the class was Thomas Herbart, born to an Englishman who had died 'outside of his native land' fighting for the Catholic persuasion in the Habsburg army.[21]

By 1780, the requirement of coming from a 'good family' was explicitly added to entrance requirements, 'all things being equal' (caeteris paribus), but students from the homes of loyal civil servants and the well-to-do bourgeoisie did not disappear. In 1786, one member of the class was a Franz Fleischhackel, the son of the court jeweller.[22] Even as the democratic upheavals of the French Revolution and its Napoleonic postscript made the Habsburg government more reactionary, the social origins of the new classes at the Oriental Academy did not wholly shift towards the traditional aristocracy. In 1803, all save one of the 32 cadets had a 'von' in his name, in several cases because they were barons or counts. Nevertheless, the emperor behind these policies, Francis i, did not want one area of the empire to dominate the student body.[23] And the search for rough equality of family background swiftly resumed. The class of 1807 had 28 boys; their respective fathers were largely bureaucrats with service titles or high technical expertise – canal construction for example. They also represented several areas in the monarchy – a lawyer's son from Prague along with a sprinkling of Hungarians and Styrians.[24]

Talent occasionally trumped even misgivings about foreigners. In April 1786, the academy's director, now Abbot Franz Höck, asked that two talented and industrious Albanian brothers from Scudari be admitted to the academy. Their greatest need seems to have been adequate clothing, a problem that Prince Kaunitz quickly remedied. He also thought the two young men worthy of special tutoring, thereby adding the expense of 54 Thalers to the perpetually strained budget of the school.[25]

From its beginnings, the Oriental Academy proved a willing and useful resource to the Habsburg government both in foreign policy and as a demonstration model for some of its more advanced social ideas. The first mission was quite natural, the second much more complex. Training linguists and diplomats for service in Eastern lands was a fairly straightforward job that required relatively little political will and imagination. Moving state officers and their heirs from somewhat lower ranges of the social hierarchy up to positions where they sat side by side with great hereditary aristocrats in advising their sovereigns called for radical changes in established perceptions of social class and its relationship to the crown. That Maria Theresa and Joseph ii both adopted and followed this policy with greater or lesser caution says much about their need for informed expertise and their willingness to nurture it.

The Oriental Academy accommodated itself to the bidding of its sovereign, regardless of how difficult the charge may have been. Such deferential co-operativeness, however, did not keep either director or faculty from deciding upon what curriculum best fulfilled the interests of the state that they served. It was such scholarly initiative that moved the institute's pedagogues to revise the course of study in ways that lay the groundwork for a nuanced and balanced view of the Turks and Islam unimaginable to the propagandists of the sixteenth or seventeenth centuries.

In linguistic matters Father Josef Franz was a perfectionist. While he gave high priority to instilling the fear of God in his charges, he gave even more instructional time to training them in the complex philology of Turkish, which has many Arabic and Persian borrowings. He also insisted that his graduates pronounce languages as idiomatically as possible. One ill-chosen word, as he said now and again, often aborted a mission. The grade report of the eight boys in the first cohort to enter the academy evaluated overall achievement and 'pronunciation' separately. Only three of them received an unqualified 'a' in the latter category.[26]

But Franz's vision of the ideal graduate only began with control of spelling, grammar and oral fluency. Neither Maria Theresa nor Kaunitz ever thought of the Oriental Academy as simply a language school. Cadets were also to learn other subjects that furthered the commercial and political position of the Habsburg monarchy in the East. Franz, however, along with the directors who followed him, read that mission very broadly. Putting the final touches on his proposal for the new school in 1753, Franz recommended that once the eight boys in the first class had acquired Turkish, they should learn the ceremonial of the Ottoman court along with 'local custom' (*Landesart*) and courtesies. Familiarity with the principles and laws of the sultan's state was essential too. Understanding these matters would make their duties far easier. Only when they had done this could they be real masters of Turkish and conversant with the 'nation' that spoke it. In fact, what applied to Turkish applied to any foreign tongue.[27]

These ideas were not unique to Vienna's political and academic communities in the eighteenth century. The very progressive universities in Halle and Göttingen, the first under control from Berlin, the second under the house of Hanover, were also approaching the study of classical Greece and Rome more contextually.[28] Nor, for that matter, were these requirements altogether new to the training of diplomats and linguists for Habsburg service. Even before they were fully qualified as translators, *Sprachknaben* in Constantinople had to get a feel for daily life in the city by shopping at local markets for provisions. Their formal studies also went beyond vocabulary and the rules of rhetoric and grammar. From the outset of their student years, they were required to study Ottoman constitutional law in appropriate depth. Habsburg officials in 1683 had seen at first hand how useful some understanding of Turkish manners and behaviour could be. A pasha's son brought by imperial dragoons before members of the imperial family would not even raise his head before them until someone spoke to him 'gently (*liebreich*) in the Turkish fashion'.[29]

Kaunitz and Maria Theresa, however, were also determined to train future translators and interpreters as cheaply as they could. Franz was therefore obliged to introduce students to the language and culture of the East outside of Constantinople. This particular constraint did not faze him in the least; he believed that if one could learn French without going to Paris one could learn Turkish in Vienna. Cosmopolitanism was as much a matter of mind-set as of location, or at least this is what he implied. It was certainly possible to drive up skilled teachers from abroad and bring them to the Habsburg capital. The first instructor for Turkish at the Oriental Academy was an Armenian called Joseph. His family name, if he had one, went unmentioned, but Franz declared that his general mastery of Eastern idioms surpassed what any linguist in Constantinople could offer. His clothing, to be sure, had the air of the 'suspect oriental' (*orientalisches Unwesen*), but he was otherwise morally sound. Franz himself recommended outfitting his charges at some point or other in the Ottoman court style imposed on foreign diplomats at the Porte.[30]

The first eight cadets at the Oriental Academy quickly became accustomed to leaping from their own culture to the Ottoman world and back again. To perfect their Turkish penmanship, they would take down Turkish proverbs read out to them in Latin, then rewrite them in Turkish scripts. Students would have had to be dull indeed not to conclude from these sessions that Christians and Muslims shared important

Suggested uniform for students at the Oriental
Academy in Vienna, c. 1806, watercolour.

sentiments and values. 'The son of a wolf is not a lamb', was a thought likely to have crossed the minds of both Balkan and Anatolian shepherds and of Europeans further west. Other Turkish sayings came close to Christian ideals: 'he who exalts himself will be humiliated', 'he who humbles himself will be exalted' or 'fear God and scorn men' (*homines erubesce*), for example. Hearing then copying out the Turkish saying 'he, who does not know how to serve does not know how to rule' might prompt a bright young person to question the routine eighteenth century conviction that the Turks were culturally prone to despotism. Folk sayings were also used to teach boys pronunciation of the 'Asiatic' and 'Constantinople' dialects.[31]

The Oriental Academy often came up short in the bureaucratic infighting of the Habsburg empire. Lax financial management and intermittent bouts with nepotism remained persistent problems. Nevertheless, the faculty stubbornly kept on training students to understand the Turks and their culture without reference to what a curricular reformer in 1771 called, 'old and mixed-up tales of witches, ghosts and castles in the air'.[32] Statistical information and the study of Ottoman political institutions were suggested as fields of study for the Oriental Academy in the mid-1770s, all to broaden student understanding of lands where they would spend the bulk of their professional lives. They were not to be just translators, as the academy's current director, Joseph Kürzbock, observed; they had to be generally knowledgeable about peoples on either side of the Habsburg–Ottoman borders. A graduate of the Oriental Academy might be called upon to introduce Turkish manners and mores to lower-level employees in consular offices who were not always expert linguists. Some idea of the history of the 'Orient' (*Morgenland*), especially of the Ottoman dynasty, would help. So would a grasp of Turkish literature that would introduce them to the written culture. Kürzbock also recommended that the cadets (*élèves*, to use his term) be thoroughly conversant with the history of the diplomatic agreements struck between Vienna and Constantinople and ready to read treaties and boundary conventions in whatever language they were written: Turkish, Latin, French, even perhaps German.[33]

A memorandum of 1786 called for expanding the curriculum to include Greek philosophy, understood in contemporary Vienna to be part of the 'Eastern' world of antiquity. Ethics received particular emphasis for the insights it would give to the customs of the peoples among whom Habsburg diplomatic personnel were to work. Students were asked to compare and contrast the moral norms of ancient times with current ideas. Philosophy also encouraged clarity of thought, a great asset in expressing oneself to others. Such exercises also trained students to get to the heart of the logical structure of texts, as all good translators should be able to do. Another curriculum memorandum of the same year remarked that the ancient Greeks had not had the last word in classical thinking. Arab philosophers had contributed much to pre-modern culture, and students at the Academy should know something about them too.

The Oriental Academy had not forgotten its primary charge of serving the political and commercial agenda of the state. Government needs clearly shaped many curricular changes through the last decades of the eighteenth century and into modern times. Along with work in philosophy, students were encouraged to learn the natural history of the Near East so that they could spot plants and animals that might be cultivated in 'our fatherland'. Modern Greek and Italian became required languages on the orders of Francis I during the Napoleonic Wars when the Habsburgs temporarily took over Venice and use of its mercantile infrastructure. Commercial law, constitutional and customary law, geography and more specialized work in history joined the syllabus as well.[34]

Nevertheless, the men putting together the course of study at the Oriental Academy by 1786 steadfastly held to their conviction that learning that combined breadth with specialization produced the most effective ambassadors, consuls, translators, interpreters and commercial negotiators. Literary studies came in for ever greater attention. Indigenous poetry was a quick and economical way to develop a student's feel for the 'genius' of the Orient and some ideas about the customs and values of its peoples.[35]

General education was even outstripping language preparation at the Oriental Academy. Only three hours a week in 1787 were spent on the latter, with French claiming almost equal time with Turkish and Arabic. On the other hand, one year each of philosophy, including physical science and logic, geography, world history and chronology, took up five hours. Entering classes at the academy did have better linguistic preparation than in the past. But it was clear that their instructors and the officials who supervised them thought that language skills were only the starting point of an appropriate education.

The texts that students had to master for examination in Oriental languages in 1791 were as historical and cultural as they were linguistic. Along with vocabulary and diction, there were Turkish songs and epigrams, the most common Turkish proverbs, the tales of Nasreddin Hogia, a classical Turkish storyteller, and some aesthetically appealing passages (*die schönsten Stellen*) from the Koran. Then there were histories of Ottoman government officials, a life of Muhammad, a history of the fifteenth-century Tatar leader Timur and a history of Nadir Shah who drove the Turks from Persia in 1730. Beyond these were narrowly professional fields to cover, for example the documentation of Ottoman–Habsburg relations.[36] The library of the Oriental Academy in 1804 attested not only to the breadth of the institute's programme, but to the interest and the commitment of men in foreign service to it. Among the several donations received that year was one from the *Internuntius* in Constantinople: a poem in Turkish on the journey of the Prophet to heaven, several works on Turkish and Arabic grammar, on geometry and engineering and on Islamic theologies.[37]

The generally liberal educational environment of Habsburg government in the latter decades of the eighteenth century certainly encouraged such a course of study. It was to be expected, therefore, that some in the reactionary circle around Francis I would take exception to the academy's intellectual environment, particularly when the Catholic faith seemed at risk. Older students, it was said in 1810, may have had all too much contact with people sympathetic to the freethinking 'spirit of the age'.[38] But the curriculum continued requiring non-language subjects like logic, metaphysics, natural science, the study of nations and peoples, law, mathematics, geography and history, all disciplines that furthered 'knowledge of the world'.[39] And while religious good behaviour counted for something during Francis's formally pious reign, the Oriental Academy did not drop intelligence and aptitude as entrance requirements. Supporting the application of his son, a commissar for the Imperial War Council (*Hofkriegsrat*) in Moravia exhausted every superlative in the German language to describe his offspring's achievements in religious studies. That done, he hastily added that the youth had a real gift for Oriental languages.[40]

A memorandum to the government done between 1811 and 1812 summarized the case for the Academy and the type of intellectual fare it offered nicely: the need for the school was unconditional given the political position of the Austrian lands and their natural connection to the Ottoman states. Its graduates would be most effective when they knew both what students ordinarily should know and the 'languages, customs, and ordinary behaviour' of the Orient.[41] The emperor himself, who conversed most comfortably in the common *Wienerisch* of his capital, was quite at home with virtuoso displays of Oriental learning on public occasions. A *Sprachknabe* from the Oriental Academy delivered oral greetings from the Oriental Academy in Turkish and German at Francis's marriage to his third empress, the Italian Maria Ludovica Beatrix, in 1808.[42]

Thus, the needs of the Habsburg government for trained and intellectually sophisticated linguists and diplomats promoted an educational experience for the few young men accepted into it that their teachers were ready and eager to support. The programme paid off for the state almost immediately. At the beginning of the nineteenth century, Austria, with its well-trained translators and interpreters, had a clear advantage over its rivals Prussia and Russia in dealing with the Porte.[43] Among the most successful of this new generation of learned civil servants was Johann Amadeus Franz *Freiherr* von Thugut, whose father supervised the Habsburg military treasury in Linz, the capital of Upper Austria. Having risked his life during the War of the Austrian Succession to get funds for Maria Theresa's armies, the elder Thugut had the kind of service record that the government acknowledged through educational preferment. In the first graduating class of the Oriental Academy, his son became an enthusiast of Turkish and Arabic literature generally. He was also, in 1758, the first graduate of the Academy to be posted to Constantinople. At first he neither translated nor interpreted, at least officially, but merely strolled around the city to familiarize himself with its folkways. Once truly fluent in Turkish, he could wear local dress without danger of being taken for a Westerner. Even after he became the director of Habsburg foreign affairs in 1793, he dropped Oriental turns of phrase and proverbs into his letters and gratefully received gifts of manuscripts and books from the East. Indeed, he asked Habsburg ambassadors and the men on their staffs to find literature and manuscripts for him when they went to the Near and Middle East. In dispatching Joseph von Hammer, a prodigiously gifted and industrious *Sprachknabe*, to Constantinople in 1799, Thugut asked the younger man to find him a copy of the *Thousand and One Nights* which, in various translations and forms, was widely ready throughout the entire eighteenth century. Some diplomats never strayed far from scholarly preoccupations at all. Bernhard *Freiherr* von Jenisch was also in the Academy's first graduating class and went to the Porte as a diplomat. Eventually, however, he edited a Persian history and became the director of the Vienna school itself. The continued updating of the Meninski dictionary was one of his lifelong causes. And at least one of the early graduates, Thomas Chabert, took the cause of understanding the Ottomans on their own terms very literally by writing a drama about Janissaries in Turkish.[44]

The impact of the educational programme of the Oriental Academy, combined with Joseph II's general policy of minimizing religious differences among peoples, thus had cultural implications that stretched far beyond the hobbies of diplomats and the intellectual idiosyncrasies of linguistically gifted alumni. It encouraged students to criticize and reject traditional and recent stereotypes of the Turks and Muslims and to think hard about assigning the erstwhile enemy a place in the human household that, at the same time, respected their religious, cultural and linguistic singularity. Though the various reworkings of the goals and of the curriculum of the Oriental Academy took place over nearly a half of a century, some of its earliest graduates absorbed the intellectual force of this instruction very early and followed its logic in ways that Habsburg governments did not wholly reject, but could not fully applaud either.

JOSEPH VON HAMMER-PURGSTALL: THE MAN AND HIS PROGRAMME

The careers of Baron Thugut and the young man whom he delegated to find a copy of the *Thousand and One Nights* for him crossed repeatedly. As director of foreign affairs for the monarchy, Thugut was for a time Joseph von Hammer-Purgstall's operational supervisor. It was the latter, however, whose impassioned commitment to the uniqueness of Islamic and Eastern cultures influenced Oriental studies throughout central Europe most profoundly. While aware of the relationship between knowledge and power that was crucial in all government thinking – the British, he said, had mastered India politically and intellectually by placing educated and meritorious men in its diplomatic service – his overriding mission was to understand Eastern cultures on their own terms rather than in the framework of values and stereotypes shaped by the West. He rejected out of hand the common European assumption of his time that knowledge of the self and knowledge of the other were more or less the same thing.

Judged by his reception from intellectuals and many civil servants in his homeland and abroad, Hammer-Purgstall succeeded brilliantly. His education was not perfect, as colleagues both malicious and constructive often pointed out. The Hungarian Ignaz Goldziher, the most notable orientalist to emerge from the Habsburg monarchy in the second half of the nine-teenth century, complained as a student that Hammer-Purgstall so dominated Austrian study of the East that it stopped in its tracks after his death in 1856. Nor were his evaluations of source materials always reliable. Nevertheless, travel and extended residence in the Near East did much to offset gaps in his linguistic and scholarly background. Historians from other nations quickly capitalized on his work. Nineteenth-century Turkish historians of the Ottoman empire drew heavily on his published research for their own writing. His awesome productivity alone turned him into an acknowledged 'colossus' among his peers, as a nineteenth-century French student of Oriental Studies put it. Even Goldziher made use of his work.[45]

Hammer-Purgstall had a lot of time at his disposal; his various govern-ment posts both abroad and at home were ordinarily no more than sinecures. Nevertheless, leisure for him was the opportunity for labour of superhuman proportions. His publication list includes his own poetry, plays and histories, and a daunting assortment of translations: Persian, Arabic and Turkish works into German and other Western languages, Latin materials into Persian, the sonnets of Edmund Spenser from English into German. He was also a prolific editor and contributor to significant contemporary periodicals throughout Europe.[46]

Born Joseph von Hammer in 1774 in Graz, the capital of Styria in south-eastern Austria, he and his family exemplified the meritocractic paradigm that Maria Theresa and Joseph II introduced to their adminis-trative personnel. Himself the son of a groundskeeper, the scholar's father picked up a legal education and became an imperial civil servant. His title of *Edler* (Sir) and the aristocratic 'von' before his surname were his rewards for administering lands that the Habsburg regime had confiscated from the Jesuits when Maria Theresa abolished the order in 1773. He was a Freemason and an agricultural progressive whose work to increase pro-ductivity in Styria dovetailed with policies in Vienna.

Like Thugut *père*, who was also eager to place his son among the 'well-born boys' sought for the Oriental Academy, Hammer senior was deter-mined that both his sons should have superior educations and positions in the Habsburg bureaucracy. Neither he nor his offspring would ever lose their loyalty to the ideals of the Habsburg reform era, particularly the idea of the career open to talent. Young Joseph was convinced of his own supe-riority from an early age, but by virtue of his intellect and not his birth. He retained a lifelong contempt for the ignorant in high places, particu-larly when they professed to know something about the Eastern languages in which he would become expert. Oriental scholarship was a calling for the gifted few. He detested Ignaz Stürmer, a future director of the Oriental

Engraving (after a sketch by Sir Thomas
Lawrence) of Joseph von Hammer-Purgstall
as a young man, *c.* 1820.

Academy, for having won his position, or so Hammer-Purgstall thought, through political connections and not mastery of Turkish.[47] Scholarly institutions were not educational but research establishments, he argued, as he sketched proposals for an Austrian Academy of Sciences in 1848.[48]

Like his regime, however, he saw no reason to upend an entire socio-economic order to realize these principles. He loved his own titles – the Purgstall added to his name after 1825 came from a noble property bequeathed to him by an aristocratic Styrian family to whom he was intensely close. Noble ladies and gentlemen grace the pages of his memoirs far more regularly than do friends and acquaintances from the middle class. Aesthetically and politically he loathed the mob rule that drove Jacobinism, its Napoleonic aftermath and the quality of a person who gained power through it. His description of the French ambassador to Constantinople, a Marshall Brune and his wife in 1803, summarized his feelings: 'Children of the revolution' – he, an erstwhile thresher whose military career had altered his physical appearance much for the better, she, the daughter of an innkeeper whose manners had never lost their origins in a tavern. Hammer-Purgstall did, however, admire people who had progressed from peasant to civil servant, yet wore their accomplishments lightly.[49]

Though his mastery of geometry left something to be desired, Joseph von Hammer entered the Oriental Academy around 1790. The range of his studies was far broader than that covered by Thugut. In 1791 he was taking a class in universal history with an Abbé Bugha, who had been appointed in 1788 to teach geography, history and mathematics. The future scholar also learned something about alternative approaches to religious dogma as well; his assigned confessor was a Kantian whose Styrian student both respected and long remembered him.[50] The young man's grasp of events both past and present quickly brought him to the attentions of his supervisors. They called upon him to analyze the meaning of a visit of an Ottoman ambassador to Vienna in 1790 that marked the end of the Austro–Turkish war.[51] Music, logic, physics, drawing and a daunting array of languages – Turkish, Arabic, Persian, French, Italian, Latin and Greek – filled out his course of study. 'I could', he said, with the irrepressible self-assurance that rubbed any number of people the wrong way, 'translate either from Turkish or Arabic into French, Italian, or English, speak Turkish like German' and be 'as one' in Arabic with the emir of Lebanon whom he met on his travels. He applied himself to required instruction in social dancing and riding with the same confidence, energy and enthusiasm. In January of 1794, he begged permission in his cramped but dainty hand to leave the academy on a Sunday afternoon for the ballroom of the *Hof burg.*[52]

But such diversions were never more than temporary distractions from his studies. By the end of his formal academic work, he was working at the suggestion of faculty members on sophisticated cultural-linguistic problems such as the etymological history of the words 'Muhammad' and 'mosque'. The centrality of Eastern poetry in the academy's curriculum had its desired effect upon him as well. He firmly believed that one could not understand peoples without knowing something of their poetry; the human capacity for rhyme and verse actually facilitated study of Islam. It was, he claimed, the highly poetic quality of the central suras in the Koran that made the text accessible to people of all beliefs. Hammer-Purgstall had a genuine knack for the genre himself. His translations of Eastern poets into German, sometimes in hexameters, sometimes into distichs, are passable even to more modern ears.[53]

Hammer-Purgstall stayed on at the Oriental Academy beyond the normal four years, waiting impatiently for an appropriate opening in state service. When he at last left for Constantinople in 1799, his primary mission was to be a translator and interpreter. Once there, however, he travelled widely. While in Egypt, he put his skills at the disposal of the British navy, which was then operating in the Mediterranean against Bonaparte. Upon his return to Vienna, his career in the government bureaucracy advanced slowly and fitfully. Indeed, it never quite lived up to his self-image and the general acclaim that his talents brought to him. Both Emperor Francis I and Prince Metternich, the imperial chancellor, feared that free expression of opinion, even of the scholarly sort, could upset the fragile political and social balance of class and ethnicity upon which the Habsburg monarchy rested. The less that was said, thought and acted upon, the more stable the system would be. Hammer-Purgstall was unsparingly sarcastic about the effects of the policy. Upon learning in 1845 that membership in a prospective Academy of Sciences might be limited to 80 learned men from Vienna, he doubted that the city could meet the quota.[54]

Hammer-Purgstall and Metternich also had quite different views about policy towards the Porte and about the threat that national unrest in the Ottoman lands posed for the sultan's rule. Hammer-Purgstall's thinking was heavily laced with bio-historical determinism. Both Islamic civilization and the Ottoman state were arch-examples to him and some of his contemporaries of how a major culture degenerates, as all cultures eventually must. It was the fate of the East to be locked in a set of self-imposed but frozen cultural stereotypes. Though it had once nurtured the various arts in the Ottoman empire, Islam had also promoted aggressive, universalistic but unsustainable ambitions. It had also discouraged the state of political freedom towards which history seemed to be moving. The Turks of the early nineteenth century were but the fading political and military spearhead of a flourishing civilization that the Arabs had begun and the Persians had adopted. All of these achievements were now, however, locked in traditional religious, political and social forms that precluded further evolution. The West, on the other hand, was in a highly dynamic phase of its historical development.[55] For Metternich, such speculative niceties were irrelevant to the needs of state.

But the tensions between the two men were overridingly personal and largely of Hammer-Purgstall's making. Irascible and relentlessly ambitious, he crossed his superiors in the Vienna foreign office very early. Briefly dispatched for consular service in the Ottoman provinces, he left in 1807, never to return to East again. Metternich pronounced him too clever for his own good. The prince-chancellor ignored Hammer-Purgstall's expertise again and again, making him at one point director of a statistical bureau charged with gathering foreign intelligence. For Emperor Francis I, the scholar was unfit to mentor the young and therefore would not be the director of the Oriental Academy. Even those not directly in the orbit of Hammer-Purgstall's career concurred. 'A bit too quick with his tongue (*vorlaut*),' commented an Austrian diplomat, Karl Friedrich von Reinhard, to Johann Wilhelm von Goethe, the day's Great Man of German letters, in 1812. No shrinking violet himself, Goethe once observed that partisanship sometimes got the better of scholarship in his Austrian colleague's work.[56]

Scholarship for Hammer-Purgstall was certainly a competitive challenge. Searching for a complete copy of the *Thousand and One Nights* while travelling in the Near East during the Napoleonic wars, he was deeply jealous of some English acquaintances who turned up with the treasure first. Though they eventually found such a book for him, he regretted that he would not be the first European to bring back the work to the continent. Nevertheless, he hastened to add, he was the first to return with the historical romance *Antar*. He longed for the various state honours that the Franciscan regime withheld from him. At last named Imperial Historian Laureate (*Reichshistoriograph*) in 1829, he did not doubt for a minute that he deserved the title, even though critics disagreed.[57] Nor did a remunerative sinecure as official court translator and interpreter satisfy him. Hammer-Purgstall tirelessly reiterated the recognition his work in Oriental studies received from foreign monarchs, among them Alexander I of Russia and King Louis Philippe of France, and from learned societies throughout the world. To cite him, emphasis and all, he was the *'first and only'* scholar on the European side of the English Channel to be made a member of the British Asian Society of Calcutta. When, towards the end of his life, the Habsburg regime at last gave him its most prestigious civil award, the Order of St Leopold, he accepted it, but most ungraciously.[58]

For all his quirks of character, or perhaps because of them, Hammer-Purgstall never lost his consuming passion for his studies and for advancing scholarship in Eastern materials generally. He laboured ceaselessly, even selflessly, to protect and expand the already sizeable collection of Orientalia in the imperial library. Hunger though he did to associate himself with those in the high offices of his government, he chose to go to Paris in 1810 without an official introduction to negotiate the return of Eastern manuscripts stolen when the French occupied Vienna. No one expected him to carry the mission off, he said, but he thought it best for Napoleon's administration to think that his sole aim was to promote study of the Eastern world and not to further the interests of the Habsburg regime.[59] He was unfailingly eager to publish the works of others if their research and writing met his standards, and he respected talents of any kind that contributed to a fuller and more authentic picture of Eastern cultures. Though himself much drawn to Persian, Turkish and Arabic poetry, he recognized that good scholars and writers in the field did not necessarily share his tastes.[60]

With Hammer-Purgstall the Oriental Academy had an exemplar of its programme – a scholar versed both in the functional skills of the translator and interpreter and the larger cultures in which Eastern languages played the central part. His experiences as a student also made it very easy to come away from his education firmly persuaded that Eastern civilizations were worthy the kind of study that the Oriental Academy provided. Though he never became its director, he had a lifelong concern for the school and its instructional standards. He defended both the institution and its intellectual integrity vigorously when he saw them under fire.[61]

The philosophical concerns of contemporary intellectuals throughout Europe also found their way into Hammer-Purgstall's thinking about the East and his passion to understand it. The widely-read German philosopher of history, Johann Gottfried von Herder, helped to convince the Austrian scholar that the antiquity of Eastern societies placed them close to the origins of humanity, thus making them all the more worthy of study. Hammer-Purgstall also subscribed to Herder's dictum that Western parallels and equivalents revealed very little about the fundamental nature of these civilizations.[62] All cultures, exotic or homegrown, had their unique values and uses, and Hammer-Purgstall was as eager to see his own thrive as he was to expand learning about the East. In 1808 Hammer-Purgstall endorsed the call of August Wilhelm Schlegel, a pre-eminent German man of letters much interested in oriental cultures, for German dramatists to take their subjects from their own history. Matthäus Collin, a leading Austrian Romantic poet, thought that Hammer-Purgstall's history of Persian aesthetic rhetoric opened the way for Germans to work their way into their past.[63]

Hammer-Purgstall's notions about the oneness of mankind stemmed from Enlightenment convictions about the universality of human reason. Contemporary Romanticism influenced him too. Very sensitive to the interplay of the rational and the irrational in human behaviour, he genuinely respected the mystic striving to be one with God that he associated with Eastern religion and literature. For him, however, such longings had a certain cognitive value. Because all men were capable of meta-rational impulses – the desire to unite oneself with God was one of them – all men could feel their way directly into this basic feature of Eastern culture and therefore learn about it without the shaping constructs of Western analogies.[64] Hammer-Purgstall himself reached an emotional comfort zone with Islamic culture and Islam as a religion early in his life; his relationship to both was as felt as it was analytical. Arriving in the Asian lands of the Ottoman empire for the first time in 1799, he kissed the ground of what he called his 'intellectual fatherland'. One of his fondest memories of Constantinople after his arrival in 1799, was drowsing back to sleep after being awakened by a chorus of muezzins calling the faithful to prayer.[65]

The ecumenical turn in contemporary theologies that stressed the interrelationships of Islam, Christianity and Judaism further reinforced Hammer-Purgstall's ideas about the mutual intelligibility of all faiths.[66] As he aged, he found certain features of Islam increasingly attractive for his own religious practice. Self-described good Catholic though he was, he became more resigned to the will of an inscrutable God. A tombstone that he erected in 1819 and that he visited frequently in his later years carried an inscription taken from Goethe's *West-ostliche Diwan* which, in turn, occurs in the second sura of the Koran: 'The East belongs to God, the West belongs to God'. A translation of Arabic prayers that he published in 1844, the year that his much-loved wife died, was, he said, suitable for devotions in any language.[67]

Hammer-Purgstall was also one of several scholars in the German-speaking world to use innovations in the study of languages and their development to enlarge historical knowledge exponentially. Such methods enabled researchers to verify documentary evidence from the past with unprecedented precision; it would become crucial to training philologists and historians alike. Students of the leading spokesman for this method, the German historian Leopold von Ranke, believed that they now could interpret the written record of earlier peoples on a level that approached true objectivity. Hammer-Purgstall endorsed both the technique and the goal throughout his life. Indeed, he owed his career to a suggested pairing of language and history. During a stay in Vienna, the great Swiss historian Johannes von Müller advised the aspiring translator to apply his linguistic talents and schooling to more wide-ranging research on the development of the Ottoman empire.[68]

Command of documentation would be one of Hammer-Purgstall's rhetorical strong points. One of his trustiest responses to criticism was to fire back a barrage of supporting data from his enormous armoury of fact.[69] Though Goethe rightly found Hammer-Purgstall socially wanting, the latter's concern for good history and its sources generally overrode his deepest feelings, positive and negative alike. Anglophile though he was, Hammer-Purgstall scornfully reviewed Sir Charles Fraser's translation of a Turkish chronicle of the Hungarian wars of the late sixteenth and seventeenth centuries. Though the work had won a prize of 25 pounds from the Oriental Translation Fund of Great Britain and Ireland, the Austrian was not impressed. The commission supervising the fund, he snapped, was as ignorant as its protégé. On the subject of what Islam borrowed from Judaism, Hammer-Purgstall recommended the work of a Jewish rabbi from Wiesbaden in Germany, Abraham Geiger, and not the writing of two scholars from the British Isles who viewed the topic through 'Presbyterian spectacles'. Geiger, in fact, was a man very much in Hammer-Purgstall's image.

A leading figure in the development of Reform Judaism, he was interested in the comparative study of his own faith and Islam. Geiger much respected the vitality of medieval Islamic thought. He was also convinced, like his Austrian advocate, that one could not study religion without some grasp of the historical environment in which it arose.

But Hammer-Purgstall did not have to admire or even like a person to see his importance to scholarship. He resented Metternich bitterly, but he rejoiced at hearing that the imperial chancellor had been wise enough to gather and pack carefully his memoirs when mobs and the dynasty drove him from Vienna during the Revolutions of 1848. The materials would, said the orientalist, be valuable for historians. The prince, moreover, would now have the time to work on them.[70]

Above all, however, Hammer-Purgstall's thinking and behaviour were representative products of the intellectual, artistic and social environment of the central Europe that was his home. The desire to present vast amounts of data about the Eastern world to the larger public was not confined to German intellectuals of the eighteenth and nineteenth centuries. Poets of the Baroque were sometimes enthusiastic encyclopedists who poured their learning into texts that their more modern successors would say were beneath such vast learning. Widely travelled throughout Habsburg and Ottoman Hungary, Lohenstein accumulated an enormous fund of information about Muslims and Turks which he included in the 'Necessary Explanations and Notes' (*Nötige Erklär=und Annmerckungen*) he attached to his vividly erotic *Ibrahim Sultan*.[71] Indeed, the playwright seemed as driven by the desire to verify his work through the accumulation of fact as were later historians.

The authentication of reality through sober accumulation of empirical data was a regnant motif in the Habsburg empire of Hammer-Purgstall's time. Not only scholars, but artists and novelists were following the programme. The passion for fact-gathering and its organization into a larger whole had their aesthetic counterpart in depictions of everyday life by contemporary Austrian painters such as Ferdinand Georg Waldmüller (1793–1865), Matthias Rudolf Toma (1792–1889) and Friedrich Gauermann (1807–62). The impact of their work, even the glossily sentimental canvases of Waldmüller, relies upon the scrupulous attention they give to the minutiae of everyday life. The writing of Adalbert Stifter, the emblematic prose stylist of the Austrian *Vormärz*, the period between the end of the Napoleonic Wars and 1848, consists of layer upon layer of microscopic details drawn from the material environment. The government found the technique quite acceptable too. Though it discouraged any philosophical speculation that threatened to stir up discord among Habsburg subjects, the Metternich regime had few objections to the recovery and editing of original sources. In fact, the prince himself actively supported such efforts.[72]

Hammer-Purgstall's willingness to look open-mindedly at the Turks and Eastern cultures also had firm roots in the Josephinian agenda that had advanced the fortunes of his immediate family. An elderly scholar stripping the scales of complacency from the eyes of the devil illustrated the cover of Sonnenfels' periodical, *Der Mann ohne Vorurtheile*. Hammer-Purgstall internalized that message for a lifetime. Few behaviours irked him more than parochial narrow-mindedness and prejudice. He bitterly resented the religious conservatism and religious obscurantism that came with it in several quarters of the post-Napoleonic Habsburg regime. 'Bigot', was the strongest epithet in his rich vocabulary of scorn; he hurled it at many, regardless of social and professional class. Preparing himself in Vienna to enter the Academy, he boarded with the Peiserstocks, a family headed by a peasant-turned-building-inspector. Though Hammer-Purgstall did not go into detail, he detested what he called the crude biases of their kind. He vigorously supported incorporating learned Jews into the mainstream of the Viennese scholarly world. Towards the end of his life and trying to establish an Asian Society in the capital, Hammer-Purgstall brought forward an initial membership list of 22 candidates. Five were Jewish, too many on general principle in the opinion of another committee member, a Professor Endlicher. Hammer-Purgstall seems to have prevailed; in a later draft, the proposed number had dropped to four, but certainly not to token membership.[73]

Enlightened free thinkers, on the other hand, he respected deeply, along with all men and women of genuine learning. An influential local friend was a fellow Styrian, Count Wenzel Gottfried von Purgstall, whose son passed the family title to Hammer-Purgstall. A close student of German idealistic philosophy, the nobleman was eager to reform the society and economy of his province. At the same time, his home in Vienna became a centre for Austrian patriots during the Napoleonic wars in which Count Purgstall fought and became a French prisoner of war. The rigours of his confinement left him with an ailment that eventually killed him in 1812. He was, however, much at home throughout Europe. He met his future wife, Lady Anne Crownstown (d. 1835), to whom Hammer-Purgstall was also very close intellectually, on a trip to England. The count had little patience with scholars whose sole concern was defending their own views against those who thought otherwise. He himself welcomed the chance to have new experiences and expressed opinions only after informing himself as fully as he could, including on sensitive political issues such as the French Revolution and Jacobinism. Like Hammer-Purgstall, he was no friend of the Terror.[74]

Experiences with cultivated Englishmen during his travels around the Middle East in 1802 and a short stay in England itself further sharpened Hammer-Purgstall's appreciation of intellectual freedom. With an excellent command of English, he thought for a short time of entering British state service. Though he decided against the move, he frequently compared the intellectual vigour of the British Isles with the small-minded pedantry that often constrained him in Habsburg service during the Napoleonic wars and after. His greatest work, a massive history of the Ottoman empire that began appearing in 1827 – basically an analysis of a great state in decline – collided squarely with Metternich's resolve to prop up the Turks against the British and Russians in the Balkans.

Circumventing censorship therefore taxed Hammer-Purgstall's bureaucratic cunning to the utmost. He submitted his study of the Ottoman empire directly to a censor on the theory that the man's spoken Turkish was so bad that he would be flattered to have an author think that he knew enough to pass on it. He would then approve it without further inspection. He contrasted the narrow-mindedness and ignorance of those passing judgement on him with his own approach to things – 'open, independent, yet quite modest [sic]'. Save for his last adjective, he lived up to that description with remarkable consistency.[75] In 1845, three years before liberal political and national revolutions broke out throughout the Habsburg lands, Hammer-Purgstall was at the centre of a group of like-minded intellectuals eager to rationalize somewhat the system of government censorship by clarifying lines of authority. They also wanted to remove the police from the process.[76]

Nevertheless, Vienna as a city inspired his commitment to Eastern culture and his enthusiastic cosmopolitanism. Its very name, he said, suggested that it should be a centre for Oriental scholarship. It was at a Church council in Vienne, a Burgundian town, where in 1311 Pope Clement v urged the study of Oriental languages in Europe. The work, in Hammer-Purgstall's view, could be continued in the like-named metropolis of central Europe. And Vienna could ill afford provincialism. With all the peoples of the earth linked in their common humanity, Hammer-Purgstall declared, it would be a serious mistake to ignore the historical impact of Asia on Europe.[77]

He therefore made a point of urging fellow historians in the Habsburg empire to respond to the interests of the world, and not only the preferences of domestic learned circles, when formulating proposals for research. In 1849, the executive committee of the fledgling Academy of Sciences in Vienna was casting around for an appropriate project to present to the new Emperor Franz Joseph. František Palacký, at that point the leading spokesman for the Czech national school of history, suggested an edition of the proceedings of the Council of Basel, the fifteenth-century Church conclave that worked out a *modus vivendi* with the Hussite movement in the kingdom of Bohemia. The product, said its supporters, would prove the value of the academy's work to scholars abroad. Hammer-Purgstall openly wondered if colleagues in Asia, Africa and America would have any interest in the subject at all. He was ready, however, to bring the attention of the world to meritorious Austrian scholars. Indeed, he did so quite unselfishly. Hammer-Purgstall was both surprised and flattered to learn that he had been made a member of the American Philosophical Society in Philadelphia. His next step, however, was to nominate a fellow Austrian and historian, Joseph von Hormayr, for election to the society in 1820.[78]

Hammer-Purgstall held on to some of the mental conventions he criticized in others who thought and wrote about Islam and the Turks. His contempt for narrow-mindedness and his drift into Eastern religious quietism as he aged did not keep him from remaining a European, firmly loyal to its culture, values and even, apparently, its cuisine. Where Turkish cooking was concerned, he accepted the distinction between taste and bigotry in his countrymen. 'Baby food', (*Kinder Koch*) sniffed guests at his daughter's wedding in 1838 upon sampling the Ottoman embassy's gifts of a crusted rice pilaf and some chopped chicken. Hammer-Purgstall uncharacteristically let the opinion go without comment.[79] By today's standards, he could be deplorably Eurocentric. Like many of his forebears abroad for the first time in the sultan's lands and the Middle East, he more than once drew parallels with the institutions, beliefs and cultural artifacts of the West to describe his experiences. As a *Sprachknabe* in 1799, he reported that his immersion in Arabic literature had revealed many correspondences in knighthood between East and West.[80]

Turks and other Easterners whom Hammer-Purgstall admired were sometimes little more than avatars of Western eighteenth-century virtues. There was an Ottoman admiralty secretary whom he met in 1802, a man, in the Austrian's opinion, of great intellectual clarity, dignity, naturalness and commitment to public service. Like most Europeans, Hammer-Purgstall sharply criticized the widespread ignorance, indolence and fanaticism he found among the Turks, including high officials who thwarted political and administrative reform. His example was an unnamed Grand Vizier who sat rooted to his chair crying out '*Inschallah*' (So God Wills) rather than fighting a fire that ravaged a suburb of Constantinople. In 1838 Hammer-Purgstall viewed a painting of the Allied Coalition's entrance into Paris at the end of the Napoleonic Wars accompanied by a Turkish ambassador in Vienna. Who, the envoy asked, were the allies and where had this procession taken place? When Hammer-Purgstall replied that the picture showed an event of only 25 years past, the ambassador said that he was a boy at the time and had heard nothing of it. To the exquisitely educated orientalist, the young man was 'good-natured, stupid, greedy and ignorant . . .'[81] While he fondly recalled muezzins' calls throughout languorous nights on the Bosporus, Hammer-Purgstall disliked Constantinople's gardens, decorated in 'deplorable Turkish fashion'. Like countless Westerners before him, he was appalled to find mature, even elderly men, abusing youthful male prostitutes in public inns.[82] The arbitrary brutality of Ottoman political culture that Europeans had long condemned repelled him too. And corruption abounded. 'Money, money, and money again leveraged all business at the Porte', he declared. In 1807, returning home from a consular position in Jassy, today in Romania, he thankfully exchanged Turkish barbarism for the European civilization that he associated with the yellow and black Habsburg imperial stripe at a border crossing.[83]

Nor could Hammer-Purgstall forget the long history of Habsburg-Ottoman antagonism. Sometimes he reminded himself of it. Passing through Wiener Neustadt in 1841, he took his daughter to the town's main church to read a tablet commemorating the death of three Habsburg military leaders against the Turks.[84] Contemporary culture in Vienna may have brought it to his mind now and again too. Popular literature continued to refer to the Austrian empire's negative experiences with Turks and Muslims generally. The vicious Turk or his generic Muslim equivalent still suffered badly when compared with the bravery and humanitarianism of the ideal Western Christian. While the European servants of the adventurers in Gleich's *Moor of Semegonda* are no models of courage, the Muslim wrongdoers are craven doubles of Kara Mustapha in Gensike's *Die Belohnte Treue* of 1783.[85] If these enmities are to be transcended at all, it is only through accepting the oneness of mankind as constructed by the *philosophes* of the eighteenth century.[86] The lecherous Turk continued to amuse. An 1820 parody of *The Magic Flute* has a black Moor groping the white Princess Pamina at the first sight of her on stage. She, in turn, compares him to 'a fly in a milk-pot', despite his effort to bleach himself. Islam could still be ridiculous. *The Beggar of Baghdad*, a brief spoof of the Panglossian side of Islamic fatalism, tells of a miserable man who has lost wealth, status, wife, children, two limbs and an eye. His comforter appears in the form of a self-identified genie from 'Muhammad's Paradise' who assures the victim that his tribulations were all for the best.[87]

The prolific Gleich continued to portray Christianity and Islam as unreconcilable blood enemies. Only conversion makes men acceptable to one another. In his *Peter Szapáry: the Hero Enslaved* (*Peter Szapary der Held im Sklavenjoche*) the eponymous Hungarian hero learns from an Ottoman commander that his capture came about with the aid of the

Prophet. Should Szapary become a Muslim, however, he would be 'the first among the first of the beloved of the ruler of all the faithful'.[88] *Muhammad the Conqueror, or the Death Bridge in Constantinople: Scenes of Love and Horror from the Bloodstained Time of the Destruction of the Greek Empire* (*Mahomed der Eroberer, oder Die Todtenbrücke in Konstantinopel. Liebes: und Gräuelscenen aus der blutbefleckten Zeit des griechischen Reiches*) opens with its hero, the Scottish Christian Roderick, rhapsodizing over the night sky of the Near East and the soft breezes, the rush of fountains and the murmuring of a glassy sea that reflects the stars above. It rapidly, however, becomes a tale of tyranny, female enslavement, Turkish indolence, drinking subterfuges, venality, cowardice and the like. That the Turks are human at all is thinkable only because the author shows Jews and more especially the Greeks behaving just as foully.[89]

Gleich's *The Turkish Siege of Vienna or Count Starhemberg's Heroism and Bravery* (*Die Belagerung Wien's durch die Türken, oder Graf Starhemberg's Heldenmuth und Tapferkeit*) rehearses the same theme even more stridently. Turks violate norms of the European Enlightenment again and again. The imperial ambassador to the Porte, Count Kaprara, 'contrary to all human rights (*Völkerrecht*)', is tossed into prison in Constantinople when the negotiations between the two courts break down before the sultan's campaign of 1683. Ottoman ferocity knows no bounds, even in defeat. When the frantic Grand Vizier Kara Mustafa realizes the hopelessness of the Ottoman position on 12 September, he orders the slaughter of 30,000 [sic] Christian slaves in his camp.[90] Gleich also reminded his audience of how close their forefathers' brush with a brutal enemy had been. He notes that one part of the city, the *Türkenschanz*, today's Nineteenth District, was once a Turkish redoubt. He also resurrected the report of those people in the high mountain ranges of Styria in 1683 who knew that the Ottoman siege of Vienna had broken only upon hearing the bells of a Te Deum coming from the church of St Augustine, adjacent to the emperor's *Hof burg*. Readers were advised that a skull with a red cord around the neck, allegedly the head of the strangled Kara Mustafa, could be seen in the city armoury.[91]

Hammer-Purgstall therefore came to his study of Islamic culture and the Eastern world in an environment that had not only still remembered its bloody history with its Muslim enemy to the south-east, but retained a template of stereotypes to sharpen those memories. That culture was, however, in the process of changing its mind, as Hammer-Purgstall's education clearly showed. From the psychological perspective, he was an unlikely person to have flourished amid such subtle tensions. Congenitally self-centred and ambitious people like himself are often hard put to choose among alternatives, all of which offer possibilities for self-gratification. He clearly could have behaved more respectfully of the Metternich government and advanced to the offices and honours that he craved and that his talents merited. That he was able to suppress these traits for a cause beyond himself – the advancement of scholarship in Eastern cultures – was in part a testimony to his self-discipline, but also to the emotional and intellectual hold that his schooling and work had on him. High self-esteem did not hurt, but it was not the only force that drove him.

On the other hand, Hammer-Purgstall sometimes exaggerated the stresses under which he laboured. His milieu was not wholly uncongenial to the highly compartmentalized structure of his character. The Vienna regime was wary of independent minds, but it had reason to encourage higher learning up to a point. Prussian Berlin, with a vigorous new university, was catching up to the Habsburg seat of government in the ongoing contest for prestige in the German-speaking world; Metternich himself was concerned to foster enough academic achievement within his emperor's lands to convince liberals at home and abroad that Vienna had a respectable intellectual life. Provided that scholarship remained uncontroversial, the chancellor and his underlings refrained from micromanaging it.

Heavily tilted towards linguistic and documentary arcana and translation, the bulk of Hammer-Purgstall's work observed the guidelines of his government quite comfortably. Nor was he implacably hostile to all that Emperor Francis I and his advisors represented. While the scholar-diplomat's ecumenical religious leanings and low regard for Catholic learning and instruction distressed Vienna's traditionalists, he could be a compelling defender of Catholic doctrine and Christian culture generally, even as he evaluated more exotic creeds quite dispassionately. The latter, he once remarked, were far better than Western thought and belief at fulfilling the instinctive longings of the human soul. Mystic union with God, the highest and deepest of spiritual drives, came more naturally to a Hindu or a Hebrew of antiquity than to Greeks or Romans in the classical age. But it was Christianity, for better or for worse, that introduced and shaped these feelings for Europeans. And it certainly had been worth defending. The defeat of the Turks before Vienna in 1683 preserved the benefits of Christian morals and education from the barbarism of the East.[92] In the end, it was his worldwide reputation that persuaded his government to treat him more carefully than other artists and intellectuals. Franz Grillparzer, a gifted contemporary playwright who had nasty encounters with censors, said with more than a touch of envy that Hammer-Purgstall could publish pretty much what he wanted.[93]

Hammer-Purgstall was not the first intellectual in the Habsburg empire to make an informed mind and sound thinking co-dependant, particularly in studying Islam and the Turks. Introducing and dedicating his *Colloquia familiara Turcico Latina seu status turcicus loquens*, published in 1672, Jacob Nagy de Harsányi, Meniniski's Hungarian counterpart, said that the data he had brought together would be especially welcome to people free of prejudice and therefore receptive to 'unvarnished truth' (*veritatem rudam*). But Hammer-Purgstall did live at the moment when high authorities in the Habsburg empire were ready to accept selected products of such ideas, if not the whole programme that lay behind them.[94]

Opinionated though he was, he knew how to present his views in the environment in which he had been schooled. From informal commentaries to major historical narratives, his thought consistently reflects conscious evenhandedness. Criticizing the chaos of Ottoman archives, he hastened to add that Italian facilities were no better.[95] Even his mischievous sense of humour could be turned to demonstrating that East and West had something to say to one another. The Muslim's water pipe, he once noted, was a boon to diplomatic conferences, allowing negotiators to recess for a puff and to collect their thoughts.[96]

His published scholarship was, among many things, an exercise in reasoned understanding. A characteristic example was his history of the first siege of Vienna. Written in 1829 to mark the 300th centenary of one of the most frightening moments in the centuries of Habsburg–Ottoman conflict, it treats the Turks and their Christian opponents impartially. For all of his dangerous ambitions, Süleyman the Magnificent was equal in talent and training to major monarchs of the Christian West in the sixteenth century: Emperor Charles v, Francis i of France, or Henry viii of England. Indeed, in Hammer-Purgstall's opinion, Süleyman may have been greater than all of them in 'power, character, high courage, love of splendour, bravery, martial spirit, and statesmanship'. He had, however, a down side: Hammer-Purgstall unsparingly criticized the wanton destruction that the Ottoman forces left behind them as they moved through Hungary in 1529. But his sources would not permit him to endorse the conventional view of European historians that the sultan's Grand Vizier, Ibrahim, had been bribed by Ferdinand i into abandoning the siege. Arrogant though he was, Ibrahim was for Hammer-Purgstall one of the best men ever to hold his office.[97]

Hammer-Purgstall's massive history of the Ottoman empire, published between 1827 and 1835, was both a realization of his philosophical credo and a compendium of information. Readers and researchers turned to it for over a century after its appearance. The project began to take shape in his mind while he was in Constantinople in 1802; he began assembling sources almost immediately.[98] The prototype of the larger work came out in 1815 as kind of handbook on Ottoman administrative and legal institutions for Habsburg officials in Eastern lands. A dozen more years, and his visions expanded mightily to include a vast array of literary materials that would become the greater part of his documentation.[99] The multi-volume history, he said, was free of any theological, political or philosophical agenda. He had started writing 'without anyone knowing from where and to where'. The sole framework of history was time and space, the specifics of which were established by the historian as he arranged his materials chronologically and geographically. The single bias to which he confessed was for governments that conducted themselves orderly and justly and furthered knowledge and benign institutions.

The introduction to the first volume reads in part as a homily on the dangers of scholarly one-sidedness, with Edward Gibbon's *Decline and Fall of the Roman Empire* as the prime case study. Hammer-Purgstall much admired the author both as an historian and prose stylist. Nevertheless, he found many lapses in Gibbon's account of the early Ottoman empire, the result, said the Austrian, of relying too heavily on one-sided and generally untrustworthy Byzantine sources. Nor were Western *Türkenschriften* in any way helpful. But the sultans' home-grown historians were unreliable too. Hammer-Purgstall notes that they could be silent on events and battles that Hungarian historians covered in great detail, 'one more proof, if it were needed, that listening to both sides produces not only fairer-minded but more complete work'. His text was therefore no apology for the Turks: it depicts the ruthless plundering and slaughter of the local population that Süleyman's forces inflicted on Hungary after the battle of Mohács as graphically as a *Türkenschrift* of the sixteenth century.[100]

Hammer-Purgstall not only had a lot to say, but an audience to listen. He found significant moral support for his work and the views behind them domestically and abroad, and, as the somewhat envious Grillparzer noted, more than enough people willing to publish it. He was often able to solicit private financing for his many projects to keep them alive at least long enough to influence oriental scholarship positively. Since the seventeenth century, European learned journals had been significant disseminators of scientific findings to the entire literate world. Vienna had yet to develop any serious counterparts, much less periodicals specialized in the study of the East.

A born editor and publicist, Hammer-Purgstall was energetic and knowledgeable enough to judge the quality of submissions wisely. He was also well connected among scholars throughout the world and could draw upon them for articles. By 1812, he was a correspondent of the Oriental Institute in Paris and the Asian Society of Calcutta. He was also dedicated to his work.

He recognized early in his career that a serious public outlet was needed to give Oriental studies the attention they deserved. In the summer of 1808, he persuaded a wealthy Polish noble who was an amateur orientalist to fund a learned periodical, the *Fundgruben des Orients* (*Sources of the Orient*). From the outset, he wanted to create an international scholarly resource – he welcomed contributions in all of the 'European learned tongues' rather than just in English, French and German. Not all disciplines would be equally represented. Because theology had good coverage in other journals, the new publication would not give it much space. But what he brought out would represent high scholarly standards. Transliterations, where required for Western audiences, were to replicate the original Arabic, Persian and Turkish words as closely as possible. Above all, they should not be Europeanisms reconfigured 'in splendid Oriental garb'.

Hammer-Purgstall took enormous pride in the series when it first came out in 1809; it delighted others too. A festive meal at a Vienna inn, the Empress Maria Theresa, brought together a motley but dedicated group of twelve Oriental amateurs. There was the versatile German man of letters, Friedrich Schlegel, and the very cultivated Russian ambassador, Count Goloffkin. The most bizarre was surely a court translator, a certain Demeter. The author of grammars for Persian and Moroccan, he was also a music lover and phrenologist. The combination of the two avocations apparently moved him to carry off Joseph Haydn's skull from its grave; not until the police intervened would he give it up.[101]

Hammer-Purgstall's professional over-commitment, which left him little time to edit, along with fiscal shortfalls, brought *Fundgruben des Orients* to an end in 1818. The total series amounted to only six folio volumes. Both English and Russian Oriental Societies offered to help keep it alive, a measure of the esteem it enjoyed. Hammer-Purgstall enjoyed the universal recognition it brought him and the opportunity it gave him to put his own values into action. All six volumes carried the lines from the second sura of the Koran that were on his gravestone: 'Say: Both East and West Belong to God/He leads whom he will to the right way'. Said himself acknowledged in his *Orientalism* that the periodical was not a first of its kind, but that it marked the beginning of the broad diffusion of scholarship on Eastern cultures.[102]

The first volume announced the journal's global reach; Asian contributors were expressly solicited. While the languages of the Islamic world were its main focus, the *Fundgruben* also accepted contributions on Hebrew and Chaldean. Though he intended the publication to be largely for scholars, Hammer-Purgstall also happily accepted submissions of travel reports about contemporary conditions in the East.[103] The world sent back its thanks. The covering letter he received from the Asian Society in Calcutta in 1813 that sent him some books dealing with Arabic and Sanskrit, also announced his honorary appointment to the organization. It also testified to the value of his work and the journal he had started.

> allow me, Sir, to express my individual admiration of that zeal, which so indefatigably prosecuted a study little cheered by public commendation, and of those talents, which have been exerted so successfully, in a path thorny and intricate, and trod but by a few engaged in enquiries whose general purport is similar to your own. I feel a lively interest in the efforts you have made to diffuse a conviction of their merit and importance, and anticipate with some hope, the most beneficial results to oriental literature and to knowledge in general.[104]

Short-lived though it was, the *Fundgruben* and the intellectual principles behind it made a mark on the Habsburg empire's thinking class, especially in Vienna itself. *Der österreichische Beobachter*, a journal of news and intellectual commentary published three times a week by Joseph Anton Pilat, who was close to the government, reprinted Turkish poetry that appeared in Hammer-Purgstall's new series. An eloquent evaluation of the series that Pilat wrote for the first cultural supplement of the *Beobachter* at the end of 1810 was largely rewritten from Hammer-Purgstall's introduction to the *Fundgruben*'s first volume.[105]

Hammer-Purgstall also had a voice in another Viennese publication that gave him page after page for his scholarly research and his opinions on Eastern scholarship along with the values he brought to it. This was the *Jahrbücher der Literatur*, one of the Habsburg regime's significant concessions to liberals and conservatives alike who longed for a local outlet that approximated the standards of other intellectual periodicals throughout western Europe. It was intended to instruct and not to entertain. Throughout the entire run of the journal – it ceased publication in 1859 – around 15 per cent of all the articles, 180 in all, dealt with oriental themes and materials, taking up 30 per cent of the actual page space. From 1830 to 1850, Hammer-Purgstall may have been the pre-eminent single contributor, either directly as an author and reviewer or as an advocate for submissions from other scholars in the field. About one-third of the editorial matter during this period covered Eastern matters.[106] Not every reader responded positively. For some liberals the *Jahrbücher* were not progressive and national enough. Writing from exile, Franz Tuvora, a confirmed anti-clerical and biting critic of Habsburg government, who brought his convictions to the Vienna Revolution of 1848, declared that the publication

> wore the mark of circumcision on its forehead. Leafing through an issue, one might as well be reading the Koran. Astounding figures abound; here and there a few German types. Lovely, very lovely. If only such scholarly luxury had a few crumbs left over to nourish the hunger for learning among the people.

For some it was just too arcane. Another exile, the Benedictine Franz Ernst Pipitz, grumbled from Zürich that the entire readership of the journal was the Oriental Academy.[107]

The high percentage of articles, reviews and travel reports dealing with the East in the *Jahrbücher* was a clear sign that the Habsburg government was no longer seriously monitoring domestic opinion about the Turks and Islam, even among the monarchy's more intellectually restless subjects. For his part, Hammer-Purgstall used the journal to publicize not only his research, but his entire intellectual agenda. As a reviewer, he pushed tirelessly for impartiality in the study of Eastern cultures and, by implication, in all scholarly undertakings. In 1832 he commended a Berlin professor, Friedrich Wilken, for incorporating the work of Eastern historians into his history of the Crusades rather than relying solely on the accounts of monks who could not see beyond their prejudices. For Hammer-Purgstall, the medieval crusaders did not divide East and West. Regardless of their motives, they created a connecting link between two cultures that was the first step towards modern ecumenical scholarship on the Eastern world. The broader the research, the fuller and more accurate the results were likely to be. 'The Koran, the Bible, the writings of Zoroaster have all received attention', he exulted in a wrap-up of Arabic, Persian and Turkish literature in 1831.[108]

The story of Islam, the Prophet and the culture that the faith and its society produced had to be constructed for him with scrupulous attention to its detail and extensive reading in its sources. The *Türkenschriften* that stiffened spines against sultans and their religion in earlier times were 'well-meant', he conceded, but for the most part 'ridiculous' efforts to deny Muhammad's teachings. Some of their authors could not even spell the Prophet's name. Equally ludicrous were their tales of his life, his physical ailments and the magnet that drew his coffin heavenward. Even his

European contemporaries, Hammer-Purgstall declared, were turning out inferior accounts of Islam and Muhammad because their supporting documentation came from only a fraction of holdings in Eastern libraries and archives. Indeed, sources readily available in the West, which he himself used extensively in his work, had never been fully exploited; a good example was the Koran itself. Scorned and maligned in Europe through the preceding centuries, it defined Muslim society, poetically, ethically, religiously and constitutionally. The full story of Mohammed and Islam, he said, would only be known when written from the best of sources.[109]

Hammer-Purgstall's Ottoman history, along with much of his output, deeply impressed his immediate contemporaries at home and abroad. They welcomed the information he put at their command and applauded the intellectual principles that guided the overall project. Moreover, they followed the latter closely in their own writing. Karl Adalbert Veith, a librarian at the University of Vienna, was among them. Like Hammer-Purgstall, he was a committed foe of prejudice and narrow-minded pedantry. He admired Johann Wilhelm Ridler, a friend of Hammer-Purgstall, who was the rector of the University of Vienna in the 1830s. Though also a government censor, Ridler judged novels from the standpoint of personal sensibilities and empathy as well as by the letter of the law.[110] Veith sympathized with scholars in any age and of any religious background when they were attacked with crude stereotypes by their intellectual establishments. He objected strenuously to disparaging epithets for Jews – 'foot draggers' (*schleppfüßig*) and 'circumcised' – that cropped up in charges of plagiarism hurled against Johannes Pauli by Geiler von Kaysersberg, an influential preacher in Strasbourg. A Franciscan monk, Pauli had converted from Judaism.[111]

Like Hammer-Purgstall, Veith could temper passion with intellectual balance, a quality that he commended wherever he found it. He criticized the Turks when criticism, in his opinion, was due. The ruins of ancient Palmyra, he remarked in 1824, bore the marks of many cultures, including a 'clumsy' (*unförmliches*) Turkish fortification. He admired academics who identified strongly with their own culture and state, yet could reach out to people beyond their own borders. An example was a professor of 'Latin philosophical literature' at the University of Vienna, Franz Hammer. Though as a philosopher he was quite conservative – he only reluctantly supported teaching Kant at the university – his vast knowledge of the old world was, in Veith's opinion, 'illuminated and clarified' (*geläutert*) by the light of a new age. Even when, according to Veith, Hammer's lectures became overtly patriotic during the Napoleonic wars, French soldiers from Alsace who understood German came to hear him and admired his courage and dedication to his fatherland.[112]

The first volume of Hammer-Purgstall's history of the Ottoman empire embodied Veith's most cherished values. Reviewing it in the *Jahrbücher* of 1828, he noted that the absence of documentation combined with a surfeit of prejudice had long deprived the subject of the study it merited. Only an author driven by the spirit of truth and real 'love' for the material could remedy such neglect; Hammer-Purgstall was clearly the man, able to find similarities between Ottoman history and civilization and their European equivalents, yet ready to acknowledge the genuine distinctiveness of each.[113]

Hammer-Purgstall's close connections with the *Jahrbücher* may have led critics writing for the journal to treat his work more than kindly. Such considerations, however, would not have come into play for a reviewer of his Ottoman history in the *Literatur-Blatt* of Stuttgart in 1834. Wolfgang Menzel, the editor and a leading critic and publicist of the day, also commended Hammer-Purgstall for his exhaustive research, a testimonial to the integrity of his work and for his 'nonpartisan' presentation. Considerable 'administrative talent' was needed to master and organize such massive documentation. Should the now-weakened Ottoman empire disappear, along with the sources to study it, Menzel was sure that Hammer-Purgstall's study would prove to be even more valuable because it had captured a picture of this 'interesting people' for 'eternity'. Hammer-Purgstall's work on Ottoman poetry was equally significant. It had all but created a field that orientalists had long dismissed because so few sources were available to them. Poetry reflected 'the spirit, temper, genius, and character' of a people and was best kept away from 'hairsplitting grammarians and verse-splitting variant-gatherers'.[114] Hammer-Purgstall would have agreed, as would have some of his old teachers at the Oriental Academy.

Hammer-Purgstall's most significant champion in promoting the study of the Ottoman empire and Eastern culture on the basis of fact and relevant source material rather than preformed opinion and imagery was Joseph von Hormayr. A publicist from the Tyrol and a fellow historian, he was both dauntingly energetic and an unabashed patriot. His prime mission was at first to use his discipline to inform his countrymen more fully about the land they were struggling to keep from Napoleon's clutches. His *History of Vienna* and the *Österreichischer Plutarch*, a set of lengthy biographical essays on major figures and rulers of the Habsburg empire, including Hungary and Bohemia, were written in this vein and very warmly received. Appearing between 1807 and 1814, both were impeccably patriotic and Christian. Passages covering the Turks and the Ottoman menace could be downright theatrical. Yet something of the critical coolness that Hammer-Purgstall brought to his own work flitters through

Hormayr's essays too. The article on Emperor Ferdinand I in the *Plutarch* credits brave, but badly supported, defenders for withstanding the Ottoman siege of Vienna in 1529. It also, however, lays great weight on difficulties that beset the Turks: heavy casualties, inadequate provisioning of the enormous force that Süleyman brought with him, pestilence and bad weather. Writing about John Hunyadi, the Hungarian defender of Belgrade in 1456, Hormayr clearly thought that Ottoman sultans were on the whole a vicious lot. Nevertheless, he pointed out that they and their military organization were clearly superior to the Byzantine empire, enfeebled as it was by corruption, effeteness and religious factionalism.

Even though he regarded Christianity and Islam as polar opposites, Hormayr readily acknowledged that the Ottoman empire had leapt from wild and nomadic beginnings to world-historical importance in three-quarters of a century. Turks were to the Byzantines what the Goths had been to the Romans. With the exception of Hunyadi and Skanderbeg, an Albanian hero who resisted the Turks fiercely in the fifteenth century, Christendom had no leaders to match the Ottoman leadership of the day. Hormayr also refrained from flag-waving during episodes in the *Plutarch* where he could have easily indulged himself. His essay on Eugene of Savoy praises its subject for saving 'the civilized world' from the Turkish threat forever, but is on balance a very sober account of the commander's military achievements and general career.[115] Even the French, who took pride in their own skills in analyzing the past, praised their Austrian colleague's precision and judicious evaluation of documents.[116]

Although he had no real expertise in Eastern cultures, Hormayr published two general periodicals that would be very helpful to Hammer-Purgstall's causes: the *Archiv für Geographie, Historie, Staats-und Kriegskunst*, more accurately retitled after a few years as the *Archiv für Geschichte, Statistik, Literatur und Kunst*, and, to a lesser extent, the *Taschenbuch für die vaterländische Geschichte*, for which Hormayr eventually split his editorial duties with a sympathetic Hungarian nobleman, Alois von Mednyánszky.

Regardless of his formal training, Hormayr was an ideal editor for Hammer-Purgstall. He too was powerfully interested in righting historical records through scrupulous and data-based research. Indeed, he was as well known for such work as his Styrian colleague. Reviewing Hormayr's collected publications in 1822, an archivist and librarian in the Styrian abbey of Admont, Albert Muchar, praised the author for his devotion to uncovering important primary sources regardless of where they were held. Though Hormayr's output was more a description of his findings than conventional narrative history, the extensive and systematic documentary appendices that he developed as part of a 'laborious critical investigation', were acclaimed by fellow scholars.[117] He also brought his concerns to the history of Habsburg-Ottoman relations. In 1823 he bemoaned the dearth of objective knowledge about Islam. He took particular exception to depicting the Prophet as a fraud and a trickster rather than as the statesman and military leader he clearly must have been to have drawn together such a faith from idolatry, Judaism and Christianity.[118]

Hormayr heaped lavish praise on Hammer-Purgstall's commitment to bringing new source material into his work. These in turn pushed the study of the Ottoman world beyond 'the limits of our conceptual structure, our customary behavior, and our salons'. He also shared Hammer-Purgstall's high regard for the insights that came from Eastern literature. Cultivating the understanding of poetry was especially important because it brought together Arab, Persian and Turkish 'outlooks and wishes, their religion and sensibilities, their enthusiasm and the level of refinement, their fantasies, their tales, their love of intellectual playfulness and comfortable leisure, the internal [dynamics of the] harem and the inviolable rank of poets, their strong passions, their routine cleansing . . .'[119] Süleyman the Magnificent, the terror and would-be conqueror of the entire world, protected poetry and therefore the more benign elements in the cultural heritage of his people at large.[120] To publicize and further knowledge of the Turks and Islam, Hormayr willingly reprinted articles from the *Fundgruben*.[121] He, Hammer-Purgstall and others often ploughed the raw material of their findings right into the *Archiv*, sometimes without explanatory comment

Like Hammer-Purgstall he was also ready to acknowledge the limitations of a given text. Reviewing Hammer-Purgstall's translation of the *Thousand and One Nights*, Hormayr found much in it that explained the values and behaviour of the 'Arabian People', even into their theological and legal practices, and their differences among themselves. Nevertheless, he warned against reading too much into imaginative tales when scanning them in comfort on one's sofa. Authors undoubtedly embellished these stories for effect. These works also had a textual history that was not always apparent immediately; these particular stories, for example, had worked their way through India and Persia before the Arabs co-opted them.[122] Hormayr also linked sound learning in Eastern studies with linguistic expertise and published work that underscored the point. In 1821, the *Archiv* ran an article that criticized misplaced syllable accents for the pronunciation of 'harem'. The cause, declared the author, was the use of English transliterations of Turkish as models for speakers of German.[123]

Hormayr's greatest service to Hammer-Purgstall, however, was to give him space in the journals, not only for his articles and reviews, but his poetry that often came with footnotes to explain classical references.[124] His often hyper-specialized scholarly commentaries on Ottoman history and bibliography are scattered throughout Hormayr's *Archiv* as well.[125] Should Hammer-Purgstall need space in the journal to defend himself against his critics, Hormayr obliged.[126]

Equally important for a man of Hammer-Purgstall's sensitivities, Hormayr admired his colleague extravagantly. The first volume of the *Archiv* of 1810 reprinted a glowing article from another journal in which Hammer-Purgstall came off as an authentic German hero for repatriating the imperial library's oriental manuscripts from France. The author described the young scholar-translator as a product of the Oriental Academy with a burning desire to learn, a poet, and a man who had mastered Turkish so completely that he could get around Constantinople in Turkish dress without being taken for a foreigner. Nor, just as Hammer-Purgstall had hoped, were his recovered treasures mere cultural trophies. The *Fundgruben* showed that these materials were really being used.[127]

Coverage of the Habsburg confrontation with the Ottomans in the *Taschenbuch* could be rather more partisan than what Hormayr published in the *Archiv*. Organized to remind readers of significant dates in Habsburg history – and world history on days when it was hard to find anything of significance that happened in the monarchy – the series respected the house of Austria faithfully. Where called for, it trotted out all of the familiar epithets that had been applied to the Turks. Religious antagonism was explicit. Muslims cry 'Allah' and Christians bellow 'Jesus, Jesus' in an article about the defence of Belgrade in 1456. Ottoman forces besieging Vienna in an essay of 1824 are 'unbelievers' belonging to what their own sources call an 'Islamic army'. Turkish-sponsored burnings, beheadings and humiliation of Christian captives abound.[128]

Nevertheless, Hormayr did not wholly abandon his general commitment to intellectual evenhandedness. The *Taschenbuch* could be critical of its own side, even in discussing Christian triumphs, including the siege of Vienna in 1683. Devout Catholic though he was, King John Sobieski of Poland was also prey to the mortal sins of vanity and envy, said one article. Religion was not the only force behind Ottoman aggression; the appetite for booty rather than their faith drove the Janissary corps. Ambition for his own empire and not the Koran inspired Kara Mustafa to argue for the second Ottoman siege of Vienna in 1683; the *Taschenbuch* notes that the *Ulema*, the advisory body to the sultan, had been very reluctant to mount another attack on the city.[129]

The effort to balance points of view on Christian–Muslim relations, and historical issues generally, was more pronounced in Hormayr's *Archiv*. Articles often criticized Ottoman government and society, but in a soberly factual tone. Whether it was the financial system, lethargic admin-istration, unpredictably arbitrary and brutal policy tactics, even the machinations of the seraglio, all were discussed cooly and dispassionately with little or no reference to religion as a cause of such problems.[130] Absence of sources alone recommended against rushing to judgement about Muslim bad behaviour. While we know, said one essay, that Caliph Omar did throw Persian books into the Tigris in the seventh century and was in general a confirmed obscurantist, one could not say for certain that his occupation of Alexandria was as destructive as some had said.[131]

Some articles weighed positives and negatives about Turks and Muslims in a single text; others were more expressly one-sided, but were offset by opinions elsewhere in the issue or in subsequent numbers. Alois Uhle, the director of a state technical school in Lemberg (Ukr.: Lv'iv) argued at length that the anarchic self-interestedness of the Polish nobili-ty contributed as much to the troubles that their erstwhile kingdom had with the Turks as the Turks themselves.[132] Closer to home but still in the countryside, Leopold Schlecht, a high school professor in Lower Austria, was certain that Islam inspired the Ottoman forces. His panegyric to Eugene of Savoy on his victory at Peterwardein in 1716 has Turks crying out 'Allah, Allah' as they charge towards Christian troops.[133] But Schlecht also showed the Turks as victims to other cruel conquerors from the East. His poem *Timur and Bajazeth* describes the suffering of a captured and allegedly caged sultan at the hands of Tamerlaine the Mongol Khan:

> Bajazet was shut inside,
> Displayed like some wild beast;
> But even though he swore and cried,
> Timur moved not the least.
> The Mongol laughed at this pain;
> Sweet revenge was his gain;
> And when he went to eat or fight,
> The cage remained within his sight.[134]

Stereotyping of the Turks in the name of loyalty to emperor and country did not guarantee a favourable review of literary works in the *Archiv*. The critic evaluating J. K. Suppantschitsch's *The Attack of the Turks on Maribor in 1529 (Der Türkensturm auf Marburg im Jahre 1529)* dismisses the 'dra-matic tale' as a poetic 'miscarriage'. Even one episode that features a woman dreaming that 'wild, ugly animals' – that is, Turks – were storming her city was not enough to rescue the piece from its sclerotic blank verse and leaden plot. Patriotic the piece undoubtedly was, but such clumsy writing did little for the fatherland. Sentimentality was no substitute for true imagination. Absent the latter, such efforts only parodied the deeds of one's ancestors.[135]

Christians, especially Catholics, could find items in the *Archiv* that reconfirmed inherited views of the Turks and Islam. Turks were still called 'unbelievers'.[136] There were unsparing accounts of Ottoman rampages around the villages of Lower Austria with hordes of peasants being hacked to death and/or strangled. Even those suffering in hospitals were not spared.[137] A splendid ruler though he was, a spiteful Süleyman the Magnificent tried to poison the city's water supply.[138] The defence of Vienna in 1529 remained a cultural conflict in which the city in the role of the protector of all Christendom against an Asiatic army. The victory was as much an act of God as were the triumphs of the medieval crusaders who, in another article, were said to have benefitted from the protection of the cross against a more numerous Muslim foe.[139]

But the journal also made it hard for readers to come away thinking that all justice was in the Christian camp and that Islam was a synonym for evil. There were the most unchristian Hungarian hussars, who stood aside from the battle for Vienna in 1529 and sold fleeing Austrians to the Turks. The taking of Constantinople in 1453 was as much a tale of Byzantine corruption, cowardice and treachery as it was of the martial prowess and fierce determination of 'Mahmoud' (Mehmet) II, the 'strangler of nations'.[140] The same sultan appears in yet another article not as a representative of Islam at all, but rather as someone who used religion only when political calculation suggested it. A Turk by his father and a Christian by his mother who raised him, the sultan joked about both faiths. Ali Pasha, a renegade Ottoman commander in the first decades of the nineteenth century who controlled the province of Albania, appears in the *Archiv* to have been vicious and ruthlessly ambitious, but not because of his religion. Other than one reference to his Muslim parents, nothing is said about his faith at all.[141] And articles in which some flag-waving might be called for are instead dominated by facts and figures about imperial and Ottoman forces, even in moments of Christian triumph.[142] The continuation of one contribution on the siege of Vienna in 1529 that is shot through with examples of Turkish bloodthirstiness is followed by another on the victory of 1683 that has no religious flourishes. A dry listing of the types of forces that the Turks brought with them is the most striking feature of the piece.[143]

The *Archiv* also offered many examples of the historical commonality of Islam and Christianity. Shared external influences shaped the development of both faiths. One essay argued that Greek philosophical speculations triggered Christian sectarian disputes as well as the Sunni–Shiite split in Islam. Islam itself was also a product of cultural interaction among the peoples who adopted it. While Arabs eventually enriched their own civilization through Persian science and literature, Persians adapted Islam to indigenous tastes – finding ways to soften prohibitions on wine, for example. Differences among all religions were respected, even as their anthropological sameness was apparent. An article on Turkish cemeteries observes that all ancient peoples, the Turks among them, honour their dead but in specific ways. That Turkish mourning practices differ from those in Christian Europe does not make them any less sincere.[144]

One piece suggested that before Europeans decry Muslim customs, they should perhaps take a deeper look into Muslim perspectives on their own behaviour. An essay that sounds suspiciously like Pezzl's eighteenth-century Moroccan urged Westerners to look again at the restrictions Islam imposes on women's freedom. Had anyone, asked the author rhetorically, ever explored the question with these women themselves? Were not the household relations of men and women in Christian and Muslim cultures more a function of economic circumstance than religion? Western couples may eat together more regularly because they do not have as many servants as are available in the East. Asian women in any case, whose husbands concerned themselves chiefly with making money and procreating, have much more control over family income than their European counterparts.[145] Europeans by no means defined humanity, even when the topic was music. Eulogizing Franz Schubert in 1829, Johann Mayrhofer, who oversaw the censorship of books in the Habsburg empire, pointed out that all peoples have their songs, the Bedouins of the desert included.[146]

To communicate effectively with another culture, one had no choice but to learn its operative customs. The point was important enough for even for a patriot like Hormayr to put his deep feelings for his land and countrymen aside. In 1815, he published an article written by DuBois Aymé, a member of the hated Napoleon's expedition to Egypt. Obviously pleased by the generally friendly reception Arab Bedouins had given him in the desert, the Frenchman thought that his mastery of the gestures, hand positions and ritual phrases appropriate to such encounters had helped him considerably.[147] It was also wise to know something of Turkish customs and preferences in order to trade with them. In 1829, Hammer-Purgstall's brother Anton published an article in the *Archiv* on clothing changes at the Ottoman court under the reform regime of Sultan Muhammad I. The essay, in his view, would interest not only the culturally curious but alert manufacturers to the textiles and garments the Porte might be ordering.[148]

Though the *Archiv*'s core authorship came largely from Vienna's progressive intellectual elite, Hormayr's editorial sweep extended to literate and scientific minds throughout the Habsburg lands. In 1820, 72 people had contributed to the journal – librarians, museum curators, people associated with the book trade in a number of capacities, physicians, academics of all sorts, local and imperial officials, including censors and military personnel, along with some who gave no professional pedigree. By its last issue in 1830, 205 people had written for the periodical, many of them several times.

Such geographic distribution of authors for the *Archiv* was fully consistent with Metternich's efforts to convince all Habsburg subjects that they had been part of a common enterprise for many centuries. The long-term struggle against the Ottoman empire was, from the editorial perspective of the *Archiv*, part of everyone's story throughout the house of Austria's lands. The volume for 1829, the tricentenary of the first Ottoman effort to take the dynasty's capital, covered several Ottoman sieges throughout the lands of the monarchy, but not in Vienna itself. The presence of authors in some of the remotest areas of the Austrian empire was above all a measure of the wide hearing that had developed for Hammer-Purgstall's plea for informed and prejudice-free judgment of Eastern cultures and the willingness of authors to submit their work to editors who espoused this programme.

The size of the *Archiv*'s readership is more difficult to gage. Available, according to its publisher, three times a week 'in all the good bookstores in Germany', it could also be purchased in monthly form.[149] By 1824 it was doing well enough to begin carrying illustrations. Initially tilted towards history, the size and contents of the journal expanded dramatically as well, presumably to satisfy the interests of a growing audience throughout the monarchy's lands. More and more pages discussed the fine arts and science and technology. The latter took in an especially wide circle of interests, inventors who might be concerned about changes in patent law, manufacturers who might like to learn about innovations in paper processing, agronomists who might be curious about a mechanical manure spreader.

The majority of Habsburg subjects were probably not philosophically addicted to informed open-mindedness and the journals that promoted it. Nevertheless, they could read popular novels or attend theatrical productions that said something about broadmindedness, at least where Muslims were part of the story. This respect for fact and its role in the story of the Habsburg empire and its relations with the Turks and Islam made its way into even sensationalist history, historical fiction and drama.[150] The cool and factual description of the siege of Vienna in Gleich's tale of the event is sharply discordant with the rest of the text. Christians and Turks in 1683 have as much in common as they differ. Neither is eager to fight forever. The Christian forces in the city are simply lucky that their enemy is equally war-weary. Kara Mustafa, Gleich notes, hoped that the imperial troops would surrender without a formal assault from the enemy. Gleich also takes full account of disagreement between the Ottoman pashas and other advisors of Kara Mustafa over the wisdom of continuing the siege when Western reinforcements arrived. Christian plundering of the huge cache of Turkish booty left behind, first by the emperor's troops, then by the heroic citizenry of Vienna is as frenzied as anything the Ottoman forces had ever done. Gleich qualifies his laudatory introduction of John Sobieski with the comment that the Pole was less than a perfect knight. The king's considerable vanity sometimes descended to petty jealousy; his ambition did not sit well with the common people, and he was ridiculously uxorious.[151]

The actual conquest of Constantinople in Gleich's novel *Muhammad the Conqueror*, while vividly written, comes off as a quite straightforward historical narrative. The futile labours of Pope Nicholas v, who tried to rouse Europe from its torpor before the menace of Islam, are explored in sober detail. Few drops of Christian blood exacted by the Muslim enemy during a massacre go unmentioned, but Gleich does not go beyond what his sources told him. Europeans of the West abandoned Greek Christendom because they had tired of past 'fanaticism' that had only stripped branches from their genealogical trees. Princes themselves were no longer willing to sacrifice millions of their subjects. Gleich also tried to present the psychological and emotional states of both Emperor Constantine and Mehmet the Conqueror in some depth, with each man having a distinctly human side.[152] Even cultural barriers fade before strong physical attraction, at least on Gleich's stage. Tucked away in the windy moralizing of his *Mohr von Semagonda* is Genoveva, a European serving girl confronting life in the harem. Nevertheless, she admits that 'even among the Moors, there are good-looking "black" men'.[153]

Should Gleich's prose have tried the patience of audiences excessively, the Viennese comic theatre taught the lesson of open-mindedness more lightly. There was, for example, *Wien, Paris, London, und Constantinopel*, a jaunty romp decked out with just about every human stereotype the Viennese ever thought of. The author, Adolf Bäuerle, one of the leading local playwrights of his day, takes his audiences on the European travels of a hatmaker, Wimpel, and a furrier, Muff. Neither of them addicted to hard labour, they believe that the wider world has more opportunities for them. Constantinople, they have heard, is a 'splendid' place where money and property are to be had. Should one be so inclined, 100 women are available without anyone caring in the least.

An unsympathetic fairy spirit appears to instruct them in the virtues of their fatherland. She condemns them to foreign travel, equipped only with magic boots, a mirror that will change their appearances at will and an iron chest that will fill with money only when they think fondly of Austria. Two others join the party, a glazier, Kitt, whose only ambition is to escape his wife – 'Satan', as he calls her – who unfortunately decides that she wants to see the Ottoman capital herself. Counterbalancing, however, the conventional images of the Turks, their sexual morals and their capital, are correspondingly negative stereotypes of the Vienna lower middle classes for whom the main protagonists in the play are the spokesmen. As the story moves West to London and Paris, they are joined by enough thieving and supercilious Frenchmen and avaricious Englishmen to convince any audience that the entire world is awash in hypocrites, petty criminals and snobs.[154]

Joseph von Hammer-Purgstall and the men who echoed his ideas about the Turks, Islam and scholarly enquiry therefore represented more than an accidental array of intellectuals committed to the improvement of Western understanding and appreciation of the East. Their activities and their views realized the logic of a long line of scholarly, political and philosophical development. Hammer-Purgstall, his teachers and colleagues were, if nothing else, added links to this historic chain of the curious. Contemporary professional innovations, aesthetic revisionism and radical philosophical retakes on the nature of man and his cultures both past and present encouraged them to try formulating and answering questions about the Orient in terms idiomatic to Eastern civilizations themselves. Frustrated though these men often were by their contemporary political environment, they believed that there was no turning away from this path in the study of the East if one wished to learn something about this part of the world and its peoples.

Hammer-Purgstall and his circle were in the end quite clearly organic products of the political and cultural environment that had fostered them. That the Habsburg regime both removed the Turks as a mortal threat to its peoples and found it politically crucial to command an objective understanding of the Ottoman state and its policies advanced the cause of oriental scholarship immeasurably. While these men complained about the policies of the regime that governed them, they were indebted to it and knew it. Even as they proselytized for the understanding of an alien culture through detailed study of its institutions, they remained loyal to their own. Addressing the members of the imperial Academy of Arts and Sciences on 29 May, 1852, Hammer-Purgstall praised the house of Habsburg for its support of language study generally since the reign of Leopold I. The name of the group before which he spoke – the 'philological-historical division' (*philologisch-historische Classe*) reflected a disciplinary commitment on the part of the ruling house. For this Franz Josef deserved a '"Long

Live the Emperor" in all the tongues of his subjects'. The orientalist, his Tyrolean publicist Hormayr and many like them believed deeply that the successful defence of Vienna in 1529 saved both the German 'fatherland' and Christendom, along with the morals and culture that informed them. This never kept them, however, from acknowledging that Süleyman the Magnificent had all of the qualifications that the sixteenth century demanded for greatness in military leaders and statesmen.[155]

Coda

A DURABLE IDEAL

Emperor Francis I and Metternich may not have admired Hammer-Purgstall, or even fully trusted him. Nevertheless, they needed his skills and talents and gave him many opportunities to realize his personal ambitions and disciplinary goals. Equally crucial to a man of Hammer-Purgstall's sensitivities was the support that his immediate civil society gave him. He never lacked external confirmation that his research, his writing and the philosophical principles that guided him were accepted and even appreciated. Though his bureaucratic career fell short of his expectations and self-image, he realized much of his overall mission. Even having been denied a formal teaching position, he encouraged others in his homeland, actively and by example, to work in the field. He also set the scholarly and philosophical agenda of orientalists in the Habsburg lands well into the twentieth century.

His most notable successor was arguably Alfred von Kremer, whose *Cultural History of the East under the Califs* still stands as the first serious historical synthesis of Islamic culture during the first two caliphates. It looks at theology, philosophy, history and literature interactively rather than as autonomous fields.[1] Even the cantankerous Ignaz Goldziher, who railed against Hammer-Purgstall's posthumous hold on oriental studies in the Habsburg lands, admired Kremer's work and used it in his own.[2]

Like Hammer-Purgstall, Kremer was the son of a jurist who had held several positions in Habsburg service and won a minor title for his performance. He was also a linguistic virtuoso: Kremer wrote as fluently in French and English as he did in German and mastered several Eastern tongues. Kremer *pére* was as ambitious for his offspring as the elder Hammer had been. He emblazoned the family coat of arms with a scale, the emblem of his own career in his government's finance ministry, and three pyramids on a bed of sand, an anticipation of young Alfred's future

calling. Kremer also studied Eastern languages at the Oriental Academy,
though he may not have enrolled for a full-time programme. His highest
earned degree was in law and came from the University of Vienna. The
legal training he received, however, was fully compatible with curricular
changes occurring at the Academy by the 1830s.[3]

Kremer, like Hammer-Purgstall, also spent the greater part of his
career in government service, though he was decidedly more successful at
it than his elder colleague. His initial appointments in the Middle East
were to consular posts in Alexandria, Cairo and Beirut; in all of these he
rose to the rank of consul-general. He represented Austria-Hungary on
the European commission overseeing the Egyptian state debt in 1876.
From 1880 to 1881 he was Emperor Franz Joseph's minister of trade for the
Austrian half of the Dual Monarchy.

Kremer had some serious disappointments. He very much wanted a
position at the University of Vienna, and his father, along with Hammer-
Purgstall, tried to have a chair created for him. Their efforts, however,
were of no avail. Kremer's year as trade minister was marred by political
battles that drove him to resign as soon as he could.[4] Nevertheless, at his
death, his son, also named Alfred, had begun the climb up the administrative ladder of the Habsburg empire.

Along with Hammer-Purgstall, Meninski and Goldziher, his immedi-
ate contemporary, Kremer was also highly acclaimed beyond the
Habsburg lands themselves. One of his major studies, the *Geschichte der
Herrschenden Ideen des Islams. Der Gottesbegriff, die Prophetie und*

Staatsidee (*The History of the Main Ideas of Islam: the Concept of God, Prophecy, and the Idea of the State*) was dedicated in part to the Asian Society of Bengal in Calcutta, which had made him a corresponding member, and the Egyptology Institute of Alexandria that gave him honorary standing. His own government bestowed high service orders too, and though the University of Vienna did not give him a professorship, it did award him an honorary doctorate. Indeed, he accumulated so many of these titles and memberships that his widow apparently despaired of listing them in his death notice in 1889.[5]

Hammer-Purgstall had given crucial support to Kremer's fledgling scholarly career. He wholeheartedly endorsed his younger colleague's application to the new imperial Academy of Sciences for funding that initially took him to the Middle East in 1850.[6] Both men held each other in high esteem, and Kremer drew heavily upon Hammer-Purgstall's work time and again for his own; they did not, however, hesitate to criticize each other for inadequate scholarship.[7]

Nevertheless, the parallel trajectories of their professional lives and the high esteem that each man held for the other only hint at the powerful affinities between them. They brought near-identical values to their research, writing and public lives. Kremer opened the *Cultural History* on a Hammer-Purgstall-like note, praising the spirit of free scholarly inquiry that he detected among parts of the Muslim middle classes from the ninth to the twelfth century. Hammer-Purgstall had himself had been deeply impressed by the culture of the period. His studies of Ottoman historians had led him to the great Arab philosopher Ibn Khaldun, whose speculations on civilizations made him, in Hammer-Purgstall's opinion, the 'Arab Montesquieu'. Kremer would remark elsewhere that this was a time when the Koran was recognized as a text constructed in part by scholars, rather than fully formed from the beginning of time to be revealed to believers. Indeed, both in background, experience and respect for critical thinking Kremer was a virtual clone of his older colleague.[8]

Although Kremer was the more philosophically rigorous of the two men, he also firmly believed that to do justice to any theme, a scholar had to explore it with sharp, unprejudiced and receptive eyes.[9] Whereas Hammer-Purgstall saw the history of civilizations as the story of organic rise and decline, Kremer saw this process as a perpetual cycle within civilizations that could always repair themselves if they paid attention to what their distinctive histories suggested. Muslims, he said, had not always been on the sidelines in the progress of learning; there were moments in their past when they had led the world in respecting intellectual freedom and general literacy. While Kremer firmly believed that mankind was divided into races whose inborn makeup inevitably conditioned their behaviour, such notions had to be applied with great care. Because Muhammad in large part was an expression of the spirit of the Arab peoples, Islam and Christianity could never be fully reconciled. Nevertheless, the two faiths could certainly live harmoniously. Hammer-Purgstall and Kremer clearly believed that all peoples, Muslims among them, were subject to the same universal laws, but in different ways. None of these questions could be clearly understood, however, if bigotry, religious fanaticism, superstition and vanity prevailed among scholars. Rigidly 'binary' polarizations of cultures had no place in their thinking.[10]

Kremer's commitment to this principle, like Hammer-Purgstall's, carried over to events of his own time. He detested the 'shameful antisemitic agitation' that was on the rise in Russia, Germany and his homeland after a disastrous collapse of the Viennese stock market in 1873. Such behaviour, in his eyes, showed that Europe had yet to leave the Middle Ages completely.[11] Kremer loathed religious and political fanaticism as intensely as Hammer-Purgstall had deplored the excesses of the French Revolution. He sharply criticized the orthodox clericalism that he believed had become the dominant strain of Islam over the course of its history. Steeped in religious literature and texts and little else, even otherwise sophisticated and well-off Muslims were intellectually unready to meet the challenges of Western technology and economic ambition. In Europe, by way of contrast, such subjects generally interested only theologians and other specialists in religious matter.[12] Like Hammer-Purgstall, he thought that religion played a fundamental role in the human make up, but so did free inquiry. Indeed, the happiest society was one in which religious belief and free inquiry were in perpetual creative tension with one another.[13]

Kremer also shared Hammer-Purgstall's commitment to high scholarly standards and his outright snobbery towards those who fell short of them. There was, for example, the French scholar who residing in Cairo for many years still thought the Arabic word for 'a pipe stem' meant 'horse'. His contempt for the superficial grasp of Eastern cultures that European tourists brought with them to Egypt was absolute. Though he gratefully acknowledged the generous support that many British subjects had given to Egyptology, he had nothing but scorn for the English traveller who insisted upon having all the comforts of home throughout the trip.[14]

Kremer also found much to fault in the society and values of the Muslim world of his day. Aside from its suffocating religious orthodoxy and the ritual hypocrisies that he thought arose in such an environment, there was the servile status of women along with the treatment of domestic animals, which he called 'truly outrageous' (*empörend*). Overloaded horses and mules that collapsed were beaten mercilessly until they rose again. The lone exceptions were cats, which the Prophet reputedly loved.

Nor, as Kremer saw it, was the Koran always a prescription for peace and harmony. Egyptian schools warned children not to befriend Christians; youngsters routinely shouted curses and maledictions at Europeans on the streets. Kremer admired Muslim scholarship, even its historical sub-variety, but it was of the medieval sort and not recent work. The latter, he thought, was shot through with poorly evaluated legend.[15]

Like Hammer-Purgstall again, however, Kremer saw many positive features in Islam and the middle Eastern societies in which it had embedded itself. He did not share Hammer-Purgstall's view that the Koran explained all of the region's history and culture, but he counted it as the central document of Muslim society. It also had much to recommend it morally and spiritually. The generosity towards the poor and beggars firmly prescribed in the text was, as he saw it, widely practiced. He found himself asking why Western scholars had lavished so much attention on the likes of Charlemagne and Alexander the Great, whose historical records were very thinly documented, compared to Muhammad, who established a worldwide religion followed even in modern times by millions of people. Islam's mystic branch, Sufism, had developed far more effective notions of the created world's reversion to the state of timeless unity and of God himself, than had the '*Deduktionen*' of Western philosophers from the Middle Ages to Kant, Schelling, Hegel and their acolytes.[16] The philosophical traditions of East and West had contributed distinctively, but equally, to world culture. Classical Greece, shot through with oriental spiritualism and mysticism though it was, had nevertheless looked at the entirety of humankind with a certain sense of detachment and even humour. The Orient on the other hand, even in Kremer's time, still served as the 'cradle' of 'asceticism, mortification of the flesh, and religious ecstasy'.[17]

Convinced empiricist though he was – as minister of trade Kremer was deeply concerned that his government did not have adequate statistical material at hand – he nevertheless brought the same romantic sensibility to his work as did Hammer-Purgstall. The latter had been much drawn to Kremer's descriptions of the Middle East's homes, orange and lemon trees in bloom. Just as a much younger Hammer-Purgstall luxuriated in the muezzin's cries through the Middle Eastern night, Kremer declared that sight and aromas of the uniquely fertile Nile valley would prompt any man to say, 'This is the most beautiful place on earth!' (*Hier ist es am schönsten auf Erden*). Watching equestrian games in Egypt, he was recalled to the Middle Ages by turbanned figures on horseback, their coats and broad robes fluttering and their fiery horses pounding through the dust. This, he said, was what it must have been like to face a Saracen horde in Spain or during the crusades.[18]

But in the end, both Kremer and Hammer-Purgstall believed that minds worked most reliably when they took account of data and not feeling alone. Some of Kremer's harshest criticisms of the Egyptian regime concerned its failure to gather serious statistical information on its economy. Westerners, he contended, were not necessarily the first people to appreciate orderly government. In a discussion of the rise and fall of great powers, he pointed out that it was Ibn Kaldun, Hammer-Purgstall's 'Arab Montesquieu', who observed that all states were constrained by the limits of time and space and that disorderly armies and finances were symptoms of decline. And Kremer, like Hammer-Purgstall, never forgot that he owed much to the culture and state that governed them and to Western civilization generally. He dutifully drove up at least one oriental manuscript for the imperial library in Vienna that wanted it. While Kremer thought little of vapid British tourists, he heartily approved of their regime's introduction of a free press in Asia, which was now publishing impressive numbers of newspapers, some either in native languages or bilingual editions. He believed that, for all its faults, the progressive side of European civilization of his time was far superior to current conditions in the Muslim world.[19]

Kremer accepted appointment as trade minister in Emperor Franz Joseph's government in part because he thought that he could do something to preserve the increasingly fragile monarchy. Like Hammer-Purgstall he was a convinced Josephinist; his prescription for the survival of the dynasty and the integrity of its state was one that his erstwhile colleague would have endorsed: vigorous and consistent support for advancement of material and spiritual well-being of the entire population through civic freedom, general prosperity and an orderly legal system. One only had to look at the increasingly feeble Ottoman empire, like his fatherland a 'mixed' state, to see how dangerous the absence of such policies could be.[20]

Reminding his audience at the Seventh International Congress of Orientalists meeting in Vienna in 1886 that Austria had introduced Europe to several products from the Orient, he noted that the East had left traces of itself all over his homeland. The more intellectual and commercial exchange there was between East and West, the more each side would benefit. It was very important that sound thinking and learning flourish in both parts of the world. Kremer had some reason for hope. He was speaking at a moment when there was an intense interest in science, medicine and technology within the Ottoman empire itself. Until the last decade of the nineteenth century, Arab intellectuals endorsed ideas of human universalism and the membership of Islamic civilizations in it. Only three years away from his death, Kremer himself was very pleased to note that Eastern scholars, journalists and writers were about to rival

Western counterparts in their work. The contributions of oriental scholars to their native cultures could pave the way for the intellectual emancipation of all their peoples. Kremer urged his audience to make sure that impartial research, reasoned criticism and the love of truth and progress lived on in the academy. In this way the West would give as much back to the East as it had received from it. He believed, as did Hammer-Purgstall, that Austria was geographically situated to be the centre of commercial and intellectual exchange between East and West. A few years before he had told yet another audience that the two cultures, for all of their differences, had taken much from one another over the centuries. The process should continue, and he urged his countrymen not to let the opportunity pass.[21]

The possibility that the Habsburg empire could learn something from contemporary Ottoman problems became academic when both sides effectively self-destructed in World War I. Born in good part out of their struggle with one another, they became allies in 1914 and met their end that way. Writing in self-imposed exile in London in 1938, yet another Austrian orientalist, Paul Wittek, concluded that the co-operation between the two multi-ethnic empires during the war said more about their decadence than about their reconciliation through common problems. He called attention once again to faith, not only as the cause of their centuries-long conflict, but as the basis of the mission that had given both empires their reason of being. Their alliance betokened a morbid atrophy of their foundational core.[22]

Nevertheless, Hammer-Purgstall and Kremer's vision of informed cross-cultural understanding from West to East, with Vienna as a centre of study, survived the collapse of the Habsburg empire in 1918. Seeking to create a cultural base for the national Austrian state established at the close of World War I, the poet, dramatist and occasional aesthetic politician Hugo von Hofmannsthal looked to the distinguishing features of Vienna once again, now the outsize capital of a very small country. In language also powerfully reminiscent of Hammer-Purgstall's introduction to the first volume of his *Fundgruben*, Hofmannsthal urged the city to persevere in its historic role as a bridge between East and West.

National cultural politics, however, were no excuses for dispensing with honest scholarship and textual criticism. Among the guiding figures behind the creation of the Salzburg Festival after World War I, Hofmannsthal was committed to fostering Austrian nationhood through awareness of its distinctive cultural heritage. While he deeply respected Ferdinand Raimund, among the most beloved of Vienna's classic comic playwrights, Hofmannsthal took exception to the dramatist's reworking of materials that came from a translation of the *Thousand and One Nights*.

The results, he thought, may have been suitable for local tastes. They were, however, far cries from the original.[23]

TO KEEP IN MIND

Hammer-Purgstall and Kremer's respect for the positive values of the European regime that they served and that brought the Ottoman state to its knees may have been too great to persuade today's critics of Orientalism that the calls of both men for an objective understanding of the East were sincere.[24] Even those who fault the Said thesis as too widely cast or even anachronistic prefer to ascribe what positive thinking there was in nineteenth-century Europe towards Islam to absence of threats from Constantinople. Implicitly ruled out is the possibility that other factors, such as the acceptance of religious pluralism or patterns of scholarship, could have encouraged this change.[25] At least one recent author has claimed that objectivity in constructing the history of East–West relations has given rise to as many myths as works written on less soaring principles.[26]

It is impossible to deny that Hammer-Purgstall and the Oriental Academy generally were charged to supply the Habsburg government with the linguistic wherewithal and some conceptual equipment it needed to deal with the Ottomans and other Muslim societies more effectively. All parties accepted the responsibility willingly.

Did, then, their scholarship add up to little more than a central European variant of the quest for power shaping the forms of knowing? Before answering this question affirmatively, one should remember that their bureaucratic work did not exhaust the scholarly goals that they had set for themselves. Their ultimate purpose was to advance the general understanding of Eastern cultures through knowledge of its texts and artifacts. Governments indeed could make use of their findings, but so could any other interested member of civil society at large. Moreover, the scrupulous concern that men like Hammer-Purgstall and Hormayr had for original texts differentiated them sharply from Said's compliant Orientalists, who respected the wishes of patrons more than the actual language of sources. One should also remember that a large part of Hammer-Purgstall's research and writing had no consistent support from government, commercial benefactors or other private funding.[27] Much of it, especially his documentary editions and literary translations, were useless to Metternich and other advisors. As much as Hammer-Purgstall resented his quasi-outsider status, it gave him the intellectual independence to choose his materials at will and interpret them along the methodological lines he endorsed.[28] Most important of all, the objectivity to which he subscribed was provisional and not absolute. Hammer-Purgstall and others like him were quite comfortable in the knowledge that new data would always compel them to rethink and revise their views routinely. Myths, even politically convenient ones, do not stand up very well under such scrutiny.

Indeed, Hammer-Purgstall and his contemporaries were often frankly critical of the intellectual and political setting in which they studied and wrote. But their complaints were largely about a specific regime that underfinanced and over supervised scholarship in their own time. In analysing the Ottoman empire and Islam as a religion, they did not reject the fundamentals of their own culture. They owed it something and gratefully acknowledged it. The defeat of the sultan in 1683 was to Hammer-Purgstall and his circle a precondition of the political and educational programmes that had informed their careers. For them to highlight the more attractive sides of the Muslim world and to suppress its nastier features at the expense of European civilization would have been a signal act of intellectual dishonesty.[29] Their purpose was to understand and appreciate Eastern cultures critically, not to disguise religious, political or social agendas by calling them scholarship.

Two centuries and many ideological sea changes separate Hammer-Purgstall and his advocates from scholars of the late twentieth and early twenty-first centuries. Nevertheless, they still share certain values. Today's historians would not disagree, either in fact or principle, that Gibbon, as Hammer-Purgstall, said, relied too heavily on Byzantine sources in his discussion of Ottoman expansion.[30] Where they differ is in the anthropological and ideological sensibility that many writers today bring to their work on Eastern cultures even as they start it. Informed empathy guided Hammer-Purgstall and his friends; their respect for fact, naive as it sounds to modern ears, kept them from the pitfalls of total subjectivity. They would not have understood those among us today who think that authenticity of a given culture depends upon its radical alienation from all others, or that imperialism's only narrative, the Ottoman chapters included, is a story of relentless victimization and oppression.[31]

Hammer-Purgstall's conviction, and Kremer's too, was that cultures did not, and indeed should not, replicate each other. With this in mind, both men and the circles that they frequented pursued what to them was a radically revisionist ambition: understanding Islamic civilization, its creed and its peoples on its distinctive terms and making accessible the texts and occasionally artifacts that were particular to this culture. Coupling this mission to the new German method of history that prescribed faithfulness to sources as the historian's highest duty and to his conviction that prejudice was the sworn enemy of clear thinking,

Hammer-Purgstall found it possible to think and feel on several levels simultaneously yet honestly. Even as he extolled the beauties of Eastern poetry and pointed out the spiritual strengths of Islam, he remained a loyal Habsburg subject of Josephinist leanings and Christian, albeit liberal, belief. In so doing, he set a standard and even the mind-set of future generations of orientalists in the Habsburg empire. His story, if nothing else, supports recent arguments that criticism of eurocentric orientalism should proceed in case-by-case discussion rather than overly broad generalizations.[32]

The emergence of Hammer-Purgstall and his intellectual comrades in a polity saturated with long-standing negative images of Turks and Muslims argues for yet another against-the-grain conclusion: that the creation of stereotypes can be the beginning of a learning process, a way-station on the road to greater understanding of, and accommodation to, the religion and culture of another.[33] Problematic though such imaging can be, it is also a normal and even productive psychological and intellectual response to first contacts with wholly alien cultural patterns and behaviour. Prevalent social and political norms can, of course, harden such images into long-standing prejudice. They can also, however, provoke greater thought and curiosity about the 'Other', especially when empirical evidence that corrects initial impressions of that 'Other' begins to pile up.[34]

The transformation of images of the Turks and their faith among the diplomats, travellers, composers, dramatists and scholars of the Habsburg empire followed this pattern. The progress of the Muslim-as-Turk from reprehensible to laughable to something more humane – from Ibrahim the Sultan to Osmin to Pasha Selim, for example – replaced one set of stereotypes with another. Nevertheless, it showed that people were actually changing their minds about Ottoman culture, however unsatisfactorily. The accumulation of information among the educated in the Habsburg empire about the customs and society of the sultan's lands took the process to a much higher level. Scholars like Hammer-Purgstall and Kremer were both the providers of that information as well as exemplars of its mental and emotional side effects. What had been an ever-present curiosity in Christian Europe about the East generally was, by the beginning of the nineteenth century, turning into systematic learning that with the application of contemporary standards of truth would heighten the objective sensibilities that scholars and educated amateurs alike brought to their study.[35]

Equally central to Hammer-Purgstall's intellectual and moral makeup and his vision of Oriental studies was the accommodationist version of tolerance that the Habsburg regime extended to Islam by the late eighteenth century. While the deeply Catholic monarchy held Islam to be theologically false in crucial areas, it was nevertheless something that an increasingly liberalized Christian polity could live with and even admire. This attitude would, to be sure, never get the intellectuals and government officials of the Habsburg empire across the very high bar that some writers set for religious toleration today. Perez Zagorin, for example, virtually rules out reason of state and political expediency, both of which moved Maria Theresa and Joseph II to reset the religious rules of their empire more flexibly, as positive forces in promoting religious toleration. Simple confessional coexistence of the sort that the Habsburg empire eventually struck with Islam and Christian Protestants by the end of the eighteenth century would certainly fail his test for true attitudinal change.[36] Assimilation is even more deplorable.

The universalization of values that converted the Terrible Turk into the on-stage icon of human magnanimity is too closely linked to European culture to satisfy advocates of authenticity at all costs, even if it leaves some cultures in permanently subordinate positions.[37] Hammer-Purgstall's ecumenical epitaph, 'to God belongs the Orient, to God belongs the Occident', meaningful though it may have been to him, is too disconnected from any genuine cultural base for it to mean much of anything, much less as a step towards real toleration.

Nevertheless, one may very well ask where the story of changing views of the Turks and Islam might have gone in the Habsburg lands without critical and qualified accommodation to the 'Other'. Such an approach in the face of a long and tense history with that 'Other', may, in the end, be the best one can practically expect from humankind.

An extended line of mental and emotional reorientation stretches from the perceptions of the Turk and the terror he wrought in Renaissance and Reformation Europe, to the doltish but recognizably human Osmin in Mozart's *Abduction*, to the rarefied cross-cultural convictions of Hammer-Purgstall and his supporters. Conditions that drove these developments along were in some ways unique to one time and one place. The Habsburg monarchy was far better positioned to guide public thinking on command than the representative Western democracies of today. But the general progression in the Habsburg lands from abiding fear of the Turks to understanding them and their faith offers an instructive chapter in the annals of human relations. That honest and rigorous teaching and scholarship could, in the end, be both the agent and the epitome of that change is reason for academics of the twenty-first century to think a little bit about the message from Vienna and the old empire's outlying lands. In defending itself from Ottoman rule and what was seen as the 'Turkish religion', the house of Austria and those who served it showed that a regime cannot only demonize an enemy and psychologically mobilize its peoples to oppose him, but emerge from the struggle able to think about that enemy and his religion remarkably free of the negativity that such contests often leave after them. A limited, but highly important group of people in the Habsburg empire had learned that a fact-based understanding of that enemy – his language, his institutions and his general culture – were more useful in conducting relations with the Turks and Islamic than were simplistic stereotypes and faith alone.

With this is mind, one can only ask if Western governments would not be better equipped to handle both present and future relations with the Muslim world if today's politicians and their educational establishments encouraged the public to think freely and critically about the religious and cultural heritages of all three Abrahamic faiths. If reasonable Europeans of the past found ways to adjust to religious diversity by knowing more about Christianity, Judaism and Islam, there is reason to hope that their successors in the twenty-first century can do so too. The process, of course, works best when all sides resolve to judge themselves and each other on the basis of fact rather than political wish lists. Such a task also calls for informed intelligence, patience, fairness and courage, qualities that are unevenly distributed among humankind. There is little to be lost, however, in trying.

References

INTRODUCTION

1 Otto Frass, *Quellenbuch zur österreichischen Geschichte* (Vienna, 1959), vol. II, pp. 161–2.

2 Anon. *Vom Türcken Erbermeliche Kleglich Zeitung Wie unser Erbfeind der Türck mit list darnach aber mit grosser Tyranney die feste Stad Falckenmor in Ungarn vier Meilen von Comorn erobert hat* (Vienna, 1587), unpaginated.

3 Almut Höfert, 'The Order of Things and the Discourse of the Turkish Threat', in *Between Europe and Islam: Shaping Modernity in a Transcendental Space*, ed. Almut Höfert and Armando Salvatore (Brussels, 2000), p. 49; Wenceslas Wratislaw of Mitrowitz (Václav Vratislav of Mitrovice), *Adventures of Baron Wenceslas Wratislaw of Mitrowitz* (London, 1862), p. 105.

4 Nabil Matar, *Turks, Moors, and Englishmen in the Age of Discovery* (New York, 1999), p. 9; Linda Colley, *Captives: Britain, Empire, and the World, 1600–1850* (London, 2002), p. 78; Frass, *Quellenbuch*, vol. II, p. 23; Franz Babinger, Robert Gragger, Eugen Mittwoch and J. H. Mordtmann, eds, *Literaturdenkmäler aus Ungarns Türkenzeit* (Berlin, 1927), pp. 21, 31.

5 Josef von Hammer-Purgstall, 'Erinnerungen aus meinem Leben, 1774–1852', *Fontes Rerum Austriacarum*, Part 2, *Diplomataria et acta*, LXX (1940), p. 222; Wolfgang Prohaska, 'Zum Bild der Türken in der Österreichischen Kunst', in *Die Türken vor Wien Europa und die Entscheidung an der Donau*, ed. Robert Waissenberger (Salzburg, 1982), p. 258; Walter Obermaier, 'Das Türkenthema in der österreichischen Dichtung', in *Türken vor Wien*, p. 326; Maximilian Grothaus, 'Zum Türkenbild der Adels-und Volkskultur der habsburger Monarchie zwischen 16. und 18. Jahrhundert', in *Das osmanische Reich und Europa 1683 bis 1789* (Vienna, 1983), pp. 64, 66–7; Maximilian Grothaus, 'Der "erbfeindt christlichen Namens", Studien zum Türkenbild in der Kultur der Habsburger Monarchie zwischen 16.u.18 Jahrhundert' (Diss., Graz, 1986), p. 114; Leopold Schmidt, 'Die Legende von der mit Pulver gefüllten Kerze. Zu einem Türkenmotiv der innerösterreichischen Wallfahrten', *Blätter für Heimatkunde*, XXIV/3 (1950), pp. 75–80.

6 *Die Presse*, 19 August 2002, p. 6; *Die Presse*, 24 August 2002, p. 2; *Wir, Österreicher. Das Bürgermagazin* (September 2006).

7 Lewis A. Coser in Maurice Halbwachs, *On Collective Memory* (Chicago, 1992), p. 24; Sean A. Forner, 'War Commemoration and the Republic in Crisis: Weimar Germany and the Neue Wache', *Central European History*, XXXV (2002), p. 515; Richard Handler, 'Cultural Theory in History Today', *American Historical Review*, CVII (2002), p. 1515.

8 Avitai Margalit, *The Ethics of Memory* (Cambridge, MA and London, 2002), p. 193; *Die Presse*, 24 August 2002, p. 2.

9 Gernot Heiß, 'Österreichs Aufstieg zur Großmacht', – sollen wir ihn heute noch feiern?' *Beiträge zur historischen Soziologie* (1982), pp. 121–5; Michael Mitterauer, 'Politischer Katholizismus, Österreichbewußtsein und Türkenfeindbild', *Beiträge zur historischen Sozialkunde* (1982), pp. 111, 115; Isabella Ackerl, *Von Türken belagert – von Christen entsetzt* (Vienna, 1983).

10 Suzanne Heine, 'Islam in Austria: Between Integration Politics and Persisting Prejudices', in *Religion in Austria*, ed. Günter Bischof, Anton Pelinka, Hermann Denz (New Brunswick, NJ, 2005), pp. 102–11; Anas Schakfeh, 'Islam in Austria', in *Religion in Austria*, pp. 155, 157; *Austrian Information*, 59 (March/April 2006), p. 10; *Die Presse*, 12 September 2006, p. 11; Robert Waissenberger, 'Orientierung im Zeitalter. Österreich und Europa vom Westfälischen Frieden bis zum Frieden von Karlowitz', in *Türken vor Wien*, pp. 7–28.

11 Schakfeh, 'Islam', p. 152.

12 Obermaier, 'Türkenthema', p. 327; Waltraud Heindl, 'Levantische Geschichten?', in *Archiv und Forschung*, ed. Elisabeth Springer and Leopold Kammerhofer (Vienna, 1993), p. 283.

13 Joseph von Hammer-Purgstall, *Geschichte des osmanischen Reiches* (Pest, 1827–35), vol. I, pp. xvii–xviii.

14 Edward W. Said, *Orientalism* (New York, 1979), pp. 17, 24; Edward W. Said, 'The Clash of Definitions', in *The New Crusades: Constructing the Muslim Enemy*, ed. Emran Qureshi and Michael Sells (New York, 2003), p. 84; Nancy Bisaha, *Creating East and West: Renaissance Humanists and the Ottoman Turks* (Philadelphia, PA, 2004), p. 6; Daniel J. Vitkus, 'Early Modern Orientalism: Representations of Islam in Sixteenth and Seventeenth Century Europe', in *Western Views of Islam in Medieval and Early Modern Europe*, ed. David Blanks and Michael Frassetto (New York, 1999), pp. 209–10, citation p. 210.

15 Ronald Grigor Suny, 'Back and Beyond: Reversing the Cultural Turn', *American Historical Review*, CVII (2002), pp. 1485–6; Said, 'Definitions', p. 79.

16 Elisabeth Young-Bruehl, *The Anatomy of Prejudices* (Cambridge, MA, 1996), pp. 4–5, 30–31.

17 See generally Edward Said, 'Definitions', pp. 68–87; John Trumpbauer, 'The Clash of Civilizations: Samuel P. Huntington, Bernard Lewis, and the Remaking of the Post-Coldwar Order', in *New Crusades*, pp. 88–130; Gerald MacLean, 'Introduction: Reorienting the Renaissance', in *Reorienting the Renaissance: Cultural Exchanges with the East*, ed. Gerald MacLean (Houndsmills and New York, 2005), p. 1.

18 Vitkus, 'Early Modern Orientalism', pp. 209–10, citation p. 210.

19 Said, 'Definitions', pp. 76, 79.

20 Two older, but still stimulating and useful studies of this questions are Gordon W. Allport, *The Nature of Prejudice* (Reading, MA, 1954), esp. pp. 9, 189–92 and the some-what more subtle Milton Rokeach, *The Open and the Closed Mind: Investigations into the Nature of Belief Systems and Personality Systems* (New York, 1960), p. 58. On the role of empathy see Partha Mitter, 'Can we ever understand alien cultures?', *Comparative Criticism. An Annual Journal*, IX (1987), pp. 13–14, 28–9.

I   AN ENEMY REAL AND IMAGINED

1 Nora Berend, *At the Gate of Christendom: Jews, Muslims, and 'Pagans' in Medieval Hungary* (Cambridge, 2001), pp. 237–44. For the development of European views of Islam and Muslims generally see John V. Tolan, *Saracens: Islam in the Medieval European Imagination* (New York, 2002).

2 William Darymple, 'Forward', in *Reorienting the Renaissance. Cultural Exchanges with the East*, ed. Gerald Maclean (Houndsmills, and New York, 2005), pp. x–xi, xiv; Gerald MacLean, 'Introduction: Re-Orienting the Renaissance', in *Reorienting*, pp. 10–12, 15–17; Viorel Panaite, *The Ottoman Law of War and Peace: The Ottoman Empire and Tribute Payers* (Boulder, CO, 2000), p. 81; Colin Imber, *The Ottoman Empire, 1300–1481* (Istanbul, 1990), pp. 15, 19, 30–6, 125–6; Tomaž Mastnak, 'Europe and the Muslims: the Permanent Crusade?' in *The New Crusades: Constructing the Muslim Enemy*, ed. Emran Qureshi and Michael A. Sells (New York, 2003), p. 206; Heath W. Lowry, *The Nature of the Early Ottoman State* (Albany, NY, 2003), pp. 45–54, 119, 131–2, 136–7.

3 Maxime Rodinson, *Europe and the Mystique of Islam* (Seattle, WA, 1987 [1980]), pp. 3–31, 37.

4 Hans Kißling, *Rechtsproblematiken in den christlich-muslimischen Beziehungen, vorab im Zeitalter der Türkenkriege* (Graz, 1974), p. 8; Wolfgang Priglinger, 'Verdrängter Humanismus und verzögerte Aufklärung. Auf der Suche nach der österreichischen Philosophie', in *Verdrängter Humanismus. Verzögerte Aufklärung*, ed. Michael Benedikt, Reinhold Knoll and Josef Rupitz (Cluj-Napoca and Vienna, 1997), vol. II, p. 37; Richard Fletcher, *The Cross and the Crescent: Christianity and Islam from Muhammad to the Reformation* (London, 2003), p. 148.

5 M. E. Yapp, 'Europe in the Turkish Mirror', *Past and Present*, 137 (November, 1992), pp. 141–2; Maximilian Grothaus, *Der 'Erbfeindt christlichen Namens'. Studien zum Türkenbild in der Kultur der Habsburger Monarchie zwischen 16. u. 18. Jh* (Diss., Graz, 1986), pp. 74–5; Robert Schwoebel, *The Shadow of the Crescent: The Renaissance Image of the Turk, 1453–1517* (New York, 1967), pp. 204, 211.

6 Schwoebel, *Shadow*, pp. 1–29; Lowry, *Ottoman State*, pp. 115–6; Caroline Finkel, *Osman's Dream* (New York, 2006), pp. 11, 56, 62–3.

7 Finkel, *Dream*, p. 50.

8 Finkel, *Dream*, p. 58; Emil Knappe, *Die Geschichte der Türkenpredigt in Wien. Ein Beitrag zur Kulturgeschichte einer Stadt während der Türkenzeit* (Diss., Vienna, 1949), pp. 4, 9, 13; Senol Özyurt, *Die Türkenlieder und das Türkenbild in der deutschen Volksüberlieferung vom 16. bis zum 20. Jahrhundert* (Munich, 1972), p. 32; Otakar Odložilík, *The Hussite King: Bohemia in European Affairs 1440–1471* (New Brunswick, NJ, 1965), pp. 152–60; Carl Göllner, *Turcica* (Bucarest and Baden-Baden, 1961–78), vol. II, pp. 104–5; Grothaus, 'Erbfeindt', p. 23; J. V. Polišenský, 'Bohemia, the Turk, and the Christian Commonwealth (1462–1620)', *Byzantinoslavica*, XIV (1953), p. 83.

9 Albert Hourani, *Islam in European Thought* (Cambridge, 1991), p. 11; Albert Hourani, *Europe and the Middle East* (Berkeley, CA, 1980), p. 9; Muhammad A. Al-Da'mi, *Mirrors and Western Soothsayers. Nineteenth-Century Literary Approaches to Arab-Islamic History* (New York, 2002), pp. 4, 7; Norman Daniel, *Islam and the West: The Making of an Image* (Oxford, 1997 [1960]), pp. 302–23; Hichem Djaït, *Europe and Islam* (Berkeley, CA, 1985 [1978]), p. 51; Lowry, *Ottoman State*, p. 9.

10 Daniel, *Islam*, pp. 302–23; Djaït, *Europe and Islam*, p. 51.

11 *Archiv*, XIX/61–2, p. 325; Robert Waissenberger, 'Orientierung im Zeitalter. Österreich und Europa vom westfälischen Frieden bis zum Frieden von Karlowitz', in *Die Türken vor Wien Europa und die Entscheidung an der Donau*, ed. Robert Waissenberger (Salzburg, 1982), p. 11.

12 Grothaus, 'Erbfeindt', pp. 176–208; Schwoebel, *Shadow*, pp. 204, 211; Carl Göllner, 'Zur Problematik der Kreuzzüge und der Türkenkriege im 16. Jahrhundert', *Revue des Études Sud-Est Européenes*, XIII (1975), p. 104; Wenceslas Wratislaw of Mitrowitz, *Adventures of Baron Wenceslas Wratislaw of Mitrowitz* (London, 1862), p. 65.

13 Colin Imber, 'Ideals and Legitimation in Early Ottoman History', in Metin Kunt and Christine Woodhead, eds, *Süleyman the Magnificent and His Age: The Ottoman Empire in the Early Modern World* (London, 1995), pp. 138–9, 143–4, 146, 152; Fred M. Donner, 'The Sources of Islamic Conceptions of War', in *Just War and Jihad: Historical and Theoretical Perspectives on War and Peace in Western and Islamic Traditions*, ed. John Kelsay and James Turner Johnson (New York, 1991), pp. 57–8; Marshall Hodgson, *The Venture of Islam* (Chicago, IL, 1974), vol. III, pp. 106–7; Gábor Agostón, 'Ideologie, Propaganda und politischer Pragmatismus. Die Auseinandersetzung der osmanischen und hasburgischen Großmächte und die mitteleuropäische Konfrontation', in *Kaiser Ferdinand I. Ein mitteleuropäischer Herrscher*, ed. Martina Fuchs, Teréz Oborni and Gábor Ujváry (Münster, 2005), p. 229.

14 Captain [Anton] Prokesch, 'Memoire über die Möglichkeit der militärischen Eroberung der europäischen Türkei durch die Russen', Vienna, Kriegsarchiv (hereafter Vienna, KA), *Memoires* 1/12, karton 1, fols. 10, 36; Ogier Ghislain de Busbecq, *Four Epistles of A. G. de Busbequius Concerning his Embassy into Turkey* (London, 1694), pp. 270, 364; Pál Fodor, 'Ottoman Policy towards Hungary, 1520–1541', *Acta Orientalia Academiae Scientiarum Hungaricae*, XXX, pp. 280–1; James Turner Johnson, *The Holy War Idea in Western and Islamic Traditions*, ed. John Kelsay and James Turner Johnson (University Park, PA, 1997), pp. 151–7; Panaite, *Ottoman Law*, pp. 17–18, 98–9, 101: Gustav Bayerle, 'The

Compromise at Zsitvatorok', *Archivum Ottomanicum*, VI (1980), pp. 26–7.

15 Tamara Sonn, 'Irregular Warfare and the Law of Rebellion in Islam', in *Cross, Crescent, and Sword: The Justification and Limitation of War in Western and Islamic Tradition*, ed. James Turner Johnson and John Kelsay (New York, 1990), p. 133; Panaite, *Ottoman Law*, pp. 82–3, 89, 94–5, 97, 128–9, 287–8, 290.

16 Eduard Skudnigg, *Bildstöcke und Totenleuchten in Kärnten* (Klagenfurt, 1977), p. 135.

17 Skudnigg, *Bildstöcke*, p. 48; Imber, *Ottoman Empire*, pp. 245–7; Priglinger, 'Humanismus', pp. 43–4.

18 Skudnigg, *Bildstöcke*, p. 48; Imber, *Ottoman Empire*, pp. 245–7; Priglinger, 'Humanismus', pp. 43–4.

19 Mark L. Stein, *Guarding the Frontier. Ottoman Border Forts and Garrisons in Europe* (London and New York, 2007), p. 21.

20 Lájos Tardy, *Beyond the Ottoman Empire: 14th–16th Century Hungarian Diplomacy in the East* (Szeged, 1978), pp. 1, 6.

21 Julius von Fárkás, ed., *Ungarns Geschichte und Kultur in Dokumenten* (Wiesbaden, 1955), p. 48; Fodor, 'Ottoman Policy', p. 287; Klára Hegyi, 'The Ottoman Network of Fortresses in Hungary', in *Ottomans, Hungarians, and Habsburgs in Central Europe: The Military Confines in the Era of Ottoman Conquest*, ed. Géza Dávid and Pál Fodor (Leiden, 2000), p. 163; Anon., *Vom Türcken Erbermeliche Kleglich Zeitung Wie unser Erbfeind der Türck mit list darnach aber mit grosser Tyranney die feste Stad Falckenmor in Ungarn vier Meilen von Comorn erobert hat* (Vienna, 1587), unpaginated.

22 Panaite, *Ottoman Law*, p. 452; Waissenberger, 'Orientierung', p. 14. On Transylvania in the sixteenth and seventeenth centuries generally see László Makkai and András Mócsy, eds, *The History of Transylvania*, vols I, II (Boulder, CO and Highland Lakes, NJ, 2002).

23 Mihnea Berindei, 'Le problème transylvain dans la politique hongrois de Süleyman Ier', in *Süleyman Le Magnifique et son temps*, ed. Gilles Veinstein (Paris, 1992), p. 505.

24 Colin Imber, *The Ottoman Empire. The Structure of Power 1300–1650* (Houndsmills and New York, 2002), pp. 256–7; Ferdinand to Johann Maria Malvezzi, 31 December 1550, in *Austro-Turcica 1541–1552*, ed. Srecko M. Dzaja (Munich, 1995), pp. 542–3, 545; Ferdinand to Johann Maria Malvezzi, 4 March 1551, in *Austro-Turcica*, p. 557.

25 Hodgson, *Venture*, vol. III, p. 115; Frass, *Quellenbuch*, vol. II, pp. 40–4.

26 Paula Sutter Fichtner, 'Aber doch ein Friede: Ferdinand I, Ungarn und die Hohe Pforte', in *Kaiser Ferdinand I*, p. 247; Panaite, *Ottoman Law*, p. 87; Memorandum of Lieutenant Ferdinand Count Nogarola to Archduke Ernst, Vienna, Kriegsarchiv, *Alte Feldakten*, 1589/6/5/, fol. 1; Domokos Kosáry, 'The Liberation of Buda and the Danube Region', *Danubian Historical Studies*, I (1987), pp. 6–7.

27 Kißling, *Rechtsproblematiken*, pp. 13, 15–16; Grothaus, '*Erbfeindt*', p. 302; Kemal Kafadar, 'The Ottomans in Europe', in *Handbook of European History 1400–1600*, ed. Thomas A. Brady, Heiko Oberman and James D. Tracy (Leiden, 1994–5), vol. I, p. 605; Josef von Hormayr, *Österreichischer Plutarch*, 1 (N.P., 1807–14), p. 118.

28 *Archiv*, XIX/61–2 (1828), pp. 324–5; Panaite, *Ottoman Law*, pp. 377–8, 383; Rhoads Murphey, *Ottoman Warfare 1500–1700* (New Brunswick, NJ, 1999), pp. 48–9; Christine Woodhead, 'The Present Terror of the World?: Contemporary Views of the Ottoman Empire c. 1600', *History*, LXXII (1987), pp. 22–3, 28; Göllner, *Turcica*, vol. II, p. 109; Ernst D. Petritsch, 'Abenteurer oder Diplomaten? Ein Beitrag zu den diplomatischen Beziehungen Ferdinands I mit den Osmanen', in *Kaiser Ferdinand I*, p. 251.

29 Stephan Gerlach, *Stephan Gerlachs deß Aeltren Tage-buch* (Frankfurt a.M, 1674) pp. 137, 191.

30 Gerlach, *Tagebuch*, pp. 393–4.

31 Gerlach, *Tagebuch*, pp. 41, 191, 215.

32 Johann Maria Malvezzi to Charles V, 5 July 1550, *Austro-Turcica*, p. 482.

33 Mitrowitz, *Adventures*, p. 43.

34 Johann Maria Malvezzi to Ferdinand, 17 December 1550, *Austro-Turcica*, p. 533; Johann Maria Malvezzi to Ferdinand, 29 March 1551, *Austro-Turcica*, pp. 565–6; Karl Teply, ed., *Kaiserliche Gesandtschaften ans Goldene Horn* (Stuttgart, 1968), pp. 312–14, 317–18.

35 Teply, *Gesandtschaften*, pp. 313–15, 319–20, 414.

36 Angelo Rachani to Ferdinand, end of November 1551, *Austro-Turcica*, p. 626; Busbecq,

Epistles, pp. 150–2, 216–17, 273; Teply, *Gesandtschaften*, pp. 390–5; Mitrowitz, *Adventures*, pp. 158–9.

37 Wolf Schreiber to Maximilian II, 23 April 1564, Vienna, Haus, Hof-und Staatsarchiv (hereafter HHStA), *Türkei* I, karton 18, Konvolut (hereafter Konv.) 2, fol. 199.

38 Caroline Finkel, 'The Treacherous Cleverness of Hindsight', in *Reorienting*, ed. Gerald MacLean, pp. 154–5; Teply, *Gesandtschaften*, p. 413; Johann Maria Malvezzi to Ferdinand, 8 October 1549, *Austro-Turcica*, p. 372; Markus Sinckmoser to Ferdinand, 8 May 1550, *Austro-Turcica*, p. 438; Johann Maria Malvezzi to Ferdinand, 26 December 1549, *Austro-Turcica*, p. 385; Busbecq, *Epistles*, p. 187.

39 Count Nicholas von Salm and Sigismund Herberstein (to Ferdinand), 16 September 1541, *Austro-Turcica*, p. 6; Johann Maria Malvezzi to Ferdinand, 21–2 August 1549, *Austro-Turcica*, p. 360; Tranquillus Andronicus to Ferdinand I (end of 1542), *Austro-Turcica*, p. 21; Johann Maria Malvezzi to Ferdinand, 11 March 1550, *Austro-Turcica*, p. 406; Johann Maria Malvezzi to Ferdinand, 22 April 1550, *Austro-Turcica*, p. 433.

40 Johann Maria Malvezzi to Ferdinand, 7 October 1550, *Austro-Turcica*, pp. 516–17.

41 Johann Maria Malvezzi to Ferdinand, 9 May 1550, *Austro-Turcica*, p. 441; Johann Maria Malvezzi to Ferdinand, 24 April 1550, *Austro-Turcica*, p. 435; Ferdinand to Johann Maria Malvezzi, 26 July 1550, *Austro-Turcica*, p. 497.

42 Johann Maria Malvezzi to Ferdinand, 19 June 1551, *Austro-Turcica*, p. 60.

43 Süleyman to the estates of Transylvania, 18–27 December 1552, in Anton C. Schaendlinger, ed., *Osmanischetürkische Dokumente aus dem Haus-, Hof, und Staatsarchiv zu Wien* (Vienna, 1983), vol. II pp. 40–41. See also Süleyman to Bank Pál, 7–16 February 1552, in *Osmanischetürkische Dokumente*, vol. II, p. 21.

44 Johann Maria Malvezzi to Ferdinand, 11 March 1550, *Austro-Turcica*, p. 405; Paula Sutter Fichtner, *Emperor Maximilian II* (New Haven, CT, 2001), pp. 127–8; Franz Babinger, 'Die türkische Studien in Europa bis zum Auftreten Josef von Hammer-Purgstalls', *Die Welt des Islams*, VII (1919), p. 107.

45 Johann Maria Malvezzi to Charles V, 5 July 1550, *Austro-Turcica*, pp. 482–3.

46 Markus Sinckmoser to Ferdinand, *c.* 7 July 1550, *Austro-Turcica*, p. 489; Johann Maria Malvezzi to Ferdinand, 18 September 1550, *Austro-Turcica*, p. 505; Panaite, *Ottoman Law*, p. 417; Géza Dávid, 'Administration in Ottoman Europe', in, *Süleyman the Magnificent*, ed. Metin Kunt and Christine Woodhead, p. 86; Fodor, 'Ottoman Policy', p. 278, note 18; Kißling, *Rechtsproblematik*, p. 19; Stein, *Frontier*, pp. 23–4.

47 Paolo Giovio to Emperor Charles V, 1531, in Frass, *Quellenbuch*, vol. II, p. 37; Göllner, *Turcica*, vol. II, p. 561.

48 Panaite, *Ottoman Law*, p. 89; Süleyman to Henry II of France, *c.* 7 January 1550, *Austro-Turcica*, pp. 389–90.

49 Gilles Veinstein, 'La voix du maitre á travers les firmans de Soliman le Magnifique', in *Soliman le Magnifique*, p. 132; Schaendlinger, *Osmanischetürkische Dokumente*, part 2, p. 67; Panaite, *Ottoman Law*, pp. 94, 98–9; Grothaus, 'Erbfeindt', pp. 325–7.

50 Busbecq, *Epistles*, p. 189; Murphey, *Warfare*, p. 157.

51 Robert Davis, 'The Geography of Slaving in the Early Modern Mediterranean', *The Journal of Medieval and Early Modern Studies*, 37 (2007), pp. 57–74; Daniel Vitkus, 'Adventuring Heroes in the Mediterranean. Mapping the Boundaries of Anglo-Islamic Exchange on the Early Modern Stage', *The Journal of Early Modern Studies*, 37 (2007), p. 80.

52 Murphey, *Ottoman Warfare*, pp. 109–10, 122; Caroline Finkel, *The Administration of Warfare: the Ottoman Military Campaigns in Hungary, 1593–1606* (Vienna, 1988), pp. 93–6, 101–3; Stein, *Frontier*, pp. 137–9; Imber, *Empire 1300–1650*, p. 265.

53 Finkel, *Administration*, pp. 101–3; Kenneth Setton, *Venice, Austria and the Turks in the Sixteenth Century* (Philadelphia, PA, 1991), p. 276; Mitrowitz, *Adventures*, pp. 200–01; Stein, *Frontier*, pp. 89–91.

54 Ferdinand Bonaventura Harrach, 'Ein Tagebuch während der Belagerung von Wien im Jahre 1683', *Archiv für österreichische Geschichte*, LXXXVI (1899), p. 248; Imber, *Empire 1300–1650*, pp. 264–5.

55 Fárkás, *Ungarns Geschichte*, pp. 71–2.

56 Kißling, *Rechtsproblematiken*, pp. 19–20; Murphey, *Ottoman Warfare*, pp. 109–10, 171.

57 Ferdinand to Sigismund Pozsgay, 13 March 1549, *Austro-Turcica*, pp. 351–2; Claudio Angelo Martelli, *Relatio Captivo-Redempti, Das isst: Eigentliche Beschreibung der Anno 1683. Von dem . . . türckischen . . . Befängnuß . . .* (Vienna, 1689), p. 27; Mitrowitz, *Adventures*, p. 151.

58 *Glaubhafte Specification der Ungarischen Christen, Manns-und Weibs, hoch-und niederen Stands Personen so wohl alt als jungen . . . in die ewige Dienstbarkeit gefänglich genommen worden.* (Vienna, 1683), unpaginated; Neck, *Osmanen*, pp. 139, 159; Harrach, 'Tagebuch', p. 248; Peter Berger, 'Finanzwesen und Staatswerdung. Zur Genese absolutistischer Herrschaftstechnik in Österreich', in *Von der Glückseligket des Staates. Staat, Wirtschaft und Gesellschaft im Zeitalter des aufgeklärten Absolutismus*, ed. Herbert Mathis (Berlin, 1981), pp. 110–11.

59 Stein, *Frontier*, p. 25.

60 Grothaus, '*Erbfeindt*', p. 297.

61 Franz Babinger, Robert Gragger, Eugen Mittwoch and J. H. Mordtmann, eds, *Literaturdenkmäler aus Ungarns Türkenzeit* (Berlin, 1927), p. 7.

62 S[alánki] G[yörgy], *Historia Cladiis Turcicis ad Nadudvar, nec non Victoriae Ungarorum . . .* (Kolosvár, 1581), unpaginated; Georg Scherer, *Ein trewhertzige Vermahnung, daß die Christen dem Türcken nicht huldigen, sondern Ritterlich wider ihn streitten sollen . . .* (Vienna, c. 1595), unpaginated; Bartoloměj Paprocký z Hlohol, *O válce turecké* (Prague, 1982), pp. 196–7.

63 Johann Maria Malvezzi to Ferdinand, 9 April 1551, *Austro-Turcica*, p. 572; Babinger, *Literaturdenkmäler*, p. 7.

64 Georg Scherer, *Ein Christliche Heer-Predig . . . so sich der Zeit in Hungern wider die Türcken gebrauchen lassen, zu einem glückseligen Sig . . .* (Vienna, 1595), unpaginated; Scherer, *Trewhertziger Vermahnung*, unpaginated.

65 Gordon W. Allport, *The Nature of Prejudice* (Reading, MA, 1954), p. 192; Norman Cigar, 'The Nationalist Serbian Intellectuals and Islam: Defining and Eliminating an Ethnic Community', in Qureshi/Sells, *Crusades*, p. 316.

66 Gerlach, *Tagebuch*, pp. 50–51, 54, 97.

67 Gerlach, *Tagebuch*, pp. 253, 384, 411–13, 516.

68 Bartolomeo Georgievitz, *Profetia dei Turchi* (N.P., 1553), unpaginated.

69 B. Georgievicz, *De turcarum moribus* (N.P., 1598), pp. 3–8; Bartholomeo Giorgievits, *La miseria così deprigioni, come anche de Christiani che vivono sotto il tributo del turco insiemeco costumi & cerimonie di quella natione* (Florence, 1551), pp. 215–16, 218; Tardy, *Beyond*, pp. 142, 147.

70 Kenneth M. Setton, *Western Hostility to Islam and Prophecies of Turkish Doom* (Philadelphia, PA, 1992), pp. 30–31, 37; Tardy, *Beyond*, pp. 142, 145–6; Almut Höfert, *Den Feind beschreiben. Türkengefahr und europäisches Wissen über das Osmanische Reich 1450–1500* ((Frankfurt, 2003), p. 213; Matthew Dimmock, *New Turkes: Dramatizing Islam and the Ottomans in Early Modern England* (Aldershot, 2005), p. 81.

71 Busbecq, *Epistles*, pp. 250, 273, 348–9, 373, 390; Barnaby Rogerson, 'A Double Perspective and a Lost Rivalry: Ogier de Busbecq and Melchior Lorck', in MacLean, *Reorienting*, pp. 88–99, misses the critical cast to Busbecq's writing on the Turks altogether.

72 Polišenský, 'Commonwealth', pp. 95–6.

73 Todd Kontje, *German Orientalisms* (Ann Arbor, MI, 2004), p. 48; Daniel Casper Lohenstein, *Ibrahim Sultan*, in *Türkische Trauerspiele*, ed. Klaus Günther Just (Stuttgart, 1953), pp. xi, xxxix, xliii, xlv, 102–7, 170–5; Grothaus, '*Erbfeindt*', pp. 41–2, 348; Daniel Casper Lohenstein, *Ibrahim Sultan* (Leipzig, 1673), frontispiece; Finkel, *Dream*, pp. 223, 233–4; Waissenberger, 'Orientierung', p. 12.

74 Erhard Pöckhl, *Newe Zeitung auß Ungern . . . welcher massen der Saswar Bascha von Siget . . . seind erlegt worden . . .* (Graz, 1587), unpaginated; Anton Mayer, *Wiens Buchdrucker-Geschichte 1482–1882* (Vienna, 1883–7), vol. I, pp. 121, 127, 176, 181, 191–2; Göllner, *Turcica*, vol. II, p. 642; Polišenský, 'Commonwealth', p. 101; Anon., *Neben dem Hatwanischen Particular . . . von Glückseliger Entsetzung der Vestung Petrinia in Crabat Landt . . .* (Prague, [1596?]), unpaginated. On the significance of the textual environment in which a given piece of writing appears, see Jonathan Sheehan, 'Enlightenment,

Religion, and the Enigma of Secularization. A Review Essay', *American Historical Review*, CVIII (2003), p. 1076.

75 E.g., Pöckhl, *Neue Zeitung*, unpaginated. See also Göllner, *Turcica*, vol. II, pp. 435, 488, 497; Woodhead, 'Present Terror', p. 21; Mayer, *Buchdrucker-Geschichte*, vol. I, p. 48; Polišenský, 'Commonwealth', pp. 101–2.

76 Grothaus, '*Erbfeindt*', pp. 299, 976–7, pl. 98–109; *Newe Zeitung und Wundergeschiecht* [sic] *so zu Constantinopel den 10. Februarii dieses 1593. Jar ofentlich am Himel gegeben worden Schützing* (Sicz [Hung], 1593), unpaginated.

77 *Sněmy české od léta 1526 až po naši dobu* (Prague, 1873), vol. II, p. 363.

78 Özyurt, *Türkenlieder*, pp. 30, 32, 112–13: Helene Patrias, *Die Türkenkriege im Volkslied* (Diss., Vienna, 1947), pp. 9, 61–2, 87, 155, 158; Grothaus, '*Erbfeindt*', pp. 312, 314–15, 336: Ivo Krsek, 'Türkische Motive in der Barockkunst der böhmischen Länder', in *Die Türken vor Wien*, p. 262; *Sněmy česke*, vol. II, p. 366; Paprocký, *Valce*, p. 368; S[alánki], *Cladiis*, unpaginated; Polišenský, 'Commonwealth', pp. 94–5.

79 Grothaus, '*Erbfeindt*', pp. 969, pl. 62–3; 970, pl. 70; 972, pl. 74, 76; Domokos Kosáry, ed, *Magyarország története képekben* (Budapest, 1971), pp. 166, pl. 1, 3; 167, pl. 6; 168, pl.1.

80 Karl Teply, 'Der Kopf des Abaza Kör Hüseyin Pasha', *Jahrbuch des Vereins für Geschichte der Stadt Wien*, XXXIV (1978), p. 175.

81 Grothaus, '*Erbfeindt*' pp. 69, 727, 960, pl.14; 967, pl.57; 968, pl. 60; 969, pl.65.

82 Krsek, 'Türkische Motive', pp. 262–3; Klára Garas, 'Die Türkenkriege und die Kunst in Ungarn vom 16. bis zum 18. Jahrhundert', in *Türken vor Wien*, pp. 285–7; Teply, 'Kopf', p. 171.

83 On the relationship between repeated practice and the creation of cultural systems, see Richard Handler, 'Cultural Theory in History Today', *American Historical Review*, CVII (2002), p. 1515.

84 Johann Casper. [Neubeck], *Zwo Christliche Sieg und LobPredigten wegen etlich Ansehlicher Victorien wider die Türken anno Domini 1593* (Vienna, 1594), pp. 33–4; Neck, *Osmanen*, pp. 130, 194; Maximilian Grothaus, 'Zum Türkenbild des Adels-und Volkskultur der habsburger Monarchie zwischen 16. und 18. Jahrhundert', in *Das osmanische Reich und Europa 1683 bis 1789. Konflikt, Entspannung und Austausch*, ed. Gernot Heiß and Grete Klingenstein (Vienna, 1983), p. 82.

85 S[alánki], *Cladiis Turcicis*, unpaginated; Neubeck, *Christliche Sieg*, pp. 24, 32.

86 Georg Scherer, *Catechismus deß Catholischen Glaubens . . . Und der Uncatholischen Lehren ware und klare Wiederlegung . . .* (Braunßberg, 1620), pp. 40–41; Todd Kontje, *German Orientalisms* (Ann Arbor, MI, 2004), p. 39; Carl Göllner, *Turcica* (Bucarest and Baden-Baden, 1978), vol. III, p. 192.

87 Neubeck, *Christliche Sieg*, forward and pp. 6, 8–9, 11, 13–20, 30, 38; Pöckhl, *Neue Zeitung*, unpaginated.

88 Knappe, *Türkenpredigt*, pp. 14, 65–66a; Georg Scherer, *Trewhertzige Vermahnung*, unpaginated.

89 Özyurt, *Türkenlieder*, p. 30; Scherer, *Christliche Heerpredigt*, unpaginated; *Taschenbuch, fur die Vaterländische Geschichte* (1811, p. 108; *Taschenbuch* (1828), pp. 31–43.

90 Scherer, *Trewliche Mahnung*, unpaginated; Scherer, *Christliche Heerpredigt*, unpaginated.

91 Neubeck, *Christliche Sieg*, forward and pp. 6, 8–9, 11, 13–20, 30, 38; Pöckhl, *Neue Zeitung*, unpaginated.

92 Gábor Ágoston, 'Habsburgs and Ottomans: Defense, Military Change and Shifts in Power', *The Turkish Studies Bulletin*, XXII (1998): p. 131; Georg Scherer, *Lob und DanckPredig wegen Glückseliger und Ritterlicher Eroberung der Haubtvöstung* [sic] *Raab . . .* (Augsburg, 1598), unpaginated.

93 Scherer, *Trewherzige Vermahnung*, unpaginated.

94 Knappe, *Türkenpredigt*, p. 136; Murphey, *Warfare*, p. 145; Harald Heppner, 'Der Lange Türkenkrieg (1593–1606): ein Wendepunkt im habsburgisch-osmanischen Gegensatz', *Journal of Ottoman Studies*, II (1981), pp. 134–6, 140, 143; Scherer, *Glückselige Eroberung*, unpaginated; John Comenius, *The Labyrinth of the World and the Paradise of the Heart* (New York, 1998), pp. 122–4.

95 Georg Scherer, *Catechismus deß Catholischen Glaubens . . . Und der Uncatholischen Lehren ware und klare Wiederlegung . . .* (Braunßberg, 1620), unpaginated.

96 *Archiv*, IX /1–3 (1818), p. 11.
97 Josef Blaskovics, 'The Period of Ottoman-Turkish Reign at Nové Zámky 1663–1685', *Archív Orientalní*, LIV (1986), p. 106; Stein, *Frontier*, pp. 38, 46.
98 Fárkás, *Ungarns Geschichte*, pp. 60–71, citation, p. 62; Murphey, *Warfare*, pp. 149–50; Wolfgang Prohaska, 'Zum Bild der Türken in der österreichischen Kunst' in *Türken vor Wien*, p. 258.
99 Gerhard Potz, 'Zur Rezeption des Naturrechts in Österreich', in *Verdrängter Humanismus*, vol. 1/2, p. 134.
100 Blaskovics, 'Nové Zámky', p. 108.
101 Walter Zrenner, 'Abraham a Sancta Clara-Jacques Bénigne Bossuet. Barockhomiletik in Österreich und Frankreich', in *Verdrängter Humanismus*, vol. 1/1, p. 219; Knappe, *Türkenpredigt*, pp. 78–117, 136.
102 Citation, Grothaus, '*Erbfeindt*', pp. 316–17. See also pp. 172–4.
103 Grothaus, 'Türkenbild', pp. 78–9; citations in Robert Kann, *A Study in Austrian Intellectual History* (New York, 1973), pp. 74–5.
104 Harrach, 'Tagebuch', pp. 86, 209–10, 212–13, 219–20, 223.
105 Josef Alois Gleich, *Geschichte der kaiserl. königl. Stadt Wienerisch-Neustadt* (Vienna, 1808), p. 100.
106 Murphey, *Warfare*, pp. 136–7; Setton, *Venice, Austria*, p. 264.
107 Ágoston, 'Habsburgs and Ottomans', pp. 131–3, 136, 138–41; Finkel, *Dream*, pp. 287, 301.
108 *Wahre und eigentliche Abbildung, der dieser Zeit von dem Türkischen Mord-Saibel höchst geängstigten doch recht Resoluten und Wehrhaften . . . Stadt Wien . . .* (Nürnberg, 1683), unpaginated.
109 Mayer, *Buchdrucker-Geschichte*, vol. I, pp. 322–33.
110 Citation, *Wahre Abbildung*, unpaginated. See also Harrach, 'Tagebuch', p. 243 and Anon., *Relation dessen was inzwischen bey Aufhebung der Belagerung der Kayserl. Residens Stadt Wienn vorgangen.* (Regensburg, 1683), unpaginated.
111 Setton, *Venice, Austria*, pp. 29, 271–3; Kosáry, 'Liberation', pp. 5–6.
112 Kosáry, 'Liberation', p. 5; Finkel, *Dream*, p. 291.
113 Setton, *Venice, Austria*, pp. 401–2; Neck, *Osmanen*, pp. 191–2; Finkel, *Dream*, p. 310.
114 Setton, *Venice, Austria*, p. 440; Franz Peikhardt, 'Dank=Rede nach der Eroberung Belgrad, und denen im Jahr 1717 erhaltenen Vorteilen', in Franz Peikhar[d]t, *Lob=Danck=und Leih=Reden.* (Vienna, 1743), pp. 207–10.
115 Françoise Karro, 'L'Empire ottoman et l'Europe dans l'opéra française et viennois au temps de Lully', *J.-B. Lully, Actes/Kongreßbericht* (1990), pp. 258–60; Karl M. Swoboda, *Barock in Böhmen* (Munich, 1964), pp. 208, 326 and pl. 136–7.
116 Karl Teply, 'Türkentaufen in Wien während des großen Türkenkrieges 1683–1699', *Jahrbuch des Vereins für Geschichte der Stadt Wien*, XXIX (1973), pp. 67–71, 74, 76–7; Mastnak, 'Europe', pp. 223–7.
117 *Archiv für Geographie, Historie, Staats-und Kriegskunst*, VIII/64–5 (1817), p. 257.
118 Finkel, *Dream*, p. 288; Anon., *Der . . . continuirte Türcken-Krieg und Christen-Sieg* (Vienna, 1696), unpaginated; Anon., *RelationsDiarium der grossen Zwischen denen kayserl. und Türkischen Krieges-Wafen . . . Feld-Slacht* [sic] *in welcher Die Unsre über die Muselmänner überauß gloriert victorisirt . . .* (Breslau, 1697), title page.
119 *Archiv*, XVII/62–4 (1826), p. 346.
120 Knappe, *Türkenpredigt*, p. 138; *Archiv*, XVII/62–4 (1826), pp. 335, 342–3.

II CONCILIATION, COFFEE AND COMEDY

1 Ludovico Maracci, *Eigentliche Beschreibung der Fahnen deß Groß- Veziers . . . sambt einer Warhaften Außlegung der Arabischen Wörter Welche die Fahne auf das allerkünstlicheste eingewebet seynd* (n.p., no date), unpaginated; Anon. *Einfältiges doch Wohlgegründetes Gedencken/Von denen seithero dem Türken u. Groß= Vezier zu Spott und Hohn In Druck heraußgegebenen Charteqven . . .* (n.p., 1684), unpaginated; Franz Peikhar[d]t, 'Dank=Rede nach der Eroberung Belgrad, und denen im Jahr 1717 erhaltenen Vorteilen', in Franz Peikhardt, *Lob=Danck=undLeich=Reden . . .* (Vienna, 1743), pp. 205, 207–10.

2 Albert Hourani, *Europe and the Middle East* (Berkeley, CA, 1980), pp. 25–6; Muhammad A. Al- Da'mi, *Arabian Mirrors and Western Soothsayers: Nineteenth-Century Literary Approaches to Arab-Islamic History* (New York, 2002), p. 11.

3 Georg Scherer, *Ein trewhertzige Mahnung, daß die Christen dem Türcken nicht huldigen, sondern Ritterlich wider ihn streitten sollen . . .* (Vienna, c. 1595), unpaginated.

4 Ivo Krsek, 'Türkische Motive in der Barockkunst der böhmischen Lände', in *Die Türken vor Wien. Europa und die Entscheidung an der Donau*, ed. Robert Waissenberger (Salzburg, 1982), pp. 263–4; Karl M. Swoboda, *Barock in Böhmen* (Munich, 1964), p. 326 and pl. 136.

5 Anton Mayer, *Wiener Buchdrucker-Geschichte* (Vienna, 1883), vol. I, p. 280; Walter Obermaier, 'Das Türkenthema in der österreichischen Dichtung', in *Türken vor Wien*, p. 326.

6 Anon., *Neues Ungarisches/Türkisches und Französisches Labet-Spiel . . . Beneben einem schönen Remedio . . .* (n.p., 1683), unpaginated.

7 Wolfgang Prohaska, 'Zum Bild der Türken in der österreichischen Kunst', in *Türken vor Wien*, pp. 252–3; Stephan Gerlach. *Stephan Gerlachs deß Aeltren Tage-buch.* (Frankfurt a. M., 1674), p. 123. The report of the Jew who laughed at Christians who prayed when the Turkish bells sounded is in a diary-like notebook of Emperor Maximilian II. It is to be found in Vienna, Haus- , Hof-und Staatsarchiv. Familienakten, II.ii, *Aufzeichnungen*, fol. 28.

8 Otto Frass, ed., *Quellenbuch zur österreichischen Geschichte* (Vienna, 1956), vol. I, pp. 149–50; Maximilian Grothaus, *Der 'Erbfeindt christlichen Namens'. Studien zum Türkenbild in der Kultur der Habsburger Monarchie zwischen 16. u. 18. Jh.* (Diss., Graz, 1986), pp. 111–14.

9 Franz Martin Pelzel [František Martin Pelcl], *Geschichte der Böhmen von den ältesten bis auf die neuesten Zeiten* (Prague, 1782), vol. I, p. 519; J. V. Polišenský, 'Bohemia, the Turk and the Christian Commonwealth, 1462–1620', *Byzantinoslavica*, XIV (1953), pp. 84–5, 88.

10 Polišenský, 'Bohemia', pp. 82–108.

11 Wenceslas Wratislaw of Mitrowitz, *Adventures of Baron Wenceslas Wratislaw of Mitrowitz* (London, 1862), pp. 8, 68; Gilles Veinstein, 'La voix du maître á travers les firmans de Soliman le Magnifique', in *Soliman le Magnifique et son temps*, ed. Gilles Veinstein (Paris, 1992), pp. 139–41.

12 Mitrowitz, *Adventures*, p. 168; Daniel Caspar Lohenstein, 'Ibrahim Bassa', in *Türkische Trauerspiele*, ed. Klaus Günther Just (Stuttgart, 1953), pp. 141–5, 147, 163–4, 182, 188–9, 208–9.

13 Karl Teply, ed., *Kaiserliche Gesandtschaften ans Goldene Horn* (Stuttgart, 1968), pp. 66–7, 120–21, 125, 413–14; Franz Babinger, Robert Gragger, Eugen Mittwoch and J. H. Mordtmann, eds, *Literaturdenkmäler aus Ungarns Türkenzeit* (Berlin, 1927), pp. 16–19; Mitrowitz, *Adventures*, pp. 66–7, 100.

14 Josef von Hammer-[Purgstall], *Wien's erste aufgehobene türkische Belagerung vom Jahre 1529* (Pest, 1829), intro.; Wolfgang Priglinger, 'Verdrängter Humanismus und verzögerte Aufklärung. Auf der Suche nach der österreichischen Philosophie', in *Verdrängter Humanismus, Verzögerte Aufklärung*, ed. Michael Benedikt, Reinhold Knoll, Josef Rupitz (Cluj-Napoca and Vienna, 1997), vol. II, p. 44.

15 Johann Maria Malvezzi to Ferdinand, 24 January 1551, in *Austro-Turcica 1541–1552*, ed. Srecko M. Dzaja (Munich, 1995), pp. 548–9; Lájos Tardy, *Beyond the Ottoman Empire: 14th–16th Century Hungarian Diplomacy in the East* (Szeged, 1978), pp. 164–5, 171, 174–7, 186; Almut Höfert, *Den Feind beschreiben. Türkengefahr und europäisches Wissen über das Osmanische Reich 1450–1500* (Frankfurt, 2003), p. 153.

16 *Archiv für Geographie, Historie, Staats-und Kriegskunst*, XX/26 (1829), unpaginated supplement.

17 Höfert, *Den Feind*, pp. 213–14; B. Georgievicz, *De turcarum moribus* (n.p., 1598), pp. 28–9, 45, 59.

18 Mitrowitz, *Adventures*, p. 32.

19 Ogier Ghislain de Busbecq, *Four Epistles of A. G. de Busbequius Concerning his Embassy into Turkey* (London, 1694), p. 157.

20 Busbecq, *Epistles*, pp. 81–2, 93–5, 157; M. E. Yapp, 'Europe in the Christian Mirror', *Past and Present*, 137 (1992), pp. 150–7; Christine Woodhead, 'The Present Terror of the World? Contemporary Views of the Ottoman Empire *c*. 1600', *History*, LXXII (1987), p. 35.

21 Busbecq, *Epistles*, pp. 60, 64–5, 83–4, 95, 157, 171, 242–3; Woodhead, 'Present Terror', p. 35; Yapp, 'Mirror', p. 149.

22 Thierry Hentsch, *Imagining the Middle East* (Montreal, 1992), pp. 61–2.

23 Polišenský, 'Commonwealth', pp. 103–4; R.J.W. Evans, 'Bohemia, the Emperor and the Porte, 1560–1600', *Oxford Slavonic Papers*, III, New Series (1970), pp. 101–2.

24 Emil Knappe, *Die Geschichte der Türkenpredigt in Wien. Ein Beitrag zur Kulturgeschichte einer Stadt während der Türkenzeit* (Diss., Vienna, 1949), pp. 137, 322; Grothaus, 'Erbfeindt', p. 102.

25 Albrecht Classen, 'The World of the Turks as Described by an Eye-Witness: Georgius de Hungaria's Dialectical Discourse on the Foreign World of the Ottoman Empire', *Journal of Early Modern History*, vol. VII (2003), p. 261 and note 16.

26 Teply, *Gesandtschaften*, p. 399; Busbecq, *Epistles*, p. 167; Babinger, *Türkenzeit*, p. 27; Mitrowitz, *Adventures*, pp. 158–60.

27 David Blanks, 'Western Views of Islam in the Premodern Period: A Brief History of Past Approaches', in *Western Views of Islam in Medieval and Early Modern Europe*, ed. David Blanks and Michael Frassetto (New York, 1999), p. 35.

28 Höfert, 'Order', in *Between Europe and Islam*, p. 43.

29 Mayer, *Buchdrucker-Geschichte*, vol. I, pp. 283, 289.

30 Höfert, *Feind*, pp. 31–2; Almut Höfert, 'Order', p. 45; Evans, 'Bohemia', p. 85.

31 Nabil Matar, *Turks, Moors, and Englishmen in the Age of Discovery* (New York, 1999), pp. 23–4, 42, 68–9.

32 Georg Scherer, *Glückseliger Lob und DanckPredig, wegen Glückseliger und Ritterlicher Eroberung der Haubtvöstung Raab* . . . (Augsburg, 1598), unpaginated.

33 Grothaus, 'Erbfeindt', p. 79; Gordon W. Allport, *The Nature of Prejudice* (Reading, MA, 1954) p. 402; Bernard Lewis, *Islam in History: Ideas Men and Events in the Middle East* (London, 1973), p. 19.

34 Georg Scherer, *Catechismus oder christlicher Unterricht im wahren Catholischen und Apostolischen Glauben zum Allgemeinen Besten* . . . revd edn (Vienna, 1752), pp. 96, 292–3, 305; Grothaus, 'Erbfeindt', pp. 173–4.

35 István Gyorgy Tóth, *Literary and Written Culture in Early Modern Central Europe* (Budapest, 2000), pp. 177–81.

36 Vienna, Kriegsarchiv (henceforth KA), Hofkriegsrat, *Kanzleiarchiv*, XV/65, fols 34–7, 42, 45, 47, 50–2; Friedrich Kornauth and Richard D. Kreutel, eds, *Zwischen Paschas und Generälen. Bericht des Osman Aga aus Tesemschwar über die Höhepunkte seines Wirkens als Diwansdolmetescher und Diplomat* (Graz/Vienna/Cologne, 1966), pp. 59–128.

37 Bartenstein to Charles VI, 20 April 1738, Vienna, HHStA, Staatskanzlei, *Vorträge*, karton 47, fol. 46; Bartenstein to Charles VI, 3 May 1738, Vienna, HHStA, Staatskanzlei, *Vorträge*, karton 47, fol. 69.

38 Karl Roider, *Austria's Eastern Question 1700–1790* (Princeton, NJ, 1982), pp. 10–17.

39 Rhoads Murphey, *Ottoman Warfare 1500–1700* (New Brunswick, NJ, 1999), pp. 128–9, 253, note 2; Hans Georg Majer, 'Zur Kapitulation des osmanischen Gran (Esztergom) im Jahre 1683', in *Südosteuropa unter dem Halbmond. Untersuchungen über Geschichte und Kultur der südosteuropäischen Völker während der Türkenzeit*, ed. Peter Bartl and Horst Glassl (Munich, 1975), pp. 194, 197–200; Rudolf Neck, *Österreich und die Osmanen* (Vienna, 1983), pp. 176, 179; Prohaska, 'Bild', p. 258; Mitrowitz, *Adventures*, p. 63.

40 Osman Aga, *Paschas und Generälen*, pp. 109–111.

41 Anon., *Das Grosse und Nachdenckliche* . . . *Manifest der Ottomannischen Pforte und gantzen Turck. Nation/An die gesamte europäische Christenheit nach dem Sie die erste Campagne in Ungarn verlohren/und keine Lust haben/die andere zu hazardiren* (n.p., 1716), unpaginated; *Capitulation der Welt-berühmten Festung Belgrad* . . . (Vienna, 1717[?]), unpaginated.

42 Bernard Lewis, *The Muslim Discovery of Europe* (New York, 1982), pp. 41–4, 50–51; H. M. Scott, *The Emergence of the Eastern Powers 1756–1775* (New York, 2002), pp. 2, 18, 140–2;

Roider, *Eastern Question*, pp. 10–17.

43 Yapp, 'Mirror', pp. 142–5; Karl Roider, *Baron Thugut and Austria's Response to the French Revolution* (Princeton, NJ, 1987), p. 20.

44 Scott, *Emergence*, pp. 245–6.

45 Count Nogarola to Archduke Ernst, Vienna, KA, *Alte Feldakten*, 1589 6/5, fol. 1; Daniel Goffman, *The Ottoman Empire and Early Modern Europe* (Cambridge, 2002), pp. 13–19, 186; Woodhead, 'Present Terror', pp. 22–8; Stein, *Frontier*, pp. 26–7.

46 Josef Blaskovics, 'The Period of Ottoman–Turkish Reign at Nové Zámky, 1663–1685', *Archív Orientalní*, LIV (1986), pp. 107, 112–13.

47 Karl Teply, *Die Einführung des Kaffees in Wien* (Vienna, 1980), pp. 12, 40; Claudio Angelo Martelli, *Relatio Captivo-redempti, Das isst: Eigentliche Beschreibung/der Anno 1683. Von dem . . . türckischen . . . Befängnuß . . .* (Vienna, 1689), pp. 109–21.

48 Johann Neiner, *Neu ausgelegten Curioser Tändl-Markt der jetzigen Welt* (Vienna and Brünn, 1734), unpaginated; Teply, *Einführung*, p. 53; Johann Pezzl, *Beschreibung der Haupt-und Residenz-Stadt Wien* (Vienna, 1816), p. 166; *Wiener Zeitung*, 27 August 1783, unpaginated.

49 Neck, *Osmanen*, pp. 112, 168; Albert Hourani, *Islam in European Thought* (Cambridge, 1991), pp. 138–9.

50 Peter Berger, 'Finanzwesen und Staatswerdung. Zur Genese absolutistischer Herrschaftstechnik in Österreich', in *Von der Glückseligkeit des Staates. Staat, Wirtschaft und Gesellschaft im Zeitalter des aufgeklärten Absolutismus*, ed. Herbert Mathis (Berlin, 1981), pp. 110–11; Frass, *Quellenbuch*, vol. II, p. 232; Manfred Sauer, 'Aspekte der Handelspolitik des "aufgeklärten Absolutismus"', in *Glückseligkeit*, p. 252.

51 Sauer, 'Aspekte', in *Glückseligket*, p. 261.

52 Diary of Valentine Baumgartner, Vienna, KA, Hofkriegsrat, *Kanzleiarchiv*, XV, fol. 32; Teply, *Einführung*, p. 108; Caroline Finkel, *Osman's Dream* (New York, 2006), p. 309.

53 Teply, *Einführung*, p. 108.

54 Teply, *Einführung*, pp. 61, 69, 104; Karl Teply, 'Johannes Diadato. Der Patriarch der ersten Armenier in Wien', *Jahrbuch des Vereines für Geschichte der Stadt Wien*, XXIII (1972), p. 32; Neiner, *Tändl-Markt*, unpaginated.

55 Babinger, *Türkenzeit*, p. 32.

56 Josef Ritter von Malfatti di Monte Treto, *Handbuch des österreichisch-ungarischen Consularwesens* (Vienna, 1879), pp. 133–5.

57 Linda Colley, *Captives: Britain, Europe and the World, 1600–1850* (London, 2002), p. 105; Sauer, 'Aspekte', p. 261.

58 *Wiener Zeitung*, 7 June 1783 and 19 July 1783, unpaginated.

59 *Wiener Zeitung*, 2 August 1783, unpaginated.

60 *Wiener Zeitung*, 22 February 1783; 26 February 1783; 1 March 1783; 5 March 1783; 15 March 1783, unpaginated.

61 Maximilian Grothaus, 'Zum Türkenbild des Adels-und Volkskultur der habsburger Monarchie zwischen 16. und 18. Jahrhundert', in *Das osmanische Reich und Europa 1683 bis 1789. Konflikt, Entspannung und Austausch*, ed. Gernot Heiß and Grete Klingenstein (Vienna, 1983), p. 87; Rainer Rückert, 'Der "Catalogus" der Wiener Porcellaine-Lotterie des Jahres 1735. Documente zur Wiener Porzellangeschichte unter Meißner Archivalien', *Keramos*, CXLV (1994), pp. 33–51; Prohaska, 'Bild', in *Türken vor Wien*, pp. 254–6; Fred Dallmayr, 'Modes of Cross-Cultural Encounter: Reflections on 1492', in *Beyond Orientalism: Essays on Cross-Cultural Encounters*, ed. Fred Dallmayer (Binghamton, NY, 1996), pp. 6–7; Rudolf Klein, '"Alla Turca" in der europäischen Musik', in *Türken vor Wien*, p. 319; Karl Teply, 'Der Kopf des Abaza Kör Hüseyin Pasha', *Jahrbuch des Vereins für Geschichte der Stadt Wien*, XXXIV (1973), p. 171.

62 Citation in Eve Meyer, 'Turquerie and Eighteenth Century Music', *Eighteenth-Century Studies*, VII (1974), p. 485. See also Meyer, 'Turquerie', p. 487; Jean-François Labie, 'Du Barbare au Philosophie', in C. Willibald Gluck, *La Rencontre imprévue ou les Pélerins de la Mecques* (Caen, 1998), p. 35; Bruce Alan Brown, *Gluck and the French Theatre in Vienna* (Oxford, 1991), p. 189; Walter Salmen, *Mozart in der Tanzkultur seiner Zeit* (Innsbruck, 1990), pp. 104–5; Richard Taruskin, *The Oxford History of Western Music* (Oxford, 2005), vol. II, p. 678; John A. Rice, *Antonio Salieri and Viennese Opera*

(Chicago, 1998), pp. 38, 393.

63 Klein, 'Alla Turca', in *Türken vor Wien*, p. 321.

64 *Wiener Zeitung*, 9 April 1783 and 16 April 1783, unpaginated; Klein, 'Alla Turca', in *Türken vor Wien*, p. 322; Alice M. Hanson, *Musical Life in Biedermeier Vienna* (Cambridge, 1985), pp. 144–5; David Benjamin Levy, *Beethoven: The Ninth Symphony* (New York, 1995), p. 147.

65 Dani Maier, 'Trois Turqueries', in Gluck, *Rencontre*, p. 30; Anton Vigano, *Mahomet und Irene: ein heroisch tragischer Ballet in drey Aufzügen* (Graz, 1788), unpaginated.

66 Colley, *Captives*, p. 130.

67 *Orientalischer Botschafter oder Auf Fried; mit Freud von Aufgang Kommender Mercurius Beym Einzug in die Kayserl. Residents=Stadt Wienn der von der Hohen Porte . . . Abgesandten Bottschaft* (Vienna, c. 1700), unpaginated.

68 Grothaus, '*Erbfeindt*', pp. 319, 736; Knappe, *Türkenpredigt*, pp. 190, 192.

69 [?] Weidmann, *Das befreyte Wien*, in *Neues Wiener Theater*, 1 (1775), pp. 4, 6, 10–12, 16–17, 37, 54.

70 Friedrich Gensicke, *Die Belohnte Treue der Wiener=Bürger oder der 12te September 1683* (Vienna, 1783), unpaginated. When the imperial army actually did occupy Belgrade in 1789, Vienna celebrated noisily. Helene Patrias, *Die Türkenkriege im Volkslied* (Diss., Vienna, 1947), p. 148.

71 Busbecq, *Epistles*, pp. 150–2.

72 Grothaus, '*Erbfeindt*', p. 960, pl.16; Hourani, *Europe and the Middle East*, p. 28.

73 Walter Preibisch, 'Quellenstudien zu Mozart's "Entführung aus dem Serail"', *Quarterly Magazine of the International Music Society*, x (1908–09), pp. 431, 436–8; Klein, 'Alla turca', in *Türken vor Wien*, pp. 319–20; Labie, 'Barbare', in Gluck, *Rencontre*, pp. 35, 37, 41; Grothaus, 'Türkenbild', pp. 86–7.

74 W. Daniel Wilson, *Humanität und Kreuzzugsideologie um 1780. Die 'Türkenoper' im 18. Jahrhundert und das Rettungsmotiv in Wielands 'Oberon', Lessings 'Nathan' und Goethe's 'Iphigenie'* (New York, 1984), p. 32.

75 Brown, *French Theatre*, pp. 212, 387, 411–12, 417; Gluck, *Rencontre*, p. 50.

76 Wilson, *Kreuzzugsideologie*, p. 21; Horst Graschitz, *Josef Haydn und Eisenstadt* (Eisenstadt, 1982), pp. 56–7; H. C. Robbins Landon and Dénes Bartha, eds, *Josef Haydn. Gesammelte Briefen* (Kassel, 1965), p. 77; H. C. Robbins Landon, *Haydn: A Documentary Study* (New York, 1981), p. 80; Werner Pieck, *Haydn. Der Große Bassa* (Hamburg, 2004), pp. 12–14; Klein, 'Alla turca', pp. 319–20.

77 Brown, *French Theatre*, p. 443; Preibisch, 'Quellenstudien', pp. 473–4.

78 Joseph Alois Gleich, *Der Mohr von Semegonda*, 2 parts (Vienna, 1805); Wilson, *Kreuzzugsideologie*, pp. 28–30; Meyer, '*Turquerie*', p. 484.

79 Gleich, *Mohr*, 2, pp. 9–12, 50–51; Preibisch, 'Quellenstudien', p. 444.

80 Friedrich Gensike, *Die Belohnte Treue* (Vienna, 1783), pp. 42–5, 48–9.

81 Daniel J. Vitkus, 'Early Modern Orientalism: Representations of Islam in Sixteenth and Seventeenth Century Europe', in *Western Views of Islam in Medieval and Early Modern Europe*, ed. David Blanks and Michael Frassetto (New York, 1999), pp. 224–5; Judith L. Schwartz, 'Cultural Stereotypes and Music in the Eighteenth Century', *Studies on Voltaire and the Eighteenth Century*, CLV (1976), pp. 2004, 2010.

82 Klára Garas, 'Die Türkenkriege und die Kunst in Ungarn vom 16. bis zum 18. Jahrhundert', in *Türken vor Wien*, p. 289; Domokos Kosáry, *Művelődés, a xvi. századi Magyarországon* (Budapest, 1983), p. 665.

83 Prebisch, 'Quellenstudien', pp. 455–6.

84 Allport, *Prejudice*, pp. 191–2; Jane O. Newman, 'Disorientations: Same-Sex Seduction and Women's Power in Daniel Casper von Lohenstein's "'Ibrahim Sultan'", *Colloquia Germanica*, xxviii (1995), p. 348.

85 Wolfgang Amadeus Mozart, *Die Entführung aus dem Serail* [libretto] (New York, 1950), p. 10; Hentsch, *Imagining*, p. 230; Ash Çurakman, 'From Tyranny to Despotism: the Enlightenment's Unenlightened Image of the Turks', *Journal of MidEast Studies*, xxxiii (2001), p. 49. Franz Xaver Süßmayer, *Soliman der Zweyte oder die drey Sultannin* (Vienna, 1807), pp. 8–13, 35.

86 Michael Potz, 'Zur Rezeption des Naturrechts in Österreich 1650–1750', in *Verdrängter*

Humanismus, vol. 1/2, pp. 133–4; Helmut Reinalter, 'Aufgeklärter Absolutismus und Josephismus', in, *Der Josephinismus. Bedeutung, Einflüsse, und Wirkungen*, ed. Helmut Reinalter (Frankfurt a. M., 1993), pp. 17–18.

87 Wolfgang Priglinger, 'Verdrängter Humanismus und verzögerte Aufklärung. Auf der Suche nach der österreichischen Philosophie', in *Verdrangter Humanismus*, vol. 11, p. 79; Ernst Wangermann, 'Reform Catholicism and Political Radicalism in the Austrian Enlightenment', in *The Enlightenment in National Context*, ed. Roy Porter and Mikulás Teich (London, 1988), p. 131.

88 Brown, *French Theater*, pp. 186–7, 189; Priglinger, 'Humanismus', p. 79.

89 Edith Rosenstrauch-Königsberg, 'Die Philosophie der österreichischen Freimaurer', in Edith Rosenstrauch-Königsberg, *Zirkel und Zentren. Aufsätze zur Aufklärung in Österreich am Ende des 18. Jahrhunderts* (Vienna, c. 1994), pp. 275–7; Edith Rosenstrauch-Königsberg, '200 Jahre Großlogen von Österreich', in *Zirkel*, p. 263.

90 Citation in Wangerman, 'Reform Catholicism', p. 139. See also Wangerman, 'Reform Catholicism', p. 131; Potz, 'Rezeption', p. 137.

91 Scherer, *Catechismus* (1620), pp. 555–7; Scherer, *Catechismus* (1752), pp. 31–2, 401, 403.

92 Rosenstrauch-Königsberg, 'Philosophie', in *Zirkel*, pp. 287, 290.

93 Johann Pezzl, *Skizze von Wien* (Graz, 1923 [1786–90]), pp. 267, 396–7.

94 Johann Pezzl, *Marokkanische Briefe. Aus dem Arabischen* (Frankfurt and Leipzig, 1784), pp. 3, 5–6, 49, 123, 134–5, 142–3, 206–7, 209–12.

95 Edward Said, *Orientalism* (New York, 1979), p. 40; Dallmayr, 'Modes', pp. 7, 32; Albert Hourani, 'Culture and Change: the Middle East in the Eighteenth Century', in Hourani, *Islam*, p. 136; Suzanne Heine, Islam in Austria: Between Integration Politics and Persisting Prejudices' in *Religion in Austria*, ed. Günter Bischof, Anton Pelinka, Hermann Denz (New Brunswick, NJ, 2005), p. 112.

96 Çurakman, 'Tyranny to Despotism', p. 49.

97 Citation in Meyer, 'Turquerie', p. 484; Edith Rosenstrauch-Königsberg, 'Die philosophie der österreichischen Freimaurer und Illuminaten', in *Verdrängter Humanismus*, vol. 11, pp. 562, 565; Jan Assmann, *Die Zauberflöte. Oper und Mysterium* (Munich and Vienna, 2005), p. 153.

98 Hentsch, *Imagining*, p. 230; Çurakman, 'Tyranny to Despotism', pp. 49, 59, 63–4; Yapp, 'Mirror', pp. 150, 152⌐3; Hichem Djaït, *Europe and Islam* (Berkeley, CA, 1995), p. 51.

99 *Wiener Zeitung*, 10 May 1783 and 10 September 1783, unpaginated.

100 *Wiener Zeitung*, 17 September 1783, unpaginated; Michael Mitterauer, 'Politischer Katholizismus, Österreichbewußtsein und Türkenfeindbild', *Beiträge zur historischen Sozialkunde* (1982), p. 115.

101 Neck, *Osmanen*, pp. 224–5; Pezzl, *Beschreibung*, pp. 12–13, 50, 317; Prohaska, 'Bild', p. 256.

102 *Wiener Zeitung*, 8 January 1783, unpaginated; *Wiener Zeitung*, 22 January 1783, unpaginated.

103 Pezzl, *Skizze*, pp. 41–2, 329–34, 437.

104 František Martin Pelcl [Pelcel], *Paměti* (Prague, 1956), p. 75.

105 Nicholas Till, *Mozart and the Enlightenment. Truth, Virtue, and Beauty in Mozart's Operas* (London, 1992), pp. 104–5; Prohaska, 'Bild', pp. 256–7; Grothaus, 'Erbfeindt', p. 160; Reinalter, 'Absolutismus', p. 19; Rice, *Salieri*, p. 359, 416, 418.

106 Gerlach, *Tagebuch*, Citation on p. 253. See also p. 405.

107 Gerlach, *Tagebuch*, pp. 163–4.

108 Said, *Orientalism*, pp. 20–21; Hentsch, *Imagining*, p. 59; Suzanne Heine, 'Islam in Austria', p. 120, note 3.

109 G. K., *Ein Soldaten Jubiläum über die Belagerung von Wienn und der dabey den 12ten Sept. 1683 über die Türken erfochtene Sieg* (Prague, 1783), pp. 1–2, 4, 7–9, 11, 14, 24–5, 30.

110 Gottfried Uhlich, *Geschichte der zweyten Türkenbelagerung Wiens* (Vienna, 1783), unpaginated; Teply, *Einführung*, pp. 58–9.

111 Gensike, *Belohnte Treue*, introduction, unpaginated.

112 Gensike, *Belohnte Treue*, pp. 23, 42.

113 Frass, *Quellenbuch*, vol. 11, p. 37; *Archiv*, 1x/1–3 (1818), p. 11; Vienna, KA, *Alte Feldakten 1683/Türkenkrieg/*, 9/1.

114 Krsek, 'Türkische Motive', p. 370; Franz Martin Pelcel (František Martin Pelcl),

Geschichte der Böhmen, vol. II, p. 833.
115 Fárkás, *Ungarns Geschichte*, p. 120; Kosáry, 'Buda', p. 8.
116 István Deák, *The Lawful Revolution: Louis Kossuth and the Hungarians 1848–1849* (New York, 1979), pp. 338–42.
117 Fárkás, *Ungarns Geschichte*, pp. 78–9.

III SERVANTS TO GOVERNMENT AND LEARNING

1 Wolfgang W. Priglinger, 'Verdrängter Humanismus und Verzögerte Aufklärung', in *Verdrängter Humanismus und Verzögerte Aufklärung*, ed. Michael Benedikt, Reinhold Knoll and Josef Rupitz (Vienna, 1992), vol. II, pp. 38–9.
2 Albert Hourani, *Islam in European Thought* (Cambridge, 1991), p. 12; Linda Colley, *Captives: Britain, Europe and the World, 1600–1850* (London, 2002), pp. 105–6; Philip Mansel, 'The French Renaissance in Search of the Ottoman Empire', in *Reorienting the Renaissance: Cultural Exchanges with the East*, ed. Gerald Maclean (Houndsmills and New York, 2005), p. 99; Matthew Dimmock, *New Turkes: Dramatizing Islam and the Ottomans in Early Modern England* (Aldershot, 2005), pp. 75–8.
3 Johannes Petheu to Maximilian II, 8 May 1564, HHStA, *Türkei* I, karton (hereafter K.) 18, Konv. (hereafter Konv.) 2, fols 213–14; Franz Babinger, 'Die türkische Studien in Europa bis zum Auftreten Josef von Hammer-Purgstall', *Die Welt des Islams*, VII (1919), p. 113; Mansel, 'French Renaissance', p. 106. Just what Mansel means when he calls it 'Europe's first school of oriental languages, established on an earlier foundation in 1796', is not altogether clear. As noted in this essay, the Vienna Oriental Academy was opened in 1754.
4 Michael Czernowitz (Zarnoujgio) to Maximilian II, 13 August 1564, Vienna, HHStA, *Türkei* I, K. 8, Konv. 4, fol. 155.
5 Karl Teply, ed, *Kaiserliche Gesandtschaften ans Goldene Horn* (Stuttgart, 1968), pp. 64–5; Karl Roider, 'The Oriental Academy in the *Theresienzeit*', *Topic*, XXXIV (1980), pp. 19–20.
6 William Montgomery Watt, *Muslim–Christian Encounters* (London and New York, 1991), p. 111.
7 Rainer Sprung and Peter G. Mayr, 'Franz Kleins Lehrtätigkeit an der k. und k. Orientalische Akademie', *Mitteilungen des Instituts für österreichische Geschichtsforschung*, XCVII (1989), p. 84; Anton Mayer, *Wiens Buchdrucker-Geschichte* (Vienna, 1883), vol. I, p. 319; Babinger, 'Türkischen Studien', pp. 114 and 115, n. 1; Roider, 'Oriental Academy', pp. 21–2.
8 Karl Teply, *Die Einführung des Kaffees in Wien* (Vienna, 1980), p. 77.
9 Joseph Benzing, *Die Buchdrucker des 16. und 17. Jahrhunderts im deutschen Sprachgebiet* (Wiesbaden, 1963), p. 460; Mayer, *Buchdrucker-Geschichte*, vol. I, pp. 302–4; Teply, *Einführung*, p. 77; Babinger, 'Türkische Studien', pp. 116–17.
10 Rudolf Neck, *Österreich und die Osmanen* (Vienna, 1983), pp. 116–17; Mayer, *Buchdrucker-Geschichte*, vol. I, pp. 303–4.
11 Babinger, 'Türkische Studien', p. 113; Kaunitz to Tassara, Vienna, HHStA, Staatskanzlei, *Interiora, Orientalische Akademie*, K. 56, Konv. B, 6 May 1777 (copy), fol. 155; Neck, *Osmanen*, p. 219. Tassara was Kaunitz's business agent.
12 Vienna, HHStA, Staatskanzlei, *Interiora*, K. 56, Konv. B, 14 November 1780, fol. 202.
13 Priglinger, 'Humanismus', p. 73; Edith Rosenstrauch-Königsberg, 'Die philosophie der österreichischen Freimaurer und Illuminaten', in *Verdrängter Humanismus*, vol. II, pp. 588–9; Dolf Lindner, *Der Mann ohne Vorurtheile. Joseph von Sonnenfels 1733–1817* (Vienna, 1983), pp. 10–15.
14 'Bene nati juventes', in Francisci Mesquien Meninski, *Institutiones Linguae Turcicae cum Rudimentis Paralellis Arabicae & Persicae* (Vienna, 1756), vol. I, p. 2.
15 Vienna, HHStA, Staatskanzlei, *Interiora, Orientalische Akademie*, K. 55, Konv. B, 20 July 1753, fols 37–9; Roider, 'Oriental Academy', p. 21.
16 Erwin Matsch, *Der auswärtige Dienst von Österreich-Ungarn 1720–1920* (Vienna, 1986), pp. 76–8; Neck, *Osmanen*, p. 215; Johann Pezzl, *Skizze von Wien* (Graz, 1923 [1786–90]), p. 266.

17 Memorandum of Pater Joseph Franz to Empress Maria Theresa, in *Von denen Orientalischen Sprachknaben*, Vienna ʜʜsᴛᴀ, Staatskanzlei, *Interiora, Orientalische Akademie* (hereafter *Interiora, Orientalische Akademie*), ᴋ. 55, April 1753, fol. 4; Babinger, 'Türkische Studien', p. 123; Sprung, 'Lehrtätigkeit', p. 86.

18 Johann Fück, *Die Arabischen Studien in Europa bis in den Anfang des 20. Jahrhunderts* (Leipzig, 1955), pp. 126–9.

19 *Interiora, Orientalische Akademie*, ᴋ. 56, Konv. ʙ, 1775–86, fols 222–3; *Interiora, Orientalische Akademie*, ᴋ. 56, Konv. ʙ, 1775–86, fols 157, 159; *Interiora, Orientalische Akademie*, ᴋ. 56, Konv. ᴄ, 1792–3, fols 102–23.

20 *Interiora, Orientalische Akademie*, ᴋ. 56, Konv. ᴀ, 1785–8, fols 27–8.

21 Johann Pezzl, *Beschreibung der Haupt-und Residenz-Stadt Wien* (Vienna, 1816 [4th edition]) pp. 190, 201–2; *Archiv für Geographie, Historie, Staats-und Kriegskunst*, x (1820), p. 627; *Orientalischen Sprachknaben, Interiora, Orientalische Akademie*, ᴋ. 55, 1753, fols 22, 37–45; *Interiora, Orientalische Akademie*, ᴋ. 55, 1 April 1754, fols 48–50; Karl Roider, *Baron Thugut and Austria's Response to the French Revolution* (Princeton, ɴᴊ, 1987), pp. 15–16.

22 *Interiora, Orientalische Akademie*, ᴋ. 56, Konv. ʙ, 1775–86, fols 75, 158; *Interiora, Orientalische Akademie*, ᴋ. 56, Konv. A, 1785–8, fol. 121.

23 *Interiora, Orientalische Akademie*, ᴋ. 57, Konv. ᴀ, 1801–05, fol. 116.

24 *Interiora, Orientalische Akademie*, ᴋ. 57, Konv. ʙ, 1806–09, fols 76–9.

25 *Interiora, Orientalische Akademie*, ᴋ. 56, Konv. ᴀ, 1785–8, fols 69, 73, 137.

26 *Interiora, Orientalische Akademie*, ᴋ. 55, Konv. ʙ, 20 July 1753, fol. 34; Vienna, ʜʜsᴛᴀ, Staatskanzlei, *Interiora, Orientalische Akademie*, ᴋ. 55, 1754, fols 48–50.

27 Babinger, 'Türkische Studien', p. 123; *Interiora, Orientalische Akademie, Von denen Orientalischen Sprachknaben*, ᴋ. 55, 1753, fol. 16; *Interiora, Orientalische Akademie*, ᴋ. 55, Konv. ʙ, 20 July 1753, fols 33–6.

28 Anthony Grafton, *Defenders of the Text. The Traditions of Scholarship in an Age of Science* (Cambridge, ᴍᴀ, 1991), pp. 216–18.

29 *Archiv*, xvıı/62–3 (1826), p. 343.

30 *Interiora, Orientalische Akademie, Von denen Orientalischen Sprachknaben*, April 1753, ᴋ. 55, fols 5–8.

31 *Interiora, Orientalische Akademie*, ᴋ. 55, 1754–5, fols 51–73, citations, fols 51–2.

32 Roider, 'Oriental Academy', pp. 23–4. Citation in Neck, *Osmanen*, p. 278.

33 *Interiora, Orientalische Akademie*, ᴋ. 56, Konv. ʙ, 1775–86, fols 68–9.

34 *Interiora, Orientalische Akademie*, ᴋ. 56, Konv. ᴀ, 1785–8, fols 106–9; Manfred Sauer, 'Aspekte der Handelspolitik des "aufgeklärten Absolutismus"' in *Von der Glückseligkeit des Staates. Staat, Wirtschaft und Gesellschaft im Zeitalter des aufgeklärten Absolutismus*, ed. Herbert Mathis (Berlin, 1981) pp. 263–4; Matsch, *Auswärtiges Amt*, pp. 77–8.

35 *Interiora, Orientalische Akademie*, ᴋ. 56, Konv. ᴀ, 1785–8, fols 106–9.

36 *Interiora, Orientalische Akademie*, ᴋ. 56, Konv. ᴀ, 1785–7, fol. 152; *Interiora, Orientalische Akademie*, ᴋ. 56, Konv. ʙ, 1791, fols 68–71.

37 *Interiora, Orientalische Akademie*, ᴋ. 57, Konv. ᴀ, 1801–5, fols 122–5.

38 *Interiora, Orientalische Akademie*, ᴋ. 57, Konv. ʙ, 1806–9, fols 95–8; Konv. ᴄ, 1810, fols 191, 194–5; *Interiora, Orientalische Akademie*, ᴋ. 57, Konv. ʙ, 1806–9, fols 95–8; *Interiora, Orientalische Akademie*, ᴋ. 57, Konv. ᴄ, 1810, fols 191, 194–5.

39 *Interiora, Orientalische Akademie*, ᴋ. 57, Konv. ᴄ, 1810, fol. 113.

40 *Interiora, Orientalische Akademie*, ᴋ. 57, ᴄ. 1799, fols 27–9.

41 *Interiora, Orientalische Akademie*, ᴋ. 57, Konv. ᴀ, 1811–12, fol. 79.

42 *Interiora, Orientalische Akademie*, ᴋ. 57, Konv. ʙ, 1806–9, fol. 98.

43 H. M. Scott, *The Emergence of the Eastern Powers 1756–1775* (New York, 2002), p. 142.

44 Babinger, 'Türkische Studien', pp. 124, n. 1–3, and p. 125; Roider, *Thugut*, pp. 11, 15–18; Joseph von Hammer-Purgstall, 'Erinnerungen aus meinem Leben, 1774–1852', *Fontes Rerum Austriacarum*, part 2, *Diplomataria et acta*, ʟxx (1940), p. 37.

45 Hammer-Purgstall in *Fundgruben des Orients*, vol. v, n.p.; Almut Höfert, 'The Order of Things and the Discourse of the Turkish Threat', in *Between Europe and Islam: Shaping Modernity in a Transcendental Space*, ed. Almut Höfert and Armando Salvatore (Brussels, 2000), p. 42; Ercümet Kuran, 'Ottoman Historiography of the Tanzimat

Period', in *Historians of the Middle East*, ed. Bernard Lewis and P. M. Holt (London, 1962), p. 424; Ignaz Goldziher, *Muhammedanische Studien* (Halle, 1888), part 1, p. 243 and part 2, pp. 368–9; Gustave Dugat, *Histoire des Orientalistes de l'Europe du XIe au XIXe Siècle* (Paris, 1868), p. xi.

46 Hammer-Purgstall, 'Erinnerungen', pp. 571–5; Robert Simon, *Ignaz Goldziher: His Life and Scholarship as Reflected in his Works and Correspondence* (Budapest, 1986), pp. 23–5.

47 Paula Sutter Fichtner, 'History, Religion, and Politics in the Austrian *Vormärz*', *History and Theory*, x (1971), pp. 35, 42–3. Hammer-Purgstall's brother Anton was also a graduate of the Oriental Academy.

48 Ingeborg Solbrig, *Hammer-Purgstall und Goethe: 'dem Zaubermeister das Werkzeug'* (Bern, 1973), p. 77.

49 Wilhelm Bietak, *'Gottes ist der Orient. Gottes ist der Okzident': Eine Studie über Joseph von Hammer-Purgstall* (Vienna, 1948), p. 34; Solbrig, 'Werkzeug', p. 47; Hammer-Purgstall, 'Erinnerungen', pp. 214, 275, 310–11. Citation p. 139.

50 *Interiora, Orientalische Akademie*, к. 56, Konv. в, 1789–91, fol. 4; *Interiora, Orientalische Akademie*, к. 56, 1791–2, fols 119–20, 157; Fichtner, 'History', p. 35.

51 Solbrig, 'Werkzeug', p. 47.

52 *Interiora, Orientalische Akademie*, к. 56, 1794, fol. 320; Solbrig, 'Werkzeug', p. 46.

53 Citation in Hammer-Purgstall, 'Erinnerungen', p. 57; *Archiv*, XII/13 (1821), p. 51; Bietak, 'Gottes', pp. 9–10, 24–5; Herbert Seidler, *Österreichischer Vormärz und Goethezeit. Geschichte einer literarischer Auseinandersetzung* (Vienna, 1982), p. 260.

54 Hammer-Purgstall, 'Erinnerungen', p. 362.

55 Bietak, 'Gottes', pp. 38–9; Klaus Kreiser, 'Clio's Poor Relation: Betrachtungen zur osmanischen Historiographie von Hammer-Purgstall bis Stanford Shaw', in *Das osmanische Reich und Europa 1683 bis 1789: Konflikt, Entspannung, und Austausch*, ed. Gernot Heiß and Grete Klingenstein (Munich, 1983), pp. 29, 33.

56 Fichtner, 'History', p. 41; Reinhard to Goethe, 7 November 1812, in Hammer-Purgstall, 'Erinnerungen', p. 502; Johann Wolfgang von Goethe, *Sämtliche Werke* (Zürich, 1977), vol. XIV, p. 957.

57 Hammer-Purgstall, 'Erinnerungen', pp. 111–12, 287.

58 Neck, *Osmanen*, pp. 227–9; Vienna, HHStA, Staatskanzlei, *Interiora, Personalia*, к. 4, Konv. *Hammer-Purgstall*, 21 August 1814, fols 26, 33; Hammer-Purgstall to the 'Ministry', 25 May 1815, Vienna, HHStA, Staatskanzlei, *Interiora, Personalia*, к. 4, Konv. *Hammer-Purgstall*, fols 35–6; Hammer-Purgstall to Count Buol von Schauenstein, 21 December 1853, Vienna, HHStA, Staatskanzlei, *Interiora, Personalia*, к. 4, Konv. *Hammer-Purgstall*, fols 26, 70–7.

59 Bietak, 'Gottes', p. 10; Solbrig, 'Werkzeug', p. 68; Hammer-Purgstall to Prince Metternich, 16 March 1810, Vienna, HHStA, Staatskanzlei, *Interiora, Personalia*, к. 4, Konv. *Hammer-Purgstall*, fol. 13.

60 *Archiv*, xv/146–7 (1824), p. 792; Solbrig, 'Werkzeug', p. 229.

61 Hammer-Purgstall, 'Erinnerungen', pp. 140, 293–4, 298.

62 Bietak, 'Gottes', pp. 38–9; Kreiser, 'Clio's', pp. 29, 33.

63 Solbrig,'Werkzeug', p. 279; Seidler, *Goethezeit*, pp. 186–7, 231.

64 Bietak, 'Gottes', pp. 9–10, 24–5.

65 Hammer-Purgstall, 'Erinnerungen', p. 40. Citation p. 44.

66 Halil Inalcik, 'The Rise of Ottoman Historiography', in *Historians*, p. 153; O. M. Dunlop, 'Some Remarks on Weil's History of the Caliphs', in *Historians*, p. 316; Kuran, 'Historiography', in *Historians*, p. 427; Hourani, *Islam*, pp. 32, 34.

67 'Gottes ist der Orient, Gottes ist der Okzident', in Bietak, 'Gottes', p. 41; Solbrig, 'Werkzeug', pp. 83, 88; Hammer-Purgstall, 'Erinnerungen', p. 348.

68 Kreiser, 'Clio's', p. 27; Fichtner, 'History', p. 38; Karl Veith, review of Hammer-Purgstall's *Geschichte des osmanischen Reiches* in *Jahrbücher der Literatur* (hereafter *Jahrbücher*), XXI (1828), p. 95.

69 For example, *Patriotisches Archiv*, XII/3 (1821), pp. 11–12.

70 Joseph von Hammer-Purgstall, *Jahrbücher*, LXI (1833), pp. 1–72; *Jahrbücher*, LXVIII (1834), pp. 10–11; Jacob Lassner, 'Abraham Geiger: a Nineteenth-Century Jewish Reformer on the Origins of Islam', in *The Jewish Discovery of Islam. Studies in Honor of*

Bernard Lewis, ed. Martin Kramer (Tel Aviv, 1999), pp. 105–6, 108, 110; Hammer-Purgstall, 'Erinnerungen', p. 386.

71 Anthony Grafton, 'The World of the Polyhistors. Humanism and Encyclopedism', *Central European History*, XVIII (1985), pp. 38–9; Daniel Kasper Lohenstein, *Ibrahim Sultan* (Leipzig, 1673), unpaginated; Jane O. Newman, *The Intervention of Philology: Gender, Learning, and Power in Lohenstein's Roman Plays* (Chapel Hill, NC, 2000), p. 11.

72 Fichtner, 'History', *passim*.

73 Hammer-Purgstall, 'Erinnerungen', pp. 21, 23; HHStA, Staatskanzlei, *Interiora, Personalia* K. 4, Konv. *Hammer-Purgstall*, fols 81, 97–8.

74 Fichtner, 'History', *passim*; Wilhelm Baum, 'Wenzel Gottfried von Purgstalls Beziehungen zu Reinhold, Kant, Schiller, und Goethe', in *Verdrängter Humanismus*, vol. II, pp. 852–66; Hammer-Purgstall, 'Erinnerungen', p. 576; Joseph von Hammer [Purgstall], ed, *Denkmal auf das Grab der beiden letzten Grafen von Purgstall*, (Vienna, 1821), pp. xxii, xlii, xlv, xlix; pp. 24–7, 29; Werner Sauer, *Österreichische Philosophie zwischen Aufklärung und Restauration* (Würzburg and Amsterdam, 1982), p. 129.

75 Hammer-Purgstall, 'Erinnerungen', pp. 126–9, 133, 437.

76 Fichtner, 'History', pp. 42–3; Hammer-Purgstall, 'Erinnerungen', pp. 354–5.

77 Hammer-Purgstall, 'Erinnerungen', p. 182; *Fundgruben*, vol. I, intro., unpaginated; *Fundgruben*, vol. II, unpaginated.

78 Hammer-Purgstall, 'Erinnerungen', p. 393; Josef von Hormayr to Hammer-Purgstall, 18 July 1820, in Hammer-Purgstall, 'Erinnerungen', p. 517.

79 Hammer-Purgstall, 'Erinnerungen', pp. 67, 326.

80 Ibid., pp. 43–4.

81 Ibid., p. 322. Citation on p. 135.

82 Ibid., pp. 41–2, 306.

83 Citation in Solbrig, 'Werkzeug', p. 57; Hammer-Purgstall, 'Erinnerungen', pp. 156, 159.

84 Hammer-Purgstall, 'Erinnerungen', p. 337.

85 Joseph Alois Gleich, *Der Mohr von Semegonda*, part 2 (Vienna, 1805), pp. 13, 17–18, 36, 62–4.

86 Gleich, *Mohr*, part 2, pp. 26, 30, 33.

87 Citation in Karl Meisl, *Die travestierte Zauberflöte* (Pest, 1820), pp. 14–15, 21; J. N. Vogl, 'Der Bettler von Bagdad', in *Taschenbuch des kaiserl. königl. privil. Leopoldstädter-Theaters* (Vienna, 1828), pp. 215–23.

88 Joseph Alois Gleich, *Mahomed der Eroberer, oder Die Todtenbrücke in Konstantinopel* (Vienna, 1841), pp. 27, 106–17; Citation in Joseph Gleich, *Peter Szapary der Held im Sklavenjoche* (Vienna, 1841), p. 55.

89 Gleich, *Mahomed der Eroberer*, pp. 3–6, 14, 17–19, 27, 29, 53, 55–6, 71, 106–17.

90 Josef Alois Gleich, *Die Belagerung Wien's durch die Türken, oder Graf Starhemberg's Heldenmuth und Tapferkeit* (Vienna, 1838), part 2, pp. 11–12, 202. Citation p. 205.

91 Gleich, *Belagerung*, part 2, pp. 202, 208, 211.

92 Josef von Hammer-Purgstall, ed, *Das arabische Hohe Lied der Liebe. Das Ist Ibnol Fáridhi's Tái'jet* (Vienna, 1854), pp. viii–ix; Joseph von Hammer-Purgstall, *Geschichte des osmanischen Reiches* (Pest, 1827–35), vol. V, pp. 415–16.

93 Franz Grillparzer, 'Erinnerungen', in *Sämtliche Werke*, (Munich, 1960–64), vol. IV, p. 209.

94 Lindner, *Mann*, pp. 71–89, 149; Jacob Nagy de Harsányi, *Colloquia familiara Turcico Latina seu status turcicus loquens* (n.p., 1672), unpaginated.

95 Hammer-Purgstall, 'Erinnerungen', p. 281; Hammer-Purgstall to Metternich [?], 4 August 1825, Vienna, HHStA, Staatskanzlei, *Interiora, Personalia*, K. 4, Konv. *Hammer-Purgstall*, fol. 50.

96 Hammer-Purgstall, 'Erinnerungen', p. 67.

97 Josef von Hammer-Purgstall, *Wien's erste aufgehobene türkische Belagerung vom Jahre 1529* (Pest, 1829), pp. 1–3, 7.

98 Hammer-Purgstall, 'Erinnerungen', p. 133.

99 Christine Woodhead, 'The Present Terror of the World? Contemporary Views of the Ottoman Empire c. 1600', *History*, LXXII (1987), p. 21, note 6.

100 Hammer-Purgstall, *Geschichte*, vol. I, pp. xxiii–xiv; Hammer-Purgstall, *Geschichte*, vol.

III, pp. 63–4; Fichtner, 'History', p. 42.

101 Hammer-Purgstall, 'Erinnerungen', pp. 183–4. Demeter's precise identification is not clear. There were three men with identical family names listed among the subscribers to the first volume of the *Fundgruben*.

102 Edward Said, *Orientalism* (New York, 1979), p. 43.

103 Hammer-Purgstall, 'Erinnerungen', pp. 285–7; Solbrig, 'Werkzeug', pp. 196–7; *Fundgruben*, vol. I, intro.

104 Vienna, HHStA, Staatskanzlei, *Interiora, Personalia*, K. 4, Konv. *Hammer-Purgstall*, 31 December 1813, fol. 26.

105 *Der österreichische Beobachter*, Supplement 1 (1810), unpaginated.

106 Silvester Lechner, *Gelehrte Kritik und Restauration. Metternichs Wissenschafts- und Pressepolitik und die 'Wiener Jahrbücher der Literatur'* (Tübingen, 1977), pp. 232, 245, 294; Fichtner, 'History', p. 43; Seidler, *Goethezeit*, p. 215.

107 Citation in Lechner, *Gelehrte Kritik*, p. 282 and note 680; Julius Marx, *Österreichs Kampf gegen die Liberalen, Radikalen und Kommunistischen Schriften* (Vienna, 1969), pp. 17–18; Waltraud Heindl, *Gehorsame Rebellen* (Vienna, 1990), p. 51.

108 *Jahrbücher*, LX (1832), pp. 199–200; *Jahrbücher*, LIV (1831), p. 72.

109 *Jahrbücher*, LXIX (1835), pp. 1–90, esp. pp. 1–4; *Jahrbücher*, LXXVI (1836), p. 258.

110 Carl Veith, *Erinnerungen an Johann Wilhelm Ridler* (Vienna, 1835), esp. p. 31; *Der Österreichischer Beobachter*, Supplements 28/29 (1810), unpaginated.

111 Karl Veith, *Ueber den Barfüsser Johannes Pauli und das von ihm verfasste Volksbuch Schimpf und Ernst* (Vienna, 1839), pp. 1–3.

112 Veith, *Erinnerungen*, pp. 10–11, 13–14. On Franz Hammer see Werner Sauer, 'Von der "Kritik" zur "Positivität"' in *Vormärz: Wendepunkt und Herausforderung*, ed. Hanna Schnedl-Bugeniček (Vienna and Salzburg, 1983), p. 35.

113 *Archiv*, 1824, XV/112 (1824), pp. 609–10; *Jahrbücher*, XLI (1828), p. 95.

114 Review of Hammer-Purgstall's *Geschichte des osmanischen Reiches*, vol. IX by Dr Wolfgang Menzel from the *Literatur-Blatt*, 64 (1834), pp. 253–56 in Vienna, Staatskanzlei, *Interiora Personalia*, K. 4., Konv. *Hammer-Purgstall*, fols 56–7.

115 Josef von Hormayr, *Österreichischer Plutarch*, 2 (n.p., 1807–14), pp. 84–105, citation p. 104. See also Hormayr, *Plutarch*, 1, pp. 117, 122 and Hormayr, *Plutarch*, 3, p. 49.

116 *Archiv*, XV/115 (1824), pp. 624–5.

117 *Archiv*, XIII/68 (1822), p. 364; *Archiv*, XIII/69–70 (1822), p. 392.

118 Josef von Hormayr to Josef von Hammer-Purgstall, 16 July 1823, 'Erinnerungen', p. 520.

119 *Archiv*, I/76–8 (1810), pp. 357–8; *Archiv*, XV/4 (1824), pp. 275–7, citation p. 275.

120 *Archiv*, XVI/152–3 (1825), p. 892.

121 *Archiv*, VI/105–6 (1815), pp. 431–2.

122 *Archiv*, XII/36 (1824), pp. 141–2; *Archiv*, XVI/34 (1825), p. 275.

123 *Archiv*, XII/3 (1821), pp. 431–2.

124 *Archiv*, VII /101–2 (1816), p. 413.

125 *Archiv*, VII/5–6 (1816), pp. 214–15; *Archiv*, VIII/53–4 (1817), pp. 137–43.

126 *Archiv*, VII/35–6 (1816), pp. 137–43.

127 *Archiv*, I/76–8 (1810), pp. 357–8.

128 *Taschenbuch* (1828), pp. 41–2; *Taschenbuch* (1824), pp. 303, 305–6, 309–11.

129 *Taschenbuch* (1824), pp. 256–8, 281.

130 *Archiv*, I/10 (1810), pp. 48–62; *Archiv*, I/11 (1810), pp. 58–60; *Archiv*, II/102–3 (1811), pp. 452–3; *Archiv*, VI/83–4 (1815), pp. 335–7, 392.

131 *Archiv*, II/92–3 (1811), p. 392.

132 *Archiv*, XX/66 (1829), pp. 517–19.

133 *Archiv*, XII/66 (1830), pp. 518–19.

134 *Archiv*, XX/90 (1829), pp. 708–9, citation p. 709. Bayezid probably died of natural causes. Caroline Finkel, *Osman's Dream* (New York, 2006), p. 30.

135 *Archiv*, XX/87 (1829), pp. 684–6.

136 *Archiv*, XVII/11 (1826), p. 58.

137 *Archiv*, XVIII/8–9 (1827), pp. 43, 278–9; *Archiv*, XI /2 (1820), p. 10; *Archiv*, XI/3 (1820), p. 14.

138 *Archiv*, XI/4 (1820), p. 18; *Archiv*, XI/5 (1820), p. 23.

139 *Archiv*, XI/2 (1820), pp. 9–10; *Archiv*, XI/3 (1820), p. 14; *Archiv*, III/101–2 (1812), pp. 324, 401.

140 *Archiv*, XI/3 (1820), p. 14; *Archiv*, I/66–7 (1810), pp. 289–93, citation p. 291.

141 *Archiv*, IV/33–4 (1813), pp. 141–6; *Archiv*, VIII/61–3 (1817), pp. 254–6.

142 For example, *Archiv*, XVI/45 (1825), p. 324.

143 *Archiv*, XI/5 (1820), pp. 25–7.

144 *Archiv*, II/92–3 (1811), pp. 392–3; *Archiv*, II/94–5 (1811), p. 401; *Archiv*, IV/42–3 (1813), pp. 86–8.

145 *Archiv*, II/102–3 (1811), pp. 450–2.

146 *Archiv*, XX/16 (1829), p. 121.

147 *Archiv*, VI/16–17 (1829), pp. 65–7.

148 *Archiv*, XX/66 (1829), p. 393.

149 *Archiv*, XII (1821), inside cover.

150 Cf. Gordon W. Allport, *The Nature of Prejudice* (Reading, MA, 1954), p. 9; Milton Rokeach, *The Open and the Closed Mind: Investigations into the Nature of Belief Systems and Personality Systems* (New York, 1960), p. 58; Partha Mitter, 'Can we ever understand alien cultures?', *Comparative Criticism: An Annual Journal*, IX (1987), pp. 13–14.

151 Gleich, *Belagerung*, part 2, pp. 192–214.

152 Gleich, *Mohamed der Eroberer*, pp. 106–17.

153 Gleich, *Mohr*, part 2, pp. 18, 36.

154 Adolf Bäuerle, 'Wien, Paris, London und Constantinopel', in *Barocktradition im österre-ichisch-bäyerischen Volkstheater*, ed. Otto Rommel (Leipzig, 1938), pp. 233–325, citation p. 238.

155 Joseph von Hammer-Purgstall, 'Vortrag über die Vielsprachlichkeit', in *Die Feierliche Sitzung der Kaiserlichen Akademie der Wissenschaften*, 29 May 1852 (Vienna, 1852), pp. 99–100; *Archiv*, XVI/152–3 (1825), p. 892.

CODA

1 Michael Batunskij, *Alfred von Kremer als einer der Begründer der Modernen Islamkunde*, Anzeiger der österreichischen Akademie der Wissenschaften, CXVI/Sonderheft 16 (Vienna, 1978), p. 245.

2 Lawrence I. Conrad, 'Ignaz Goldziher on Ernest Renan: from Orientalist Philology to the Study of Islam', in *The Jewish Discovery of Islam, Studies in Honor of Bernard Lewis*, ed. Martin Kramer (Tel Aviv, 1999) pp. 143, 167; Alfred von Kremer, *Culturgeschichte des Orients unter den Chalifen* (Vienna, 1875–7), vol. I, pp. iv–vi, viii–ix; Ignaz Goldziher, *Muhammedanische Studien* (Halle, 1880), parts 1 and 2, *passim*.

3 Vienna, Haus, Hof,-und Staatsarchiv, Staatskanzlei, *Interiora, Orientalische Academy*, Karton 58, folder *Vorträge betreffend das Lehrpersonale*, fols 6–7; Waltraud Heindl, 'Beamtentum, Elitenbildung und Wissenschaftspolitik im Vormärz', in *Vormärz: Wendepunkt und Herausforderung*, ed. Hanna Schnedl-Bubeniček (Vienna and Salzburg, 1983), pp. 50–1.

4 William Jenks, *Austria under the Iron Ring 1879–1893* (Charlottesville, VA, 1965), pp. 65, 67–8.

5 Austrian Academy of Sciences, *Allgemeine Akten*, 998/1889.

6 Batunskij, *Islamkunde*, p. 245.

7 Alfred von Kremer, *Geschichte der Herrschenden Ideen des Islams. Der Gottesbegriff, die Prophetie und Staatsidee* (Leipzig, 1868), pp. 121, 129, 236; Alfred von Kremer, *Über das Budget der Einnahmen unter der Regierung des Harun Alrasid* (Vienna, 1887), p. 1 and note 3; Alfred von Kremer, ed. *History of Muhammad's Campaigns by Aboo 'Abd Ollah Mohammad 'Bin Omar Al-Wa 'dy* (Calcutta, 1856), pp. 4–6, 8–9; Batunskij, *Islamkunde*, pp. 255–6; *Sitzungsberichte der kaiserlichen Akademie der Wissenschaften, Phil.-hist. Classe*, XIII/5 (1844), pp. 485–6.

8 Alfred von Kremer, *Culturgeschichte des Orients unter den Chalifen* (Vienna, 1875–7), vol. I, pp. iv–vi; Kremer, *Herrschenden Ideen*, p. 464, note 23 and p. 465; Birgit Schaebler, 'Civilizing Others: Global Modernity and the Local Boundaries (French, German,

Ottoman, and Arab) of Savagery', in *Globalization and the Modern World*, ed. Birgit Schaebler and Leif Stenberg (Syracuse, NY, 2004), pp. 16–17.

9 Batunskij, *Islamkunde*, p. 246, note 9; Alfred von Kremer, *Aegypten. Forschungen über Land und Volk während eines zehnjärigen Aufenthalts* (Leipzig, 1863), pt. 1, p. vi.

10 Kremer, *Culturgeschichte*, pp. viii, ix; Batunskij, *Kremer*, pp. 250, note 10, 251–2; Kremer, *Campaigns*, p. 3; Alfred von Kremer, *Culturgeschichtliche Beziehungen zwischen Europa und dem Oriente* (Vienna, 1876) Lecture 24 November 1875, p. 1; Schaebler, 'Civilizing Others', pp. 4–5.

11 Kremer, *Herrschenden Ideen*, p. xi; Alfred von Kremer, *Die Nationalitätsidee und der Staat. Eine culturgeschichtliche Studie über den Einfluß der nationalen Ideen, besonders auf Staaten mit gemischter Bevölkerung* (Vienna, 1885), p. 4, note 1.

12 Kremer, *Aegypten*, part 2, p. 330–31; Alfred von Kremer, *Mollâ-Shâh et le spiritualisme orientale* (Paris, 1869), p. 51.

13 Kremer, *Herrschenden Ideen*, p. 320; Kremer, *Aegypten*, part 2, pp. 330–1.

14 Kremer, *Aegypten*, pp. viii–ix, xi.

15 Kremer, *Herrschenden Ideen*, p. 84; Kremer, *Aegypten*, pp. 70–1, 76, 90–1; Kremer, *Campaigns*, p. 3.

16 Kremer, *Aegypten*, p. 76; Kremer, *Campaigns*, p. 1; Kremer, *Herrschenden Ideen*, 113–16.

17 Kremer, *Mollâ*, pp. 1–2.

18 Kremer to ?, 22 July 1880, Austrian National Library, Autographen Sammlung, *Sammlung Otto Frankfurter*, 240/3–1; Kremer, *Aegypten*, pp. 198, 239–40; *Sitzungsberichte der kaiserlichen Akademie der Wissenschaften, phil.-hist. Klasse*, XIII/5 (1854), pp. 484–5.

19 Kremer, *Aegypten*, p. x; Kremer, *Beziehungen*, pp. 1, 5–6; Kremer, *Nationalitätsidee*, p. 188; Alfred von Kremer to Freiherr A. von Munek, 7 January 1860, Austrian National Library, Autographen Sammlung, *Teilnachlaß Friedrich Halm*, 1186/10–1. Munek was the director of the imperial library.

20 Kremer, *Nationalitätsidee*, pp. 135–6, 139.

21 Alfred von Kremer, *Discours Prononcé a la Séance du 27 Septembre 1886 du Septième Congrès International des Orientalistes.* (Vienna, 1886), pp. 14–22; Schaebler, 'Civilizing Others', pp. 18–19, 23–4.

22 Paul Wittek, *The Rise of the Ottoman Empire* (Rpt: New York, 1971), pp. 3–6.

23 Wolfgang Köhler, *Hugo von Hofmannsthal und 'Tausend und eine Nacht'* (Bern, 1972), pp. 39, 41, 57.

24 Pierre Zagorin, *How the Idea of Religious Toleration Came to the West* (Princeton, NJ, 2003) p. 9. See also Hichem Djaït, *Europe and Islam* (Berkeley, CA, 1995 [1978]), p. 51.

25 William Montgomery Watt, *Muslim-Christian Encounters. Perceptions and Misperceptions* (London and New York, 1991), p. 109; Nancy Bisaha, *Creating East and West: Renaissance Humanists and the Ottoman Turks* (Philadelphia, PA, 2004), p. 6. See also generally Robert Irwin, *Dangerous Knowledge: Orientalism and its Discontents* (Woodstock and New York, 2006). While Irwin's treatment on p. 81 of Hammer-Purgstall is both superficial and inaccurate, his book examines central European orientalism more fully than do comparable studies.

26 María Rosa Menocal, 'The Myth of Westernness in Medieval Literary Historiography', in *The New Crusades: Constructing the Muslim Enemy*, ed. Emran Qureshi and Michael Sells (New York, 2003), p. 249.

27 Edward Said, *Orientalism* (New York, 1979), pp. 5, 13–15, 20–1, 42. See also Ranjit Guha, *Dominance without Hegemony: History and Power in Colonial India* (Cambridge, MA, 1997).

28 Lewis, *Islam in History*, p. 22. See also Almut Höfert, *Den Feind beschreiben. Türkengefahr und europäisches Wissen über das Osmanische Reich 1450–1500* (Frankfurt, 2003), p. 167.

29 Cf. Yohanan Friedman, *Tolerance and Coercion in Islam: Interfaith Relations in the Muslim Tradition* (Cambridge, 2003), pp. 3–4.

30 For example, Zachary Lockman, *Contending Visions of the Middle East: The History and Politics of Orientalism* (New York, 2004), pp. 1–66.

31 On the suppression of the self and total alienation see Fred Dallmayr, 'Gadamer,

Derrida, and the Hermeneutics of Difference', in *Beyond Orientalism: Essays on Cross-Cultural Encounters*, ed. Fred Dallmayr (Binghamton, NY, 1996), p. 58.

32 Francesco Gabrieli, 'An Apology for Orientalism', in *Orientalism: A Reader*, ed. A. L. Macfie (New York, 2000), p. 81.

33 Contrast with Thierry Hentsch, *Imagining the Middle East*, trans. Fred A. Reed (Montreal, 1992) and Lockman, *Contending Visions*, pp. 1–61. See also David Blanks, 'Western Views of Islam in the Premodern Period: A Brief History of Past Approaches', in *Western Views of Islam in Medieval and Early Modern Europe*, ed. David Blanks and Michael Frassetto (New York, 1999), pp. 34–5.

34 Mitter, 'Alien Cultures', pp. 12–13, 28–9.

35 Bernard Lewis, *Cultures in Conflict: Christians, Muslims and Jews in the Age of Discovery* (New York, 1995), p. 78; Conrad, 'Goldziher', pp. 139–40; Maxime Rodinson, *Europe and the Mystique of Islam*, trans. Roger Veinus (Seattle, WA, 1987 [1980]), pp. 3–31, 55–6, 70.

36 Zagorin, *Toleration*, pp. 9–13.

37 Dallmayer, 'Modes of Cross-Cultural Encounter: Reflections on 1492', in *Beyond Orientalism*, pp. 6, 32.

Select Bibliography

Allport, Gordon W., *The Nature of Prejudice* (Reading, MA, 1954)

Benedikt, Michael, Reinhold Knoll and Josef Rupitz, eds, *Verdrängter Humanismus. Verzögerte Aufklärung* (Cluj-Napoca and Vienna, 1997–)

Berend, Nora, *At the Gate of Christendom: Jews, Muslims and 'Pagans' in Modern Hungary* (New York, 2001)

Bisaha, Nancy, *Creating East and West: Renaissance Humanists and the Ottoman Turks* (Philadelphia, PA, 2004)

Bischof, Günter, Anton Pelinka and Hermann Denz, eds, *Religion in Austria* (New Brunswick, NJ, 2005)

Blanks, David and Michael Frassetto, eds, *Western Views of Islam in Medieval and Early Modern Europe* (New York, 1999)

Brown, Bruce Alan, *Gluck and the French Theatre in Vienna* (Oxford, 1991)

Colley, Linda, *Captives: Britain, Europe and the World, 1600–1850* (London, 2002)

Dallmayr, Fred., ed., *Beyond Orientalism. Essays on Cross-Cultural Encounters* (Binghamton, NY, 1996)

Daniel, Norman, *Islam and the West. The Making of an Image* (Oxford, 1997 [1960])

Deák, István, *The Lawful Revolution. Louis Kossuth and the Hungarians 1848–1849* (New York, 1979)

Djaït, Hichem, *Europe and Islam*, trans. Peter Heinigg (Berkeley, CA, 1995 [1978])

Fichtner, Paula Sutter, *Emperor Maximilian II* (New Haven, CT, 2001)

Friedman, Yohanan, *Tolerance and Coercion in Islam. Interfaith Relations in the Muslim Tradition* (Cambridge, 2003)

Goffman, Daniel, *The Ottoman Empire and Early Modern Europe* (Cambridge, 2002)

Göllner, Carl, *Turcica*, 3 vols (Bucarest and Baden-Baden, 1961–78)

Grothaus, Maximilian, *Der 'Erbfeindt christlichen Namens'. Studien zum Türkenbild in der Kultur der Habsburger Monarchie zwischen 16. u. 18. Jh.* (Diss., Graz, 1986)

Hanson, Alice M., *Musical Life in Biedermeier Vienna* (Cambridge, 1985)

Heiß, Gernot and Grete Klingenstein, eds, *Das osmanische Reich und Europa 1683 bis 1789. Konflikt, Entspannung und Austausch* (Munich, 1983)

Hentsch, Thierry, *Imagining the Middle East*, trans. Fred A. Reed (Montreal, 1992)

Hodgson, Marshal, *The Venture of Islam*, 3 vols (Chicago, 1974)

Höfert, Almut, *Den Feind beschreiben. Türkengefahr und europäisches Wissen über das Osmanische Reich 1450–1500* (Frankfurt, 2003)

Hourani, Albert, *Europe and the Middle East* (Berkeley, CA, 1980)

——, *Islam in European Thought* (Cambridge, 1991)

Imber, Colin, *The Ottoman Empire 1300–1481* (Istanbul, 1990)

——, *The Ottoman Empire, 1300–1650: The Structure of Power* (New York, 2003)

Johnson, James Turner, *The Holy War in Western and Islamic Traditions* (University Park, PA, 1997)

——, and John Kelsay, eds, *Cross, Crescent, and Sword: The Justification and Limitation of War in Western and Islamic Tradition* (New York, 1990).

Kelsay, John and James Turner Johnson, eds, *Just War and Jihad: Historical and Theoretical Perspectives on War and Peace in Western and Islamic Traditions* (New York, 1991)

Kißling, Joachim, *Rechtsproblematiken in den christlich-muslimischen Beziehungen vorab im Zeitalter des Türkenkrieges* (Graz, 1974)

Kontje, Todd, *German Orientalisms* (Ann Arbor, MI, 2004)

Kramer, Martin, ed., *The Jewish Discovery of Islam: Studies in Honor of Bernard Lewis* (Tel Aviv, 1999)

Kunt, Metin and Christine Woodhead, eds, *The Ottoman Empire in the Early Modern World* (London and New York, 1995)

Landon, H. C. Robbins, *Haydn: A Documentary Study* (New York, 1981)

Lewis, Bernard, *The Muslim Discovery of Europe* (New York, 1982)

——, and P. M. Holt, eds, *Historians of the Middle East* (London, 1962)

Lockman, Zachary, *Contending Visions of the Middle East: The History and Politics of Orientalism* (Cambridge, 2004)

Levy, David Benjamin, *Beethoven: the Ninth Symphony* (New York, 1995)

Lindner, Dolf, *Der Mann ohne Vorurtheile. Joseph von Sonnenfels 1733–1817* (Vienna, 1983)

Macfie, A. L., ed., *Orientalism: A Reader* (New York, 2000)

Mathis, Herbert, ed., *Von der Glückseligkeit des Staates. Staat, Wirtschaft und Gesellschaft im Zeitalter des aufgeklärten Absolutismus* (Berlin, 1981)

MacLean, Gerald, ed., *Reorienting the Renaissance: Cultural Exchanges with the East* (Houndsmills and New York, 2005)

Murphey, Rhoads, *Ottoman Warfare 1500–1700* (New Brunswick, NJ, 1999)

Murray, Stephen O. and Will Roscoe, eds, *Islamic Homosexualities: Culture, History, and Literature* (New York and London, 1997)

Neck, Rudolf, *Österreich und die Osmanen* (Vienna, 1983)

Newman, Jane O., *The Intervention of Philology: Gender, Learning, and Power in Lohenstein's Roman Plays* (Chapel Hill, NC, 2000)

Özyurt, Senol, *Die Türkenlieder und das Türkenbild in der deutschen Volksüberlieferung vom 16. bis zum 20. Jahrhundert* (Munich, 1972)

Panaite, Viorel, *The Ottoman Law of War and Peace: the Ottoman Empire and Tribute Payers* (Boulder, CO, 2000)

Pieck, Werner, *Haydn. Der Große Bassa. Biographie* (Hamburg, 2004)

Qureshi, Emran and Sells, Michael A., eds, *The New Crusades: Constructing the Muslim Enemy* (New York, 2003)

Rice, John A., *Antonio Salieri and Viennese Opera* (Chicago, 1998)

Rodinson, Maxime, *Europe and the Mustique of Islam*, trans. Roger Veinus (Seattle, WA, 1987 [1980])

Roider, Karl, *Austria's Eastern Eastern Question 1700–1790* (Princeton, NJ, 1982)

——, *Baron Thugut and Austria's Response to the French Revolution* (Princeton, NJ, 1987)

Rokeach, Milton, *The Open and the Closed Mind. Investigations into the Nature of Belief Systems and Personality Systems* (New York, 1960)

Rosenstrauch-Königsberg, Edith, *Zirkel und Zentren. Aufsätze zur Aufklärung in Österreich am Ende des 18. Jahrhunderts* (Vienna, c. 1994)

Said, Edward W., *Orientalism* (New York, 1979)

Schaebler, Birgit and Leif Stenberg, eds, *Globalization and the Muslim World* (Syracuse, NY, 2004)

Schwoebel, Robert, *The Shadow of the Crescent: the Renaissance Image of the Turk, 1453–1517* (New York, 1967)

Scott, H. M., *The Emergence of the Eastern Powers 1756-1775* (New York, 2002)

Simon, Robert, *Ignaz Goldziher: His Life and Scholarship as Reflected in his Works and Correspondence* (Budapest, 1986)

Solbrig, Ingeborg, *Hammer-Purgstall und Goethe: 'dem Zaubermeister das Werkzeug'* (Bern, 1973)

Stoye, John, *The Siege of Vienna* (London, 1964)

Swoboda, Karl M., *Barock in Böhmen* (Munich, 1964)

Taruskin, Richard, *The Oxford History of Music*, 6 vols (Oxford, 2005)

Teply, Karl, *Die Einführung des Kaffees in Wien* (Vienna, 1980)

Till, Nicholas, *Mozart and the Enlightenment: Truth, Virtue and Beauty in Mozart's Operas* (London, 1992)

Tolan, John V., *Saracens. Islam in the Medieval European Imagination* (New York, 2002)

Veinstein, Gilles, ed., *Süleyman Le Magnifique et son temps* (Paris, 1992)

Waissenberger, Robert, ed., *Die Türken vor Wien. Europa und die Entscheidung an der Donau* (Salzburg, 1982)

Watt, William Montgomery, *Muslim-Christian Encounters: Perceptions and Misperceptions* (London/New York, 1991)

Wilson, W. Daniel, *Humanität und Kreuzugsideologie um 1780. Die 'Türkenoper' im 18. Jahrhundert und das Rettungsmotiv in Wielands 'Oberon', Lessings 'Nathan' und Goethe's 'Iphigenie'* (New York, 1984)

Zagorin, Perez, *How the Idea of Religious Toleration Came to the West* (Princeton, NJ, 2003)

Acknowledgements

This work could never have been completed without much-needed help from many sources. Miriam Levy, Howard Louthan, Bruce MacIntire and Karl Roider, busy people all, read through various parts of the manuscript, criticized it thoughtfully and offered bibliographical suggestions that filled in serious gaps in my own reading. They were also generous with their encouragement at moments when I very much needed it. Gabor Vermes and Leonard Gordon gave me greater perspective on Hungarian affairs and the development of orientalism respectively. Members of Columbia University's external seminars on Law and Politics and Eighteenth Century Studies heard papers based on some of the materials incorporated into the present text and had many useful questions and suggestions. Waltraud Heindl put her vast learning in the bureaucratic history of the Habsburg empire and her practical experience in Austrian archives and scholarly institutions at my disposal. Mag. Petra Aigner was of enormous help in driving up crucial material in the archive of the Austrian Academy of Arts and Sciences as were Csilla Bíró of the Széchényi National Library of Hungary, Dr Ibolya Gerelyes of the Hungarian National Museum and Mag. Walter Öhler of the Museum of the City of Vienna. A chance encounter in the Austrian National Library with Dr Anna Blaschek saved me a great deal of time in my work on Alfred von Kremer, who appears towards the end of the study. Without the patient co-operation from the staffs of the Augustinian Reading Room in the Austrian National Library, the Austrian State Archives in Vienna and the Middle East and Asian Reading Room of the New York Public Library I would not have advanced far in the project at all.

Funds from the Austrian Cultural Forum Book Prize, which I won in 2002, underwrote several months of research in Vienna. I shall never forget the hospitality of Waltraud Heindl and Walter Langer to whom this book is dedicated. I am also deeply grateful for the unflagging moral and technical support of Edward Fichtner.

Photo Acknowledgements

The author and publishers wish to express their thanks to the below sources of illustrative material and/or permission to reproduce it.

Courtesy of the Austrian Academy of Arts and Sciences, Vienna: p. 132; by permission of the Austrian State Archives, Vienna: pp. 126, 164; courtesy Citygallery, Prague: p. 70; courtesy of the Cultural Office of the Market Community of Perchtoldsdorf: p. 10; by permission of the Hungarian National Museum, Budapest: pp. 86, 87, 98; reprinted from Paul Magocsi, *Atlas of East Central Europe*, © 2002, by permission of the University of Washington Press: pp. 20, 72, 116; by permission of the Museum der Stadt Wien: pp. 22, 34, 59, 62, 65, 68, 95; photo General Research Division, The New York Public Library (Astor, Lenox and Tilden Foundations) p. 132.

Index